An
Anthology of Musical Criticism

AN ANTHOLOGY
OF MUSICAL CRITICISM

COMPILED BY

NORMAN DEMUTH

1947
LONDON
EYRE & SPOTTISWOODE

THIS BOOK FIRST PUBLISHED IN 1947 IS
PRINTED IN GREAT BRITAIN BY ROBERT MACLEHOSE AND CO. LTD.
THE UNIVERSITY PRESS, GLASGOW
FOR EYRE AND SPOTTISWOODE (PUBLISHERS) LIMITED
15 BEDFORD STREET, LONDON, W.C. 2

The introduction of a new kind of music must be shunned as imperilling the whole state; since styles of music are never disturbed without affecting the most important political institutions.

The new style gradually gaining a lodgment, quietly insinuates itself into manners and customs; and from these it issues in greater force, and makes its way into mutual compacts; and from compacts it goes on to attack laws and constitutions, displaying the utmost impudence, until it ends by overturning everything, both in public and in private.

PLATO, Republic IV, 424 C.

TABLE OF CONTENTS

viii

——Mr. (Robert) Newman supported by his accomplished conductor, Mr. Henry J. Wood, has done wonders on behalf of good music. On Sat., Feb. 10th there was a singular novelty—nothing less than an attempt to illustrate the career of Napoleon on the pianoforte.

'Monthly Musical Record,' March 1900

PREFACE

This is not a made-up book of sayings about music which have appeared in literature other than that of music. It is literally 'An Anthology of Musical Criticism', a panorama of the progress of taste and judgment in this country. Nothing has been quoted simply because it mentions the word 'music'; qualification for inclusion has depended entirely upon the statement of definite opinions, assessments, or the reflection of certain fashions.

What is criticism? Is it merely an expression of personal opinion or a judgment delivered *ex cathedra*? Has it any value and does it wield any influence on both composers and popular taste? Does it require a highly cultivated musical knowledge or can it be written by anyone who 'likes music'? Do critics necessarily like music? Can it be unprejudiced by personal feelings? Do the criticised care what anyone may say about their works?

The answers to all these questions may be found herein.

The swans of yester-year are indeed the geese of to-day. It is interesting to note that nearly all those composers now considered established and inevitable received 'bad notices' in their own days. Indeed, the number of bad notices at times became quite embarrassing and at one stage it seemed impossible to find any constructive and unqualified praise. This must always be the case with those who have anything vital to say; it is only those who are content to sit on the sandbanks instead of floating with the current who can be assured of early recognition. That which is immediately acceptable, proves, in the end, to be worthless. It is from a collection such as this that we are able to find a yard-stick, and the expressions of all ages in the volume are instructive also from the historical angle. It would appear that critics are nearly always wrong!

The question of inclusion and exclusion has rested on whether the writer has had something interesting, constructive, destructive, or individual to say. The trouble with most of the reading has been that of repetition and bald statement. Leaving aside all considerations of literary standard, many estimable writers have merely echoed in so many words what others have said, and have contributed nothing either new or important. Biographies have proved disappointing in this respect; most of them have concentrated on biographical facts and have included little, if any, reasoned assessment.

Newspaper criticism has not played the large part the reader might have expected, except when critics have collected their wisdom in book form. The exception is that on Wagner when the critics do not seem to have been limited by the exigencies of time or space and have had their tirades (and I use the word advisedly) printed in full —so often newspaper criticism is not the complete statement of the writer and has been written under circumstances preventing due and mature consideration.

In order to break the long series of opinions on composers a number of articles have been interpolated on generic subjects which reflect the spirit and taste of the age, and whose literary standard is often higher than that of the genuine musical criticism. With what authority these Daniels come to judgment is not always clear, but in each one selected there is an expression of opinion and assessment.

Generally speaking, therefore, the book shows how times and opinions alter—the fact that they differ is not very important, and although a certain amount of this difference of opinion has been inevitable, there has been no intention to provide a collection of pro's and con's.

Sources are varied and the chase has often been exciting. The sources naturally increased in scope and number as time went on.

The fifteenth, sixteenth, and seventeenth centuries have

been limited to Epitaphs, Dedications, and old books and Diaries. Thomas Morley's *A Plaine and Easie Introduction to Practicall Musicke* has given me many a laugh and it is a pity that more of it was not apposite. Its quaint format and phraseology are the kind of things which make a learned book human—'But, stay; who is this approaching? Why, it is my worthy pupil——.' This opens a new approach from master to student. We find also the first attempt to use music for purposes ulterior to mere listening, in Robert Burton's *Anatomy of Melancholy*, with its meticulous quotation of every authority.

The original spelling has not always been reproduced; some of the quotations have been discovered in modernised form, but when the original did not seem too unintelligible, no attempt has been made to spoil a good thing.

The Diarists are most illuminating for their reflections on the times, and their candour is all the more valuable for its never having been intended for publication; hence they were untroubled by the laws of libel and slander.

Addison and Steele reflect cynically the fashions of their day, many of which could be applied to the present time. Colley Cibber on the Opera, Dean Swift with his pungent criticism of the political and social dangers of 'The Beggar's Opera', the gleeful verbal criticism of the singer who couldn't sing it, the appeals of Cathedral Chapters for new organists—all these make up with no little humour the picture of music and the musical world in those centuries.

The eighteenth century sees criticism becoming increasingly erudite and informed. The histories of Hawkins and Burney, biassed against everything not of their own centuries, bring a keen assessment and considerable authority to the subject. Letters show how music began to be an element of significance in daily life. William Tansur gives his description of what a Master of Music should be—perhaps giving the solution, too, of why that degree is held by so few at Cambridge to-day! The Hon. Daines Barrington puts Mozart through an examination much as he might give a performing animal; Dr. Johnson pontificates through his Boswell; Charles Lamb glories in not having an ear for music; William Hazlitt follows in the paths of the cynical Addison—all these lead up to the beginnings of professional criticism and to the publication of the first books of panoramic events and surveys.

The nineteenth century launches the first regular musical journals—the *Harmonicon*, the *Quarterly Musical Magazine*, the *Musical World*. These give us startling opinions on the composers we now call 'the classics' and extreme laudation of many whose names are now museum pieces. From these beginnings we reach the musical journals which engaged the best writers in the country— *Monthly Musical Record, Musical Opinion, Musical Times* and others which not only led but often directed public opinion, leading to the time when a musical degree was the sign manual of a composer and the holding of a professional appointment an armour against adverse opinion; here the love of officialdom and official positions reaches a remarkable height. Amateurs write for publication and not for the sole delectation of their friends, whether they know anything about music or not— surveys of periods, note-books, some enlightened, others not in the slightest degree so.

Then we come to the first professional critics and the use of the editorial 'we'. H. F. Chorley, J. W. Davison, George Hogarth, Henry Smart—all blest with pens the venom of which makes the poison of an asp seem almost harmless; all hiding behind that editorial 'we', and none of them seemingly qualified in any way as musicians, Henry Smart excepted—an organist. There is no doubt about their loves, hates, and utter ineptitude for the task.

The first Programme Notes, in which Sir George Macfarren (so limited in most directions but so open-minded in others) did his best to provide something like an elementary form of aesthetics; to be succeeded by Joseph Bennett who had the happy knack of quoting other people, a habit imitated by others in later years and one which procures a reputation for erudition; Sir George Grove weighing in with due veneration for Beethoven, and his editorship of the mighty *Dictionary of Music and Musicians* by means of which so many have become musicians 'by the Grace of Grove'; in their writings and others of the period we read of the early struggles to understand Schumann and Brahms.

At the latter end of the century Sir Hubert Parry and Sir W. H. Hadow bring us to the first serious books on aesthetics in which music is treated as one of the liberal arts and sciences and the musician himself is looked upon as rather more than the leader of the band. The subject becomes more and more worth while and eventually becomes one upon which anyone can write with no very extensive knowledge. A high literary standard is set once for all and a reasoned thought is brought to all criticism.

After 1894 the journals cease to be the sole channels, and we leave them as mines of information and turn to them, as well as to the many books, for enlightened assessments of an ever-increasing literary standard. As against mere musical reporting and journalism, journals increase in number and devote themselves to musical studies. These twentieth century publications—*Sackbut, Dominant, Music Review, Music and Letters, Chesterian* —have editors of discernment and distinction who attract the best pens in the country to their service. As music becomes more and more 'fashionable', so theories grow up and are propounded, some reasonable, others preposterous and polemic. The verbiage becomes exceedingly flowery and correspondingly obscure, and the actual meaning ever more uncertain. Such writers as these do not appear in this Anthology.

Edwin Evans, Cecil Gray, Eric Blom—these three names alone are typical of the skill and knowledge which the criticism of music to-day necessitates.

Not enough composers have been born since 1900 to warrant a separate section. Few of those who have been born since the beginning of the century have become established. I have, therefore, taken my own age (47) as an average and included those who I myself remember in the flesh as well as in the music under the heading 'Living Memory'.

Perhaps these pages will make the reader sit up and take notice. We might take warning from the earlier Daniels and think.... 'An Anthology of Musical Criticism' compiled in 2045 has such possibilities that it makes one regret the remote chance that will occur of reading it.

ACKNOWLEDGEMENTS

Every attempt has been made to trace the owners of the rights of everything in the book. If any infringement is found, an assurance is given that the attempt was well and truly made, an apology offered, and a promise made that after due substantiation, the fault will be amended in future editions. The present (1944-1945) situation has in some cases made it impossible to trace the whereabouts of certain authors. No doubt any 'displaced persons' who find themselves omitted from this acknowledgement will communicate with the publishers in order that recognition may be given later on.

It is with regret that three names are omitted.

Mr. George Bernard Shaw will not consent to the use of any of his writings still available in print in his own editions.

Mr. Ernest Newman does not wish to appear.

The literary executors and musical friends of the late Sir Donald Tovey fear a repetition of the ill-nature which they say greeted the publication of Sir Donald's writings in book form, and think that inclusion of them here will lead to still further misunderstanding.

The assistance given by those included in the Anthology has been most generous, and in every case the source and date of the extract has been clearly stated.

During the period of research and compilation I have received and gratefully acknowledge unstinted help from:

My wife, whose skill at deciphering my hand-writing and whose speed and accuracy on the typewriter improved correspondingly with the progress of the book.

Mr. John Graber who read through the typescript and made various useful suggestions.

Mr. Stock, Librarian of the Royal Academy of Music, who gave me the benefit of his wide knowledge of the early literature and who unearthed several treasures from the R.A.M. Library, which were indispensable.

Miss Banner, Librarian of the Royal College of Music, who emerged triumphantly from an air-raid shelter (presumably) with two books which filled an obvious gap and for which I had almost given up the search.

The librarians and staffs of various public libraries who dug up forgotten volumes from cellars and other not easily available places, and who climbed innumerable ladders to find books-behind-books in their willing endeavours to help the good work along, in most cases not knowing for what purpose the hunt was up.

Miss Rose Standfield, who lent me the files of *The Harmonicon* from her late father's library, also the files of *Music and Letters* and *The Monthly Musical Record*, and a room in which I spent many hours on research work.

Mr. R. D. Gibson and Mr. Maurice Jacobson, who lent me the files of *The Chesterian* and the *Sackbut* respectively.

Mr. Henry Boys, who read the proof sheets and gave many valuable opinions.

Acknowledgements are made to

The Trustees of the following deceased Authors for permission to quote from writings the rights of which are the property of the estates:
The late Sir W. H. Hadow,
The late Mr. Edwin Evans (Mrs. Netta Evans),
The late Sir Hubert Parry (Lady Ponsonby of Shulbrede),
The late Dr. W. G. Whittaker (Mr. Edward Pollitzer),
The late Mr. Bernard van Dieren (Mrs. F. van Dieren),
The late Mr. Samuel Butler.

The following Societies, Authors, and Authors' Representatives:
Gramophone Co., Henry Boys, 'Notes on Mahler's Ninth Symphony.'
Royal Musical Association, Sir W. H. Hadow (Trustees), Paper on 'Parry'.

Sir Hubert Parry (Lady Ponsonby of Shulbrede), Paper on 'Monteverde'.

Sir George Macfarren, Paper on 'Bach'.

Royal Philharmonic Society, Joseph Bennett, Programme Note.

Sir George Macfarren, Programmes Notes.

Royal Society, Paper by the Hon. Daines Barrington on 'Mozart'.

Paper by Dr. Charles Burney on 'Samuel Wesley'.

Anonymous communication on 'Dr. William Crotch'.

The Editors, Proprietors, Authors, and Authors' Representatives, of the following musical journals (where a general acknowledgement is made, the complete rights of all quotations are the property of the journal).

The Editor of *Musical Opinion*.

The Editor of *The Musical Times*, Edwin Evans (Mrs. Netta Evans), 'Vaughan Williams'.

The Editor of *Scrutiny*, W. H. Mellers, 'The Composer and Civilisation: Albert Roussel'.

The Editor of *The Listener*, Constant Lambert, 'Tchaikowsky'.

The Editor of *Music and Letters*, Gerald Abraham, 'Tchaikowsky: Some Centennial Reflections.'

Eric Blom, 'His Favourite Device'.

'Verdi as Musician'.

A. E. Brent-Smith, 'Purcell'.

Rev. Dr. E. H. Fellowes, 'William Byrd'.

Sir John McEwen, 'Beethoven's Third Period'.

Messrs. J. & W. Chester, Ltd., Proprietors of *The Chesterian*.

Messrs. J. Curwen & Sons, Ltd., Proprietors of *The Sackbut*.

J. H. Elliot, 'Elgar and England'.

Cecil Gray, 'Bela Bartok'.

'Three Modern Italian Composers'.

Messrs. Methuen & Co., Ltd., J. A. Fuller-Maitland, *Brahms.*

W. J. Turner, *Variations on the Theme of Music.*

A. E. Brent-Smith, *Studies and Caprices.*

Messrs. Nelson & Sons, Ltd., Rev. Basil Maine, *New Paths in Music.*

Messrs. Novello & Co., Ltd., Sir George Grove, *Beethoven and His Nine Symphonies.*

Sir Hubert Parry, *Summary of Musical Art.*

Oxford University Press, E. Dannreuther, *Oxford History of Music,* Vol. VI.

Sir George Dyson, *The New Music.*

Rev. Dr. E. H. Fellowes, *The Heritage of Music,* Vol. II.

J. A. Fuller-Maitland, *Oxford History of Music,* Vol. IV.

Cecil Gray, *A Survey of Contemporary Music. Predicaments.*

Sir W. H. Hadow, *Oxford History of Music,* Vol. V. *Beethoven's Op.* 18 *Quartets.*

Gustav Holst, *The Heritage of Music,* Vol. I.

Samuel Langford, *Musical Criticisms.*

Sir Hubert Parry, *Oxford History of Music,* Vol. III.

Ernest Walker, *A History of Music in England.*

W. G. Whittaker, *Bach's Cantatas.*

Tom S. Wootton, *The Heritage of Music,* Vol. II.

E. J. Dent, *Mozart's Operas.* (2nd Ed:)

Edwin Evans, Bernard van Dieren, Richard Capell, Herbert Antcliffe, 'Essays from *The Dominant*'

A. E. F. Dickinson, *An Introduction to the Music of Vaughan Williams.*

Messrs. Kegan Paul & Co., Ltd., Sir Hubert Parry, *The Art of Music.*

Messrs. Putnam & Co., Ltd., Sir Hubert Parry, *Johann Sebastian Bach.*

Messrs. Seeley Service & Co., Ltd., Sir W. H. Hadow, *Studies in Modern Music.*

An
Anthology of Musical Criticism

I consider that criticism is useless, I would even say that it is harmful. . . . Criticism generally means, the opinion some man or other holds about another person's work. How can that opinion help forward the growth of art? It is interesting to know the ideas, even the erroneous ideas, of geniuses and men of great talent, such as Goethe, Schumann, Wagner, Saint-Beuve, and Michelet when they wish to indulge in criticism; but it is of no interest at all to know whether Mr. So-and-so likes, or does not like, such-and-such dramatic or musical work.

VINCENT D'INDY, *Revue d'art dramatique,*
Feb. 5th, 1899

The
Fifteenth and Sixteenth Centuries

A canon in three parts hath a resemblance to the Holy Trinity, for as they are three distinct parts comprehended in one; the leading part hath reference to the Father, the following part to the Son, and the third to the Holy Ghost.

ELWAY BEVIN, 15?–16?, *A Briefe and Short Introduction to the Art of Musick*

ON JOHN DUNSTABLE (?–1453)

THOMAS MORLEY

We must take heed of separating any part of a word from another by a rest, as some dunces haue not slackt to do; yea, one whose name is Johannis Dunstaple (*sic*) (an ancient English author) hath not only diuided the sentence, but in the verie middle of a word hath made two long rests . . . , in a song of foure parts vpon these words, 'Necsiens virgo mater virum.' . . .

For these be his own notes and words, which is one of the greatest absurdities which I haue seen committed in the dittying of musick.

A Plaine and Easie Introduction to
Practicall Musicke, 1597

ON DR. CHRISTOPHER TYE
(?1497–1572 or 3)

WILLIAM ROWLEY

Doctor, I thank you and commend your cunning.
I oft have heard my father merrily speak
In your high praises; and thus His Highness saith:
England one God, one Truth, one Doctor hath
For musick's art, and that is Dr. Tye,
Admired for skill in musick's harmony.

Dialogue, in a play, between Prince Edward
—afterwards Edward VI—and Dr. Chris-
topher Tye, 1613

ON THOMAS TALLIS (1505 to 10—1585)

DR. CHARLES BURNEY

Though the melody of the Cathedral Services was first adjusted to English words by Markbeck (*sic*), yet Tallis enriched it with harmony. Indeed, the melody used by

Tallis is not exactly similar to that of Markbeck, it is only
of the same kind; consisting of fragments of the ancient
ecclesiastical canto fermo. But the harmony in which he
has clothed it is admirable: and the modulation being so
antique, chiefly in common chords or fundamental
harmony to each note of the diatonic scale often where the
moderns have sixths, sevenths, and their inversions,
produces a solemn and very different effect in music that
has been composed during the present century.

History of Music, 1776

JOHN MARBECK (1523–1585)

Destitute bothe of learning and eloquence, yea, and
such a one as in maner never tasted the swetnes of learned
letters, but altogether brought up in your highnes
College at Wyndsore in the study of musicke and pliyng
on organs, wherin I consumed vainly the greatest part of
my life.

Dedication to Edward VI, *Concordance*

SIR JAMES MELVIL (1535–1617)

. . . she (Queen Elizabeth) asked 'what kind of exer-
cises she (Mary of Scotland) used? I answered that when
I received my despatch, the queen was lately come from
the Highland-hunting; that when her more serious affairs
permitted, she was taken up with reading of histories; that
sometimes she recreated herself with playing on the lute
and virginals. She asked, if she played well; I said,
reasonably for a woman. The same day, after dinner, my
lord of Hunsden drew me up to a quiet gallery, that I
might hear some music, (but he said that he durst not
avow it), where I might hear the queen play upon the
virginals. After I had hearkened awhile, I took by the

tapestry that hung before the door of the chamber, and seeing her back was toward the door, I entered within her chamber, and stood a pretty space, hearing her play excellently well. But she left off immediately as soon as she turned about and saw me. She appeared to be surprised to see me, and came forward, seeming to strike me with her hand, alleging, she used not to play before men, but when she was solitary, to shun melancholy. She asked, how I came there? I answered, as I was walking with Lord Hunsden, as we passed by the chamber door, I heard such a melody as ravished me, whereby I was drawn in ere I knew how; excusing my fault of homeliness, as being brought up in the court of France where such freedom was allowed; declaring myself willing to endure what kind of punishment her majesty should be pleased to inflict upon me for so great an offence. Then she sat down low upon a cushion, and I on my knee by her; but with her own hand she gave me a cushion to lay under my knee, which at first I refused, but she compelled me to take it. She enquired whether my queen or she played best? In that I found myself compelled to give her the praise.

Memoirs, pub. 1683

WILLIAM BYRD (1542 or 43–1623)

Reasons briefly set down by the auctor, to perswade everyone to learne to sing.

First, it is a knowledge easely taught, and quickly learned where there is a good Master, and an apt Scoller.

2. The exercise of singing is delightfull to Nature & good to preserve the health of Man.

3. It doth strengthen all the parts of the brest, & doth open the pipes.

4. It is a singular good remedie for a stutting & stammering in the speech.

5. It is the best meanes to procure a perfect pronunciation & to make a good Orator.

6. It is the onely way to know where Nature hath bestowed the benefit of a good voyce: which guift is so rare, as there is not one among a thousand, that hath it: and in many, that excellent guift is lost, because they want Art to expresse Nature.

7. There is not any Musicke of Instruments whatsoever, comparable to that which is made of the voyces of Men, where the voyces are good, and the same well sorted and ordered.

8. The better the voyce is, the meeter it is to honour and serve God there-with: and the voyce of man is chiefly to be imployed to that ende.

omnis spiritus laudet Dominum.

Since singing is so good a thing
I wish all men would learne to sing.

Psalmes, Sonets, & songs of Sadnes and pietie, made into Musicke of five parts, Preface, 1588

ON WILLIAM BYRD

THOMAS MORLEY

. . . the most excellent Musician Maister William Birde.
. . . in all loue and affection to you most addicted.

A Plaine and Easie Introduction to Practicall Musicke, 1597

THOMAS PEACHUM
HENRY PEACHAM
(Variously spelt)

For Motets and musicke of pietie and devotion, as well as for the honour of our nation as for the merit of the man,

I preferre above all others our Phoenix, Mr. William Byrd, whom in that kind, I know not whether any may equal.

Compleat Gentleman, 1622

DR. CHARLES BURNEY

Crowded and elaborate as is the harmony, and uncouth and antiquated the melody, of all the pieces in this collection by various composers, there is a manifest superiority in those of Bird (*sic*) over all the rest, both in texture and design. In a later age his genius would have expanded in works of invention, taste, and elegance; but, at the period in which he flourished, nothing seems to have been thought necessary for keyed-instruments, except variations to old tunes, in which all the harmony was crowded, which the fingers could grasp, and all the rapid divisions of the times, which they could execute. Even nominal 'Fancies' were without fancy, and confined to the repitition of a few dry and unmeaning notes in fugue, or imitation. Inversion was so young and feeble as to be unable to go alone, and the old chants of the church, or tunes of the street, were its leading-string and guides.

History of Music, 1776

REV. DR. E. H. FELLOWES

Byrd himself claims to have framed his music 'to the the life of the words', and he made his claim good, for the words and their exact meaning were always the foremost thing in the composer's mind, and he succeeded in a wonderful measure in finding musical phrases which exactly fitted the rhythm of the words and expressed their meaning. Then, again, Byrd could build up magnificent long musical phrases; no better example of such a phrase could be given than at the beginning of the three-voice Sanctus, the bass-part of which must always give an intense thrill to the singer as he performs it; and glorious long phrases, showing great beauty of curve, are to be found over and over again in the 'Great' Service and, of course, in the motets. And in spite of the very limited scope for modulation prevailing in those days, Byrd could secure wonderful effects by this device. Nothing, for example, could be more exactly expressive, without the least suggestion of theatrical effect such as later composers contrived to produce than the phrase 'And was crucified' in the Creed of the 'Great' Service.

Music and Letters, April 1923

It is impossible to overestimate his influence and importance in the history of keyboard music. It is not too much to say that he is the father of it. Himself a brilliant executant, he could write with a masterly appreciation of technical effect....

... the quality of his work marks him off very clearly as standing on a higher plane than the best of his contemporaries, among whom Farnaby, Bull, and Gibbons were conspicuous, and he did more than any of them to develop the scope and design of this class of composition, as well as to create a keyboard technique.

The Heritage of Music, Vol. II, 1933

THOMAS MORLEY (1557–*circa* 1603)

Supper being ended and Musicke bookes (according to the custome) being brought to the table, the mistresse of the house presented me with a part, earnestly requesting me to sing; but when, after many excuses, I protested unfainedly that I would not, every one began to wonder. Yes, some whispered to others, demanding how I was brought up; so that, upon shame of my ignorance, I goe now to seeke out mine old friend, master Gnorimus, to make myselfe a scholler.

A Plaine and Easie Introduction to Practicall Musicke, 1597

ON THOMAS MORLEY

SIR JOHN HAWKINS

As a practical Composer he has doubtless shown great
abilities; he was an excellent harmonist, but did not
possess the faculty of invention in any very eminent
degree.

*A General History of the Science and
Practice of Music,* 1776

DR. CHARLES BURNEY

Thomas Morley, a disciple of Bird, Bachelor of Music,
one of the Gentlemen of Queen Elizabeth's Chape.,
acquired more celebrity by his treatise, entitled *A
Plaine and Easie Introduction to Practicall Musicke,* than
by his performance or compositions, though eminent
for both.

If due allowance be made for the quaintness of the
dialogue and style of the times, and the work be considered as the first regular treatise on Music that was
printed in our language, the author will merit great
praise for the learning and instruction it contains. At
present, indeed, its utility is very much diminished by the
disuse of many things which cost him great pains to
explain; and new modulations since his time, which, to
render intelligible, require a more recent elementary
treatise. Yet though this work is redundant in some par-
ticulars and deficient in others; it is still curious and
justly allowed to have been excellently adapted to the
wants of the age in which it was written. However, its
late republication in the original form, 'totidem verbis',
whatever honour it may reflect on the memory of the
author, somewhat disgraces later times, which have not
superseded this by producing a better and more complete
book of general instructions in English, after the lapse of

A2   D.M.C.

so many years, and the perpetual cultivation and practise of the art in our country, both by native musicians and foreigners.

History of Music, 1776

EPITAPH

ON JOHN WYNAL, ORGANIST AT YORK MINSTER, *circa* 1573

Musician and logician both
John Wynal lieth here
Who made the organs erst to speak
As if, or as it were.

ROBERT BURTON (1576–1639)

Many and sundry are the means which philosophers and physicians have prescribed to exhilarate a sorrowful heart, to divert those fixed and intent cares and meditations, which in this malady so much offend; but in my judgement none so present, none so powerful, none so apposite as a cup of strong drink, mirth, music, and merry company. Ecclus. xl. 20. 'Wine and music rejoice the heart.' Rhasis, cont. 9. Tract 15. Altomarus, cap. 7, Aelianus Montaltus, c. 26, Ficinus, Bened. Victor. Faventinus are almost immoderate in the commendation of it; a most forcible medicine Jacchinus calls it; Jason Pratensis, 'a most admirable thing, and worthy of consideration, that can so mollify the mind, and stay those temptuous affections of it.' 'Musica est mentis medicina maestae', a roaring-meg against melancholy, to rear and revive the languishing soul; 'affecting not only the ears, but the very arteries, the vital and animal spirits, it erects the mind, and makes it nimble.' Lemnius, insti. cap. 44. This it will effect in the most dull, severe, and sorrowful souls, 'expel grief with mirth, and if there be any clouds, dust, or dregs of cares yet lurking in our thoughts, most powerfully it wipes them all away,' Salisb. polit. lib. cap. 6, and that which is more, it will perform all this in an instant: 'Cheer up the countenance, expel austerity, bring in hilarity (Girald Camb. cap. 12, Topog. Hiber) inform our manners, mitigate anger'; Atheneaus (Dipnosophist. lib. 14, cap. 10), calleth it an infinite treasure to such as are endowed with it: 'Dulcisonum reficit tristia corda melos,' Eobanus Hessus. Many other properties Cassiodorus epist. 4. reckons up of this our divine music, not only to expel the greatest griefs, but 'it doth extenuate fears and furies, appeaseth cruelty, abateth heaviness, and to such as are watchful it causeth quiet rest; it takes away spleen and hatred', be it instrumental, vocal, with strings, wind, etc. 'Quae a spiritu, sine manuum dexteritate gubernetur etc.'; it cures all irksomeness and heaviness of the soul. Labouring men that sing to their work, can tell as much, and so can soldiers when they go to fight, whom terror of death cannot so much affright, as the sound of trumpet, drum, fife, and such like music animates; 'metes enim mortis' as Censorinus informeth us, 'musica depellitur.' 'It makes a child quiet', the nurse's song, and many times the sound of a trumpet on a sudden, bells ringing, a carman's whistle, a boy singing some ballad tune early in the street, alters, revives, recreates a restless patient that cannot sleep in the night etc. In a word, it is so powerful a thing that it ravisheth the soul, 'regina sensuum', the queen of the senses, by sweet pleasure (which is a happy cure) and corporal tunes pacify our incorporeal soul, 'sine ore loquens, dominatum in animam exercet', and carries it beyond itself, helps, elevates, extends it. Scaliger, exercit. 302, gives a reason of these effects, 'because the spirits about the heart take in that trembling and dancing air into the body, are moved together and stirred up with it,' or else the mind, as some suppose harmonically composed, is roused up at the tunes of music. And, 'tis not only men that are so effected, but almost all other creatures. You know the tale of Hercules, Gallus, Orpheus, and Amphion, 'foelices animas' Ovid calls them, that could 'saxa movere sono testudinis, etc.', makes stocks and stones, as well as beasts and other animals, dance after their pipes; the dog and hare, wolf and lamb; 'vicinumque lupo proebuit agna latus; clamosus graculus, stridula cornix, et Jovis aquila,' as Philostratus describes it in his images, stood all gaping upon Orpheus; and 'trees pulled up by the roots came to hear him, Et comitem quercum pinus amica trahit.'

Arion made fishes follow him, which as common experience evinceth, are much affected with music. All singing birds are much pleased with it, especially night-ingales, if we believe Calcagninus; and bees amongst the rest, though they be flying away, when they hear any tingling sound, will tarry behind. 'Harts, hinds, dogs, bears, are exceedingly delighted with it.' Scal. exerc. 302. Elephants, Agrippa adds, lib. 2, cap. 24, and in Lydia, in the midst of a lake there be certain floating islands (if ye will believe it), that after music will dance.

But to leave all declamatory speeches in praise of divine music, I will confine myself to my proper subject: besides that excellent power it hath to expel many other diseases, it is a sovereign remedy against despair and melancholy, and will drive away the devil himself. Canus, a Rhodian fiddler, in Philostratus, when Apollonius was inquisitive to know what he could do with his pipe, told him, 'That he would make a melancholy man merry, and him that was merry much merrier than before, a lover more enamoured, a religious man more devout.' Ismenias the Theban, Chiron the centaur, is said to have cured this and many other diseases by music alone; as now they do those, saith Bodine that are troubled with St. Vitus' Bedlam Dance. Timotheus the musician compelled Alexander to skip up and down, and leave his dinner (like the tale of the Friar and the Boy) whom Austin de civ. Dei, Lib. 17, cap. 14, so much commends for it. Who hath not heard how David's harmony drove away the evil spirits from king Saul, 1 Sam. xvi, and Elisha when he was much troubled by importunate kings, called for a minstrel, 'and when he played, the hand of the Lord came upon him', 2 Kings iii? Censorinus de natali cap. 12, reports how Asclepiades the physician helped many frantic persons by this means, 'Phreneticorum mentes morbo turbatas'—Jason Pratensis, cap. de Mania, hath many more examples, how Clinias and Empedocles cured some desperately melancholy, and some mad, by this our music. Which because it hath such excellent virtues belike Homer brings in Phemius playing, and the Muses singing at the banquet of the Gods. Aristotle, Polit. L.8. c.5, Plato, de legibus, highly approve it, and so do all politicians. The Greeks, Romans, have graced music, and made it one of the liberal sciences, though it be now become mercenary. All civil Commonwealths allow it: Cneius Manlius (as Livius relates) anno ob urb. cond 567, brought first out of Asia to Rome singing wenches, players, jesters, and all kind of music to their feasts. Your princes, emperors, and persons of any quality, maintain it in their courts; no mirth without music. Sir Thomas More, in his absolute Utopian commonwealth, allows music as an appendix to every meal, and that throughout, to all sorts. Epictetus calls 'mensam mutam praesepe' a table without music a manger; for 'the concert of musicians at a banquet, is a carbuncle set in gold; and as the signet of an emerald well trimmed with gold, so in the melody of music in a pleasant banquet.' Ecclus xxxii 5, 6. Louis the Eleventh, when he invited Edward the Fourth to come to Paris, told him that as a principal part of his entertainment, he should hear sweet voices of children, Ionic and Lydian tunes, exquisite music, he should have a ——, and the Cardinal of Bourbon to be his confessor, which he used as a most plausible argument: as to a sensual man indeed it is. Lucian in his book 'de saltatione', is not ashamed to confess that he took infinite delight in singing, dancing, music, women's company, and such like pleasures: 'and if thou (saith he) didst but hear them play and dance, I know thou wouldst be so well pleased with the object, that thou wouldst dance for company thyself, without doubt thou wilt be taken with it.' So Scaliger ingenuously confesseth, exercit. 274. 'I am beyond all measure affected with music, I do most willingly behold them dance, I am mightily detained and allured with that grace and comeliness of fair women, I am well pleased to be idle amongst them.' And what young man is not? As it is acceptable and conducing to most, so especially to a melancholy man. Provided always, his disease proceed not originally from it, that he be not some light inamorato, some idle phantastic, who capers in conceit all day long, and thinks of nothing else, but how to make jigs, sonnets, madrigals, in commendation of his mistress. In such cases music is most pernicious, as a spur to a free horse will make him run himself blind or break his wind. 'Incitamentum enim amoris musica', for music enchants, as Menander holds, it will make such melancholy persons mad, and the sound of those jigs and hornpipes will not be removed out of the ears a week after. Plato for this reason forbids music and wine to all young men, because they are for the most part amorous, 'ne ignis addatur igni', lest one fire increase another. Many men are melancholy by hearing music, but it is a pleasing melancholy that it causeth; and therefore to such as are discontent, in woe, fear, sorrow, or dejected, it is a most present remedy. Otherwise, saith Plutarch, 'Musica magis dementat quam vinum': music makes some men mad as a tiger; like Astophos' horn in Ariosto; or Mercury's golden wand in Homer, that made some wake, others sleep, it hath divers effects: and Theophrastus right well prophesied, that diseases were either procured by music or mitigated.

The Anatomy of Melancholy,
Music a Remedy, Mem. 6, Sub. 3

ON DR. JOHN BULL (?1562–1628)

DR. CHARLES BURNEY

... possessed as he was of such extraordinary powers of execution on keyed-instruments, I have been frequently astonished in perusing Dr. Bull's lessons at the few new and pleasing passages which his hand suggested to his pen. It has been said, that the late Dr. Pepusch preferred Bull's compositions to those of Couperin and Scarlatti, not only for harmony and contrivance, but air and modulation: an assertion which rather proves that the Doctor's taste was bad, than Bull's music good. Though I should greatly admire the hand as well as patience, of any one capable of playing his compositions; yet, as Music, they would afford me no kind of pleasure: 'Ce font des notes', and 'rien que des notes'; there is nothing in them which excites rapture. They may be heard by a lover of Music with as little emotion as the clapper of a mill, or the rumbling of a post-chaise.

History of Music, 1776

VERSE ROUND THE FRAME OF THE
PICTURE IN THE MUSIC SCHOOL, OXFORD
The bull by force in field doth reigne,
But Bull by skill good will doth gayne.

ON JOHN DOWLAND (?1563–1626)

DR. CHARLES BURNEY

It has frequently happened that a great performer has been totally devoid of genius and cultivation necessary for a composer and on the contrary, there have been eminent composers whose abilities in performance have been very far from great. Close application to the business of a composer equally enfeebles the hand and the voice, by the mere action and a facility of committing to paper musical ideas, clothed in good harmony, be not early acquired, even supposing that genius is not wanting, the case seems hopeless, as I never remember the difficulties of composition thoroughly vanquished, except during youth.

History of Music, 1776

ON MONTEVERDE (1567–1643)

DR. CHARLES BURNEY

... it was not only by the use of these discords that he improved music, for by quitting ecclesiastical modulation in his secular productions, he determined the key of each movement, smoothed and phrased the melody, and made all his parts sing in a more natural and flowing manner than had been done by any of his predecessors. In the first set of Monteverde's madrigals the composition is not only correct, and simple, but so dry and fanciless, as to threaten no attempts at such new harmonies, and effects, as would bring about a revolution in the art. And it seems to have been by design, and in his dramatic experiments at the expression of words, that he ventured to violate ancient rules, and miligate (*sic*) against prejudice and pedantry: for neither his Church Music, nor the two first books of his madrigals, contain any licences that would offend or surprise orthodox ears, even in the fifteenth century. But in his fifth and last book of madrigals, almost every species of discord and modulation is hazarded, for the use of which the boldest composers of modern times have been often thought licentious.

History of Music, 1776

SAMUEL BUTLER

Formerly all discords were prepared, and Monteverde's innovation of taking the dominant seventh unprepared was held to be cataclysmic, but in modern music almost any conceivable discord may be taken unprepared. We have grown so used to this now that we think nothing of it, still, whenever it can be done without sacrificing something more important, I think even a dominant seventh is better prepared.

It is only this preparation of discords which is now less rigorously insisted on; their resolution—generally by the climbing down of the offending note—is as necessary as ever if the music is to flow on smoothly.

This holds good exactly in our daily life. If a discord has to be introduced it is better to prepare it as a concord, take it on a strong beat, and resolve it downwards on a weak one. The preparation being often difficult or impossible may be dispensed with, but the resolution is still 'de rigueur'.

Note Books

SIR HUBERT PARRY

It is noteworthy that the devices which arouse attention in Monteverde's work because of their being such marked departures from the traditions of the old choral music recur very often—the device of reiteration most frequently of all. But also there is a family likeness about his ways of taking vivid discords, his novel resolutions of suspensions, his extreme use of strongly accented appoggiaturas, anticipations, and pedal notes. Like his finest madrigals, they give the impression that he was not only ardent for dramatic expression, but an intellectualist of a high order. He hit upon a device which widened the scope of human expression,—just as a man of genius would hit upon some device in an undeveloped machine, and then incorporate it into his system and go on building more inventions on it. Yet, unlike so many superficial revolutionaries, he retained the sense of what had been discovered or invented by his predecessors. It becomes almost quaintly humorous in connection with the Church modes. The attitude of mind generated by them is most prominent in the madrigals, both in progressions and closes, the latter of which are sometimes very lame and ineffective in consequence. These influences, however, survive even into the works of his age, such as the 'Incoronazione de Poppea', and the effect is often felicitous, for the influence of the modes saved the world for a time from the reiterations of tonic and dominant which became so wearisome in the formal procedure of later times. True it is that Monteverde was unconsciously gravitating in that direction: but though the baneful influence of the theatre on the intrinsic quality of his work is obvious as time goes on, he did not yet adopt the cheap devices of the hack opera composer, but aimed, like Wagner later, at the continuity of melodic movement.

It is very important to have a clear and exact view of Monteverde's position in relation to orchestration, as more 'travellers' tales' have been told about that department of his work than about almost anything in music. The greater part of his stage works have come down to us in the depressingly uninteresting form of a voice part and a bass. The whole of the interest centres on the voice part; and very often that amounts to next to nothing. What the instruments did which accompanied the voices is a mere matter of guess-work. There are hardly any scored instrumental accompaniments to solos in the early part of his career except in the big solos in 'Orfeo' and in the 'Combattimento di Tancredi e Clorinda' of 1624. The one movement which seems to claim recognition as an experiment in orchestral effect is the famous Toccata at the beginning of 'Orfeo'. But in order to understand the claims made for it, it is essential to realise the special conditions under which the work was written.

There were no recognised and established orchestras in those days: and there can be little doubt that for the band in the performance of 'Orfeo' in 1607 Monteverde had to take whatever instruments were available in Mantua, just as Peri had to do in Florence some years earlier. Anyone in the town who had any reputation as a performer no doubt wanted to take part, and he collected a marvellous and ungainly combination of instruments. Among the performers there must have been some efficient professionals, some of whom probably played on at least two different instruments—though not at the same time. There was no question of balance and proportion. The sum total of sound would be wildly barbarous. The bowed stringed-instruments were twelve viols, three gambas, two double-basses, and two little violins. There were two harpsichords, two lutes, and two harps. The great mass of sound was provided by five trombones, two cornetti, one clarino, and three trumpets. There were two little flutes, and two instruments called 'organo di legno'. As far as can be made out he never uses them all at once: and some of the instruments have no parts provided for them, but only directions in the score where they are to play. The Toccata is scored for several brass instruments and string basses. It is remarkable as an undisguised attempt to solve the special problem of a preparatory summons to attention before the beginning of a stage piece. It indicates an extraordinary vivacity of mind in Monteverde; as if he had foreseen the behaviour of an audience as they collect in theatres and the bustle and irresponsible talk while they settle down; as if he said, 'I don't care a fig what they do. I'll let them know something is going to happen by making a barbarous noise which they can listen to or not—but at all events I will make it difficult for them to keep up their cackling.' The Toccata is a touch of genius in that respect; and is indeed one of the most quaintly barbarous pieces of music in existence. Trumpets, big and little, bray out harsh passages, some with conjunct diatonic motion, some in arpeggios, some with Monteverde's favourite repeated notes; while the lower instruments tug away persistently at the tonic and fifth above on the strong accents of the bar. It is much like a showman outside a booth asking the company to come in and sit down. The showman is often very amusing, and so is Monteverde. But to refer to it as a sort of anticipation or counterpart of the introduction of Wagner's 'Rheingold' is absurdly misleading. The only thing it has in common with that romantic passage is its being all on one chord. It has no special relevance to the drama which has to follow it, whereas the introduction to 'Rheingold' portrays the deeps of the Rhine; it is very short, and the introduction to 'Rheingold' is long. What is much more to the point is that it is a conspicuous illustration of the device which Monteverde found out of giving decisive character by making a movement almost all on one chord; which he employed also in his 'Combattimento' and in the 'Ritorno d' Ulisse', and passed on to his foremost pupil, Cavalli, who made use of it with much effect in the incantation scene in 'Medea'.

Apart from these barbarous effects, the Toccata does not afford any inference at all with regard to Monteverde's being the fountain-head of modern orchestration. The effects are of the same order produced by town bands (mainly of wind instruments) all over Europe long before Monteverde's time.

But neither do the other instrumental movements afford much that can be called instrumentation in the modern sense. There are many ritornellos and symphonies, which are no more than short passages of instrumental music which punctuate all through. There does not seem to be any idea of variety either of mass or colour; and there are hardly any traces of instrumental style. The musical material is almost without significance, and has little or no relevance to the context. It seems as though Monteverde regarded them merely as elements in the formal design, and purposely avoided making them significant in order not to distract the mind from the more essential vocal portions of the work. The sum total of impressions that the majority of these movements produce is portentious heaviness, crudity, and dullness. Monteverde was not inspired by such interstices in the dramas, and did not trouble himself to produce anything which had either intrinsic interest, relevance, or character. Consequently, with only rare exceptions—the most noteworthy being in the 'Combattimento'—there is nothing which suggests Monteverde's having laid the foundations of modern orchestration. The chief indications of his having any notions of colour effects are in the directions which allocate special groups of instruments to special characters. . . . The arrangement of having special groups of instruments for special scenes may have been partly dictated by the convenience of the performers. And there does seem to have been some vague idea of relevance of colour to situation; . . . But the procedure does not amount to much more than simple adaptation of crude resources such as any child might have attempted with a birthday party of mouth-organs and tooth-combs and banjos and kitchen furniture. . . .

Monteverde belonged to that strongly defined order of composers who are not so much impelled by the mere delight of music itself as by the opportunities it offers to interpret vividly emotions, moods, human feelings, dramatic situations, pathetic incidents, and exhilarating joys. They are the musicians who instinctively feel music's sphere in the scheme of things. They are never apt to give us tunes which are delightful in themselves: they do not supply us with inspiring examples of absolute music: but they delve into human life and feeling, and get their highest inspirations from their keen sympathy with their fellow creatures and their insight into them.

All Monteverde's conspicuous achievements are interpretative. Left to himself, with no human circumstance to inspire him, he merely made music against the grain. His sinfonias, and ritornellos and ricercars are devoid of significance and charm. He had hardly any instinct for dance movements. But he had a deep feeling for human situations; for the strong type of emotional states. He was also, to judge from his finest Madrigals, a man of keen intellect.

He found music in a state which hardly admitted of strong secular feeling; and his dramatic sense and intelligence sought out means to expand art in that direction, and to find the way to express dramatic essentials. And the result of his ardent efforts makes him one of the most significant figures in the story of music.

> *The Significance of Monteverde,* a paper read before the Royal Musical Association on Feb. 16th, 1916

THOMAS WEELKES (1575–1623)

My Lord, in the Coledge of Winchester, where I live, I have heard learned men say, that some Philosophers have mistaken the soule of man for an Harmonie: Let the president of the error be a priviledge for mine, I see not, if soules doe not partly consist of Musicke, how it should come to passe, that so noble a spirit as yours, so perfectly tuned to so perpetuall a Tenor of excellencies as it is, should descend to the notice of a qualitie lying single in so low a personage as my selfe. But in Musicke the Base part is no disgrace to the best eares attendauncie. I confesse my conscience is untoucht with any other arts, and I hope, my confessione is unsuspected, many of us Musitians thinke it is as muche praise to be some what more then Musitians, as it is for golde to bee some what more then golde, and, if Jack Cade were alive, yet some of us might live: unlesse we should think, as the Artisans, in the Universities in Poland and Germany think, that the Latin tongue comes by reflection. I hope your Lordship will pardonne this presumption of mine, the rather, because I know before Nobilitie I am to deal sincearely; and this small facultie of mine, because it is alone in mee, and without the assistance of other more confident sciences, is the more to bee favored, and the rather to bee received into your honors protection, so shall I observe with as humble and as true an heart, as hee, whose knowledge is as large as the worlds creation, and as earnestly pray for you, to the worlds Creatore.

Dedication, 5-*part Madrigals*, 1600

ON ORLANDO GIBBONS (1583–1625)

DART (Translation)

To Orlando Gibbons of Cambridge, born among the muses and music; organist of the Chapel Royal; emulating by the touch of his fingers, the harmony of the spheres; composer of many hyms which sound his praises no less than that of his Maker; a man of integrity whose manner of life and sweetness of temper v'yed with that of his art: being sent for to Dover to attend the nuptials of King Charles and Mary, he died of the small pox,[1] and was conveyed to the Heavenly choir on Whitsun Day, anno 1625. Elizabeth, his wife who bore him seven children, little able to survive such a loss, to her most deserving husband hath, with tears, erected this monument.

History and Antiquities of the Cathedral Church of Canterbury, 1726

ON MR. JNO. JENKINS (1592–1678)

HON. ROGER NORTH

In his fancys his points were for the most part elegant & wrought with no small Industry yet easy & familiar, But never insipid as had bin then lately ye musick chiefle in request. His early compositions, done in his full strength, and being likely to pass among his owne faculty, were his best, and parcells of them may yet be extant in some gentlemen collections, whereof the greatest part would bear ye test of ye present time, if a violent pre-

[1] Gibbons died of apoplexy.

judice did not propossess it, the greatest disadvantage of his works is, that most of his early pieces are 1st, and his latter consorts chiefle remain; And those were calculated for low hands litle better than scollars who were not composers of anything more masterly. & for ye same reason, they were moulded In ye way of Lessons rather than fancys. But in all that plaineness, adapted to ye true modes of conducting ye keys is to be observed a genuine air, according to ye true modes of conducting ye keys & changing, as might be owned. In consirt at this day, & If in the performance by a good moderne hand an agreeable spirit were infused, as ye manner is at present, and an ample Orchester to set it off, the most ordinary of his music would make a lively appearance.

But to doe the right in shewing what was most amiss in ye manner of Mr. Jenkins, It was wholly devoid of fire & fury, such as the Itallians musick affects, In their stabb & stoccatas, which defect is onely excusable upon ye humour of the times, those were pleased with ye sedate, which these will not bear, and for that matter, as to recall virtue, or goodness of the musick, I referre to what hath bin sayd. Another more considerable failing is the manner of movement, which he & his contemporarys used & others since. It was chiefly (as it were) going up & downe staires, and had less of the sault or itterations then ye Itallians have. In which respect it must be allowed the latter style is better as more conforme to mens ordinary behaviour. And it may be alledged also as a defect, that Jenkins did not dash upon Harsh notes, as ye Itallians doe, which makes their consorts more Saporite, then the musick was when the parts did but hunt one and other, from concord to concord, as to that, its allowed ye English rules of composition did not permit such freedoms but Jenkins used his discords allwais properly & with sincopation, according to law, yet In that he dared more & rather outwent then came short of his contemporarys. But to conclude Mr. Jenkins was a very gentile

& well bred gentleman, and was always, not onely wellcome, but greatly valued by ye familys wherever he had taight & converst.

The Musical Grammarian, circa 1728

ON HENRY LAWES (1595–1662)

JOHN MILTON

Harry, whose tuneful and well measur'd Song
  First taught our English Musick how to span
  Words with just note and accent, not to scan
  With Midas' Ears, committing short and long;
Thy worth and skill exempts thee from the throng,
  With praise enough for Envy to look wan;
  To after age thou shalt be writ the man,
  That with smooth aire couldst humor best our tongue.
Thou honour'st Verse, and Verse must send her wing
  To honour thee, the Priest of Phoebus Quire
  That tun'st their happiest lines in Hymn, or Story.
Dante shall give Fame leave to set thee higher
  Than his Casella, whom he woo'd to sing
  Met in the milder shades of Purgatory.

To Mr. H. Lawes, on his Aires

DR. CHARLES BURNEY

I have examined with care and candour all the works I can find of this composer, which are still very numerous and am obliged to own myself unable, by their excellence, to account for the great reputation he acquired, and the numerous panegyrics bestowed on him by the greatest poets and musicians of his time. His temper and conversation must certainly have endeared him to his acquaintances and rendered them partial to the productions, and the praise of such writers as Milton and Waller is durable fame.

History of Music, 1776

ON THOMAS KINGSTON, ORGANIST OF LINCOLN CATHEDRAL (1599–1616)

CHAPTER OF LINCOLN CATHEDRAL

He is verye often drunke and by means thereof he hathe by unorderlye playing on the organs putt the quire out of time and disordered them.

The Seventeenth Century

He who in the present time wants to make a profit out of his music betakes himself to England.

MATTHESON, *Neu-eröffnete Orchester* 1713

ON WILLIAM INGLOTT, ORGANIST
AT NORWICH CATHEDRAL 1608–1621

Here William Inglott, Organist, doth rest,
Whose art in Music this Cathedral blest;
He passed on Organ, Song, and Virginall.
He left this life at age of sixty-seven,
And now 'mongst Angels all sings first in Heaven.
His fame flies far, his Name shall never die,
See, Art and Age here crown his memorie.

ON DR. BENJAMIN ROGERS (1614–1698)

DR. CHARLES BURNEY

It is to be feared that instead of weeping, the wicked
lovers of modern music would now laugh, if they were to
hear the quaint and starched strains, and see on paper the
ruffs and roll-ups of honest Ben Rogers at the Opera
House or professional concert, Hanover Square. But,
alas, what is the secular music that thirty years have not
wrinkled, withered, and rendered superannuated!

History of Music, 1776

ON CHRISTOPHER GIBBONS (1615–1676)

ANTHONY À WOOD

His compositions for instruments whether in 2, 3, or 4
parts, have been highly valued and were, 30 years ago,
always first called for, and played as well in the public
music schools as in private chambers: and Dr. Wilson,
the professor, the greatest and most curious judge of
Music that ever was, usually wept when he heard them
well performed, as being wrapt up in an ecstasy; or, if you
will, melted down; while others smiled, or had their hands
and eyes lifted up; at the excellence of them.

MS. Memoirs

ON CAPTAIN COOKE (?1616–1672)

ANTHONY À WOOD

... was esteemed the best musician of his time to sing to the lute, till Pelham Humphrey, his scholar, came up, after which he died of grief.

MS. Memoirs

JOHN EVELYN (1620–1706)

March 4th, 1656. This night I was invited by Mr. Roger L'Estrange to hear the incomparable Lubrier on the violin. His variety on a few notes and plain ground, with that wonderful dexterity, was admirable. Though a young man, yet so perfect and skilful, that there was nothing, however cross and perplexed, brought to him by our artists, which he did not play off at sight with ravishing sweetness and improvements, to the astonishment of our best masters. In sum, he played on the single instrument a full concert, so as the rest flung down their instruments, acknowledging the victory. As to my own particular, I stand to this hour amazed that God should give so great perfection to so young a person. There were at that time as excellent in their profession as any were thought to be in Europe, Paul Wheeler, Mr. Mell, and others, till this prodigy appeared. I can no longer question the effects we read of in David's harp to charm evil spirits, or what is said some particular notes produced in the passions of Alexander, and that King of Denmark.

May 5th, 1659. ... next day, to see a new Opera, after the Italian way in recitative music and scenes, much inferior to the Italian composure and magnificence; but it was prodigious that in a time of such public consternation such a vanity should be kept up or permitted. I, being engaged with company, could not decently resist the going to see it, though my heart smote me for it.

Jan. 11*th*, 1662. I dined at Arundel House, where I heard excellent music performed by the ablest masters, both French and English, on theorbos, viols, organs, and voices, as an exercise against the coming of the Queen, purposely composed for her chapel.

June 9*th*, 1662. I heard the Queen's Portugal music, consisting of pipes, harps, and very ill voices.

Dec. 21*st*, 1662. Instead of the ancient, grave, and solemn wind music accompanying the organ, was introduced a concert of twenty-four violins between every pause; after the French fantastical light way, better suiting a tavern or playhouse than a church. This was the first time of change, and now we no more heard the cornet which gave life to the organ; that instrument quite left off in which the English were so skilful. I dined at Mr. Povey's, where I talked with Cromer, a great musician.

Oct. 5*th*, 1664. To our Society. There was brought a new-invented instrument of music, being a harpsichord with gut-strings, sounding like a concert of viols with an organ, made vocal by a wheel, and a zone of parchment that rubbed horizontally against the strings.

Nov. 14*th*, 1668. I heard Sir Edward Sutton play excellently on the Irish Harp; he performed genteely, but not approaching my worthy friend Mr. Clark, a gentleman of Northumberland, who makes it execute lute, viol, and all the harmony an instrument is capable of; pity it is that it is not more in use; but, indeed, to play well, takes up the whole man, as Mr. Clark has assured me, who, though a gentleman of quality and parts, was yet brought up to that instrument from five years old, as I remember he told me.

Jan. 5*th*, 1673. I saw an Italian opera in music, the first that hath been in England of this kind.

Nov. 19*th*, 1674. I heard that stupendous violin, Signor Nicholao (with other rare musicians), whom I never heard mortal man exceed on that instrument. He had a stroke so sweet, and made it speak like a concert of several instruments. He did wonders upon a note, and was an excellent composer. Here was also that rare lutenist, Dr. Wallgrave; but nothing approached the violin in Nicholao's hand. He played such ravishing things as astonished us all.

Dec. 2nd, 1674. At Mr. Slingsby's, Master of the Mint, my worthy friend, a great lover of musick. Heard Signor Francisco on the harpsichord, esteemed one of the most excellent masters in Europe on that instrument; then came Nicholao with his violin, and struck all mute, but Mrs. Knight, who sung incomparably, and doubtless has the greatest reach of any English woman; she had been lately roaming in Italy, and was much improved in that quality.

Nov. 20th, 1679. I dined with Mr. Slingsby, Master of the Mint, with my wife, invited to hear musick, which was exquisitely performed by four of the most renowned masters: Dr. Prue, a Frenchman, on the lute; Signor Bartholomeo, an Italian, on the harpsichord; Nicholao on the violin; but, above all, for its sweetness and novelty, the viol d'amore of five wire strings played on with a bow, being but an ordinary violin, played on lyre-way, by a German. There was also a flute douce, now in much request for accompanying the voice.

Sept. 23rd, 1680. Came to my house some German strangers and Signor Pietro, a famous musician who had been long in Sweden in Queen Christina's Court; he sung admirably to a guitar, and had a perfect good tenor and base, and had set to Italian composure many of Abraham Cowley's pieces which showed extremely well.

Jan. 27th, 1682. After supper, came in that famous treble, Mr. Abel newly returned from Italy; I never heard a more excellent voice; one would have sworn it had been a woman's, it was so high, and so well and skilfully managed, being accompanied by Signor Francesco on the harpsichord.

Feb. 7th, 1682. My daughter, Mary, began to learn

music of Signor Bartholomeo and dancing of Monsieur Isaac, reputed the best masters.

Jan. 27*th*, 1685. I dined at Lord Sunderland's, being invited to hear that celebrated voice of Mr. Pordage, newly come from Rome; his singing was after the Venetian recitative, as masterly as could be, and with an excellent voice both treble and bass; Dr. Walgrave accompanied it with his theorbo lute, on which he performed beyond imagination, and is doubtless one of the greatest masters in Europe on that charming instrument. Pordage is a priest, as Mr. Bernard Howard told me in private.

Jan. 28*th*, 1685. . . . after dinner the same Mr. Pordage entertained us with his voice, that excellent and stupendous artist, Signor John Baptist, playing to it on the harpsichord. My daughter Mary being with us, she also sung to the great satisfaction of both the masters, and a world of people of quality present.

She did so also at my Lord Rochester's the evening following, where we had the French boy so famed for his singing, and indeed he had a delicate voice, and had been well taught. I also heard Mrs. Packer (daughter to my old friend) sing before His Majesty and the Duke, privately, that stupendous bass, Gosling, accompanying her, but hers was so loud as took away much of the sweetness. Certainly never woman had a stronger or better ear, could she possibly have governed it. She would do rarely in a large church among the nuns.

Mar. 10*th*, 1685. She (Evelyn's daughter) had an excellent voice, to which she played a thorough-bass on the harpsichord, in both which she arrived to that perfection, that of the scholars of those two famous masters, Signors Pietro and Bartholomeo, she was esteemed the best; for the sweetness of her voice and management of it added such an agreeableness to her countenance, without any constraint or concern, that when she sung it, it was as charming to the eye as to the ear; this I rather note, because it was a universal remark, and for which so many noble and judicious persons in music desired to hear her, the last being at Lord Arundell's, of Wardour.

April 19th, 1687. I heard the famous singer, Cifaccio, esteemed the best in Europe. Indeed, his holding out and delicateness in extending and loosing a note with incomparable softness and sweetness was admirable; for the rest I found him a mere wanton, effeminate child, very coy, and proudly conceited, to my apprehension. He touched the harpsichord to his voice rarely well. This was before a select number of particular persons whom Mr. Pepys invited to his house; and this was obtained by particular favour and much difficulty, the Signor much disdaining to show his talent to any but princes.

May 30th, 1698. I dined at Mr. Pepys, where I heard the rare voice of Mr. Pule, who has lately come from Italy, reputed the most excellent singer we had ever had. He sung several compositions of the late Dr. Purcell.

Diary

THOMAS MACE (*circa* 1620–*circa* 1710)

Abundance of people of the best rank and quality being shut up in the city, namely, lords, knights, and gentlemen of the countries round about, besides the souldiers and citizens, who, all or most of them, came constantly every Sunday to hear public prayers and sermon, the number was so exceeding great, that the church was (as I may say) even cramming and squeezing full. Now here you must take notice that they had then a custom in that church (which I hear not of in any other Cathedral which was) that always before the sermon, the whole congregation sang a psalm, together with the quire and the organ; and you must also know, that there was then a most excellent-large-plump-lusty-full-speaking organ which cost (as I am credibly informed) a thousand pounds. This organ I say, (when the psalm was set before the sermon), being let out into all its fullness of stops, together with the quire, began the psalm. But when that vast-conchording-unity of the whole congregational-chorus, came (as I may say) thundering in, even so it made the very ground shake under us; (oh the unutterable ravishing soul's delight!) in the which I was so transported, and wrapt up into high contemplation, that there was no room left in my whole man, namely, body and spirit, for any thing below divine and heavenly raptures.

On the Psalm singing at York Cathedral (*sic*), during the Siege, from *Music's Monument*, 1676

Let the parish clerk be taught to pulse or strike the common psalm-tunes for a trifle—20s., 30s., or 40s., (a year). This will lead to business for the clerk for he will be so doated on by all the pretty ingenuous children and young men of the parish that they will beg a shilling from their parents for a lesson on how to pulse the psalm-tune, which they may learn in a week or a fortnight's time very well, and so in a short time the parish will swarm with organists, and no parent will grutch the money so given.

On the Value of paying Musicians, from *above*

JOHN PLAYFORD (1623–1686 or 7)

It is observed that of late years all Solemn and Grave Musicke is much laid aside, been esteemed too heavy and dull for the light heels and Brains of this Nimble and wanton Age; Nor is any Musick rendered acceptable, or esteemed by many, but what is presented by Forreigners; Not a City Dame though a Tap-Wife, but is ambitious to have her Daughters Taught by Monsieur La Novo Kickshawibus on the Gittar, which Instrument is but a new (old) one used in London in the time of Q. Mary.

Preface to *Musick's Delight on the Cithren*, 1666

SAMUEL PEPYS (1633–1703)

June 6th, 1661. . . . I went down by water to Greenwich and eat and drank and heard musique at the Globe, and saw the simple motion that is there of a woman with a rod in her hand keeping time to the musique while it plays, which is simple, methinks.

March 18th, 1662. This day my tryangle, which was put in time yesterday, did please me very well; Ashwell playing upon it pretty well.

Sept. 14th, 1662. To White Hall chapel, where sermon almost done, and I heard Capt. Cooke's new musique. This the first day of having viialls and other instruments to play a symphony between every verse of the anthems; but the musique more full than it was the last Sunday, and very fine it is. But yet I could discern Capt. Cooke to overdo his part at singing, which I never did before.

Nov. 22nd, 1663. The anthem was good after sermon, being the fifty-first psalme, made for five voices by one of Capt. Cooke's boys, a pretty boy. And they say there are four or five of them that can do as much. And here I first perceived that the King is a little musicall, and kept good time with his hand all along the anthem.

July 22nd, 1664. . . . and one slovenly and ugly fellow, Signor Pedro, who sings Italian songs to the theorbo most neatly; and they spent the whole evening in singing the best piece of musique counted of all hands in the world, made by Signor Charissimi, the famous master in Rome. Fine it was indeed, and too fine for me to judge of.

Sept. 9th, 1664. After dinner my wife and Mercer and Tom and I, sat till eleven at night, singing and fiddling, and a great joy it is to see me master of so much pleasure in my house. The girle plays pretty well upon the harpsichon, but only ordinary tunes. My Boy, a brave boy, sings finely . . . .

Dec. 6th, 1665. Here the best company for musique I ever was in, in my life, and I wish I could live and die in it, both for musique and the face of Mrs. Pierce, and my wife, and Knipp, who is pretty enough; but the most excellent, mad-humoured thing, and sings the noblest that ever I heard in my life, and Rolt, with her, some things together, most excellently. I spent the night in an ecstasy, almost . . . .

Dec. 9th, 1665. To Mr. Hill, and sang, among other things, my song of 'Beauty retire', which he likes, only except against two notes in the base, but likes the whole very well.

June 18th, 1666. To my Lord Ballassis, by invitation, and there dined with him, and his lady and daughter; and at dinner there played to us a young boy, lately come from France, where he had been learning a year or two on the viallin, and plays finely. But it was pretty to see how passionately my Lord's daughter loves musick.

July 30th, 1666. Thence home; and to sing with my wife and Mercer in the garden; and coming in, I find my wife plainly dissatisfied with me, that I can spend so much time with Mercer, teaching her to sing, and could never take the pains with her, which I acknowledge; but it is because that the girl do take musick mighty readily, and she do not, and musick is the thing of the world that I love most, and all the pleasure almost that I can now take. So to bed, in some little discontent, but no words from me.

Nov. 10th, 1666. Mr. Temple's wife, after dinner, fell to play on the harpsicon, till she so tired everybody, that I left the house without taking leave, and no creature left standing by her to hear her.

Dec. 26th, 1666. To the Duke's house, to a play. It was indifferently done, Goenell not singing, but a new wench, that sings naughtily.

Jan. 23rd, 1667. . . . I did see the organ, but I do not like it, it being but a bauble, with a virginal going to it: so I shall not meddle with it.

Jan. 24th, 1667. We continued dancing and singing; and among other things our Mercer unexpectedly did happen to sing an Italian song I know not, of which they two sung the other two parts—two that did almost ravish me, and made me in love with her more than ever with her singing.

Feb. 12*th*, 1667. With my Lord Brouncker to his house, there to hear some Italian musique; and here we met Tom Killigrew, Sir Robert Murray, and the Italian Signor Baptista, who hath proposed a play in Italian for the opera . . . and here he did sing one of the acts. He himself is the poet as well as the musician; which is very much, and did sing the whole from the words without any musique and played all along upon a harpsicon most admirably, and the composition most excellent. The words I did not understand, and so know not how they are fitted, but I believe very well, and all in the recitativo very fine. But I perceive there is a proper accent in every country's discourse, and that do reach in their setting of notes to words, which, therefore, cannot be natural to any body else but them; so that I am not so much smitten with it as, it may be, I should be, if I were acquainted with their accent. But the whole composition is certainly most excellent; . . . I confess I was mightily pleased with the musique. . . . My great wonder is, how this man do to keep in memory so perfectly the musique of the whole act, both for the voice and the instrument too. I confess I do admire it: but in the recitativo the sense much helps him, for there is but one proper way of discoursing and giving the accents.

Feb. 13*th*, 1667. Discoursed most about plays and the opera, where, among other vanities, Capt. Cooke had the arrogance to say that he was fain to direct Sir W. Davenant in the breaking of his verses into such and such lengths, according as would be fit for musick, and how he used to swear at Davenant and command him that way, when W. Davenant would be angry and find fault with this or that note—a vain coxcomb he is, though he sings and composes so well.

Feb. 16*th*, 1667. They sent two harpsicons before; and by and by after tuning them, they began; and, I confess, very good musique they made: that is, the composition exceeding good, but yet not at all more pleasing to me than what I have heard in English by Mrs. Knipp, Capt. Cooke and others. Their justness in keeping time by practice much before any that we have, unless it be a good band of practiced fiddlers.

March 1*st*, 1667. Being returned home, I find Greeting, the flageolet-master, come, and teaching my wife; and I do think my wife will take pleasure in it, and it will be easy for her and pleasant. So to the office, and then before dinner making my wife to sing. Poor wretch! Her eare is so bad that it made me angry, till the poor wretch cried to see me so vexed at her, that I think I shall not discourage her so much again, but will endeavour to make her understand sounds, and do her good that way; for she hath a great mind to learn, only to please me.

April 7*th*, 1667. To walk in the Park, and heard the Italian musick at the Queen's Chapel, where composition is fine, but yet the voice of eunuchs I do not like.

Oct. 1*st*, 1667. To White Hall; and there in the Boarded Room did hear the musick with which the King is presented this night by Monsieur Grebus, the master of his musick; both instrumental—I think twenty-four violins—and vocall; an English song upon Peace. But, God forgive me! I never was so little pleased with a concert of musick in my life. The manner of setting the words, and repeating out of order, and that with a number of voices, makes me sick, the whole design of vocall musick being lost by it.

Dec. 10*th*, 1667. Met Mr. Hingston, the organist—and, asking him many questions, I do find that he can no more give an intelligent answer to a man that is not a great master in his art, than another man. And this confirms me that it is only the want of an ingenious man that is master in musick, to bring musick to a certainty, and ease in composition.

Feb. 27th, 1668. With my wife to the King's House, to see 'The Virgin Martyr' . . . But that which did please me beyond any thing in the whole world was the wind musick when the angel comes down, which is so sweet that it ravished me, and, indeed, in a word did wrap up my soul so that it made me really sick, just as I have formerly been when in love with my wife; that neither then, nor all the evening going home, and at home, I was able to think of any thing, but remained all night transported, so as I could not believe that ever any musick hath that real command over the soul of a man as this did upon me; and makes me resolve to practise wind-musick, and to make my wife do the like.

May 7th, 1668. . . . and thither comes Bannister with a song of hers that he hath set in Sir Charles Sedley's play for her, which is, I think, but only meanly set; but this he did, before us, teach her, and, it being but a slight, silly short ayre, she learnt it presently. But I did get him to prick me down the notes of the Echo, in 'The Tempest', which did please me mightily.

April 10th, 1668. So to Duck Lane, and there kissed bookseller's wife, and bought Legend. So home, coach. Sailor. Mrs. Hannam dead. News of peace. Conning my gamut.

May 18th, 1668. And which made it the worse was, that there never was worse musick played—that is, worse composed, which made me and Captain Rolt, who happened to sit near me, mad.

Diary

ON PELHAM HUMPHREY (1647–1674)

SAMUEL PEPYS

Nov. 15th, 1667. Home, there find, as I expected, Mr. Caesar and little Pelham Humphrey, lately returned from France, and is an absolute Monsieur, as full of form and confidence, and vanity, and disparages everything, and everybody's skill but his own. But to hear how he laughs at all the King's musick here, at Blagrove and others, that they cannot keep time nor tune, nor understand anything; and that Grebus, the Frenchman, the King's master of the musick, how he understands nothing, nor can play on any instrument, and so cannot compose: and that he will give him a lift out of his place; and that he and the King are mighty great.

Nov. 16th, 1667. To White Hall, where there is to be a performance of Pelham's before the King. The company not come .... There got into the theatre-room: and there heard both the vocall and instrumentall musick; where the little fellow stood keeping time; but for my part, I see no great matter, but quite the contrary in both sorts of musick.

ON DR. JOHN BLOW (1648–1704)

EPITAPH

His own musical compositions (especially his Church Music) are a far nobler monument to his memory than any other that can be raised for him.

DR. CHARLES BURNEY

I am as sorry to see, as to say, how confused and inaccurate a harmonist he was, but it is necessary to speak of an artist so celebrated and honoured by his contemporaries, to dissemble his faults would surpass candour and incur the censure of ignorance and partiality; for it is as much the duty of an historian to blame as to praise, when justice and integrity require it. Indeed, upon whatsoever subject a man writes, he should aspire at nothing so much as speaking the truth, if he wishes for the approbation of his conscience which is not only the most comfortable of all praise, but luckily the most within his own power.

There are strokes of pathetic and subjects of fugue in Blow's works that are admirable; yet I have examined no one of them that appears to be wholly unexceptionable, and free from crudities in the counterpoint. Of the two-part anthem with choruses 'Lord, how are they increased' the first movement is very plaintive and expressive but there are licences in the Harmony which look and sound quite barbarous. Indeed these crudities are so numerous as to throw a doubt on his learning as well as genius. Whether they are notes of passion, effusions of an unruly spirit, or of ignorance, and affectation, I will not venture to determine; but to my ears, they have the full effect of jargon and want of principles.

It does not appear that Purcell whom he did himself the honour to call his scholar or Croft or Clarke, his pupils, ever threw notes about at random in this manner or insulted the ear with lawless discords which no concords can render tolerable.

In an anthem 'Turn then unto me, O Lord', printed by Henry Playford in the second collection of 'Divine Harmony' there are so many wanton violations of rule, particularly in the last chorus, that it would be endless to point them out; but they seem such as no rule, authority, or effect can justify: 7ths resolve on the 8th ascending and descending 2nds treated with as little ceremony as 3rds. Indeed I never saw so slovenly a score in print; and it may in general be said of his faults in counterpoint, that there are unaccountable millions of them to be found in his works.

He has been celebrated by Dr. Boyce for his 'success in cultivating an uncommon talent for modulation', but how so excellent a judge of correct and pure harmony could tolerate his licence or reconcile them to his monumental character, and the additional praise he has himself bestowed upon him, is as unaccountable as anything in Blow's compositions, considering that knowledge and known probity of the late worthy editor of our Church Music.

History of Music, 1776

SIR JOHN HAWKINS

... in the songs for two, three, and four voices, the harmony is such as it became so great a master to write; but in the article of expression, in melody, and in all the graces and elegancies of this species of vocal composition, it is evidently defective.

A General History of the Science and Practice of Music, 1776

EDWARD FITZGERALD

... June is recompensing us for all, and Dr. Blow may be said to be leading the great Garden Band in full Chorus.

Letter to F. Tennyson, June 12th, 1845

ON JOHN BERKENSHAW (?–?)

JOHN EVELYN

Aug. 3rd, 1664. To London; a concert of excellent musicians, especially one Mr. Berkenshaw, that rare artist who invented a mathematical way of composure very extraordinary, true as to the exact rules of art, but without harmony.

Diary

SAMUEL PEPYS

Feb. 24th, 1662. Long with Mr. Berkenshaw in the morning at my musique practice, finishing my song of 'Gaze not on swans' in two parts, which pleases me well, and I did give him £5 for this month or five weeks that he hath taught me, which is a great deal of money, and troubled me to part with it.

Feb. 27th, 1662. Come Mr. Berkenshaw and in our discourse we fell to angry words, so that in a pet he flung out of my chamber, and I never stopped him, being intended to put him off to-day, whether this had happened or not, because I think I have all the rules that he hath to give.

Diary

DR. CHARLES BURNEY

The translator, John Birkenshaw, seems to have been a kind of musical adventurer with sufficient literature and science to have imposed on the fellows of the Royal Society, by a long and splendid advertisement, to which admission was given in the Philosophical Transactions, for the year 1672, page 5153. In this advertisement is given the plan of a treatise on Music, which seems never to have been published. It is drawn up with a scientific air, but promises too much; not only what this author never performed, but what never has nor ever will be performed by any other. As an apology for so peremptory an assertion, the musical reader is desired to pause and consider the following proposition, which constitutes the fifth article of his advertisement.

'An easy way is by this author inserted for making airy tunes of all sorts by a certain rule, which most men think impossible to be done, and the composing of two, three, four, five, six, and seven parts, which by the learner may be done in a few months, viz.: in two months he may exquisitely and with all the elegancies of Music, compose two parts; in three months three parts; and so forward, as he affirms many persons of honour and worth have often experienced, which otherwise cannot be done in many years.'

History of Music, 1776

ON HENRY PURCELL (1656 or 9–1695)

JOHN DRYDEN

What has been wanting on my part has been abundantly supplied by the Excellent Composition of Mr.

Purcell; in whose person we have at length found an Englishman equal with the best abroad. At least my Opinion of him has been such, since his happy and judicious Performances in the late Opera, and the Experiences I have had of him, in the setting of my three Songs for this Amphitryon; To all which, and particularly to the Composition of the Pastoral Dialogue, this numerous Quire of Fair Ladies gave so just an Applause on the Third Day.

Dedication to *Amphitryon*, 1690

There is nothing better, than what I intended, than the Musick; which has arrived at a greater perfection in England, than ever formerly; especially passing through the artful hands of Mr. Purcell, who has composed it with so great a genius, that he has nothing to fear but an ignorant, ill-judging audience. But the numbers of poetry and vocal musick are sometimes so contrary, that in many places I have been obliged to cramp my Verses, and make them rugged to the Reader, that they may be harmonious to the Hearer; of which I have no reason to repent me, because these sorts of Entertainments are principally designed for the ear and the eye; and therefore, in reason, my art on this occasion ought to be subservient to his.

Dedication to *King Arthur*, 1691

EPITAPH

Here lyes Henry Purcell Esqre, who left this Lyfe and is gone to that Blessed Place where only his Harmony can be exceeded.

HON. ROGER NORTH

Orfeus Britanicus, Mr. H. Purcell, who unhappily began to show his great skill before the reform of musick al Italiano, and while he was warm in the pursuit of it, Dyed, but a greater musical genius England never had.

Musical Grammarian, circa 1728

. . . during a short life, and in an age almost barbarous for every species of music but that of the Church, manifested more original genius than any musician under similar circumstances, that my enquiries into the history of the art have yet discovered in any part of Europe . . .

. . . perhaps he had a few lessons in composition from Dr. Blow, which were sufficient to cancel all the instructions he had received from other masters, and to occasion the boast inscribed on the tomb-stone of Blow, that he had been 'Master to the famous Mr. Henry Purcell'.

But there is nothing more common than this petit-larceny among musicians; if the first master has drudged eight or ten years with a pupil of genius, and it is thought necessary, in compliance with fashion or caprice that he should receive a few lessons from a second, he instantly arrogates to himself the whole honour of the talent and cultivation of his new scholar, and the first and chief instructor is left to sing 'sic vos non nobis'. . . .

The complete service of Purcell, in B flat, printed by Boyce, is a most agreeable and excellent piece of counter-point, of which the modulation frequently stimulates attention by unexpected transitions, yet of so sober a kind as never to give the ear the least uneasiness . . . and then the crudities of the sharp 3rd, 4th, and 5th, as have been elsewhere censured, occur; which, I hope, in spite of my reverence for Purcell, the organists of our cathedrals scruple not to change for better harmony. These two or three combinations, like some words which his likeness Shakespeare tried unsuccessfully to render current, have been rejected by posterity; and it is in vain to attempt at forcing them upon the public by the mere weight of authority. The ear will patiently bear very rough usage from an artist who in general makes it such ample amends; however, there are limits beyond which it is unsafe to exercise cruelty of all kinds, and the auricular sense will be deadened, disgusted, or rendered indifferent to Music's powers, by too harsh treatment. . . .

Exclusive admirers of modern symmetry and elegance may call Purcell's taste barbarous; yet in spite of superior cultivation and refinement, in spite of all the vicissitudes of fashion, through all his rudeness and barbarism, original genius, feeling, and passion are, and ever will be, discoverable in his works, by candid and competent judges of the art.

History of Music, 1776

SIR JOHN HAWKINS

Whatever encomiums may have been bestowed elsewhere . . . it is certain that we owe to Purcell the introduction amongst us of what we call the fine air, in contradistinction to that narrow, contracted melody which appears in the compositions of his predecessors.

A General History of the Science and Practice of Music, 1776

SIR HUBERT PARRY

Purcell's work covers more ground than that of any other composer of the century. He attempted every branch of art then known, and even developed some which can hardly be said to have been known till he mastered them; and there was no department in which he did not excel. He easily learned the secrets of the composers who preceded him, and swept the methods of all different branches into his net. Though in some respects he seems to have more natural kinship with Monteverde than with any other composer, he was equally master of the instrumental style of the French Opera, the style of the Italian sonata-writers, and the methods of dealing with a chorus which had been Carissimi's peculiar glory. Probably no composer except Schubert has ever had a readier fund of melody; and it always rings true and characteristic of the country to which he belonged. And inasmuch as he possessed also a great power of expression of a serious and dramatic order—as illustrated for instance in the scene of the Witch of Endor, and in Bess of Bedlam —it may be confessed that his outfit was among the most comprehensive ever possessed by a composer. But the tragic fact cannot be ignored, that the essentially English attitude towards art which Purcell represented in his highest achievements for church, concert room, or theatre, led to no ulterior development. Handel possibly profited by the example of his admirable and vigorous treatment of histrionic chorus-writing; but no one followed up the possibilities of his superb conception of scenes for solo voices. The most brilliant moment in the history of seventeenth-century music thus remained outside the general evolution of European art. The style was too individual and too compromising to appeal to foreigners, and the advance which, mainly owing to Purcell's genius, had seemed phenomenal, came to a sudden standstill at his death. At once virile and intense, marked by not a few points of doubtful taste, the English music of the last quarter of the seventeenth century remains a supremely interesting but isolated monument of unfulfilled promise.

The Music of the Seventeenth Century,
Oxford History of Music, Vol. III, 1902

GUSTAV HOLST

It is surely unnecessary nowadays to dwell on Purcell's gift of melody. According to some it is excelled only by Mozart's. Others hold that Purcell's best melodies—and how numerous they are!—are inferior to none. In addition to his gift of melody there are his sense of harmony, his feeling for orchestral colour, his humour, his intensity, his lyrical power. We can witness their steady growth to perfection as we compare Purcell's earlier with his later works. Yet all these details of composition were subordinate to his amazing power of dramatic characterisation.

This power has been possessed by very few opera

composers. Indeed, many do not seem to have been aware of the necessity of cultivating it. They have thought it more important to study the idiosyncracies of the particular opera singers engaged for a production than to consider the dramatic foundation on which to build the music. Musical characterisation is usually looked upon as a modern factor in opera. One instinctively thinks of Wagner. Both Purcell and Wagner used all their gifts of melody and harmony, all their mastery of orchestral colour, to give life to their characters and situations. But while Wagner painted huge scenes, each consistent in itself and at the same time part of a vaster whole, Purcell was content to paint little cabinet pictures.

But in one way Purcell is a finer stage composer than Wagner: his music is full of movement—of dance. His is the easiest music in all the world to act. Only those can realise fully the truth of this who have experienced the joy of moving to Purcell's music, whether in the ballroom or on the stage or in the garden; but especially in the garden.

At the end of his life Purcell was master of every branch of musical technique. In all essentials of opera writing, save that of dramatic concentration, he had left 'Dido' far behind. But 'Dido' still remains his one opera.

If he has never been sufficiently praised for 'Dido', neither has he been blamed sufficiently for this artistic crime. Any producer of practical ability and imagination will find it easy to make a success of 'Dido'. 'The Fairy Queen', 'King Arthur', and 'Dioclesian' offer almost insuperable difficulties. They are too dramatic for the concert platform, too incoherent for the stage. Producers must be prepared to cut, to alter the disposition of some numbers, to make discreet changes in the words of others, and, above all, to toil and struggle for a scheme that will inform the work with a semblance of dramatic unity.

That success is possible the Cambridge production of 'The Fairy Queen' in 1920 proved beyond reasonable doubt. It also proved—and Purcell's countrymen were sadly in need of the proof—that England has produced at least one great dramatic composer.

The Heritage of Music, Vol. I, 1927

ALEXANDER BRENT SMITH

In spite of patchiness, in spite of inequalities, Purcell's individual numbers, his rhapsodic solos, his unaccompanied anthems, and of course 'Dido', will stand for all time, and only in the greatest moments of subsequent composers shall we find passages worthy to stand beside them. To have written one or two works which have no rivals except in the greatest works of their class is in itself a passport to Parnassus. If we measure Purcell by the quantity of flawless works, then indeed he must occupy a very lowly position, but if we measure him by the quality of the few acknowledged masterpieces then we may look for him high upon those sacred slopes where we shall most certainly find him; and Schubert, Gluck, and Bach are of his company.

Music and Letters, April, 1937

STEPHEN JEFFRIES (1662–1712)

Organist at Gloucester Cathedral

ON HEARING AN AMATEUR SINGER (WHOM HE DID NOT WISH TO EMPLOY) MAKE A MISTAKE IN AN ANTHEM.

'He can't sing it.'

Vocal criticism—told by Sir John Hawkins in his *General History of the Science and Practice of Music*, 1776

ON STEPHEN JEFFRIES

Mr. Subdean pronounced against Mr. Stephen Jeffries, Organist of this Church, his second monition to depart this Church, for that he, the said Stephen Jeffries, did upon Thursday last in the morning (being Thanksgiving day) immediately after the sermon ended and the blessing given, play over upon the organ a common ballad in the hearing of 1500 or 2000 people, to the great scandal of religion, prophanation of the Church, and grievous offence of all good Christians. And further, because though Dr. Gregory (the Senior Prebendary of this Church) did immediately express his great detestation of the same to Mr. Deighton, the Chaunter of this Church, and Mr. John Tyler, the senior singingman of this Church, informing them of the unspeakable scandal that universally was taken at it, and that they immediately acquainted the said Stephen Jeffries therewith, yet he, the said Stephen Jeffries, in direct despite to religion and affront to the said Dr. Gregory, did after evening prayer, as soon as the last Amen was ended, in the presence and hearing of all the congregation, fall upon the same strain, and on the organ played over the same common ballad again, insomuch that the young gentlewomen invited one another to dance, the strangers cryed it were better that the organs were pulled down than they should be so used, and all sorts declared that the Dean and Chapter could never remove the scandal if they did not immediately turn away so insolent and profane a person out of the Church.

Chapter Minute Book, Gloucester
Cathedral, Feb. 8th, 1688

ON PRE-RESTORATION
CHURCH COMPOSERS

THOMAS TUDWAY (*circa* 1650–1730)

The standard of Church music begun by Mr. Tallis, Mr. Byrde, and others was continued for some years after the Restoration and all composers conformed themselves to the pattern which was set them.

His Majesty, who was a brisk and airy prince, coming

to the crown in the flower and vigour of his age, was soon, if I may say so, tired with the grave and solemn way which had been established by Tallis, Byrde, and others, ordered the composers of his chapel to add Symphonies etc. with instruments to their anthems; and thereupon established a select number of his private music to play the symphony and ritornelles which he had appointed. . . .

The old masters of music, Dr. Child, Dr. Gibbons, Mr. Low, etc., organists to His Majesty, hardly knew how to comport themselves with these new-fangled ways, but proceeded in their compositions according to the old style, and therefore there are only some services and full anthems to be found.

Dedication to second volume
MS. Collection of English Church Music

ON ASSESSING MUSIC

HON. ROGER NORTH (1653–1734)

. . . as to ye point of Better or wors Intrinsically reason may determine, but humour must governe & pronounce, for the states of Humanity are Infinitely various, and admitt of all degrees of good & evill, Important or frivolous, sane or distracted. And it must be granted that musick which excores the best, most Important & sane thinking and acting is in true Judgement the best musick, and this will fall upon the ecclesiasticall style, which hath already ye suffrage of most skilfull musicians. But it is very possible that the thoughts of some folks may run upon a dance, ye hurry of football play, ye madfolks at bedlam or mortall Battells at Bear Garden, all which Bizzarie ye masters of musick will undertake to represent, and many persons that doe not well distinguish between real good & evill, but are hurried away by caprice, as in a whirlewind, think such musick ye best; & despise those who are not of ye same opinion and (as ye rabble) crye, it is brave sport. But that is not ye standard, and as to these in naming vivaldi (tho he hath his fellows) I have instanced enough; so I conclude, setting aside ye singular humor of men & times, that musick which agrees most with ye best actions of civilised harmanity is ye best musick. And how much of it will fall to ye share of former times and of these (for better or wors will fall on both) must be left to the candid & skilfull (yet can judge as well as hear) to pronounce.

Musical Grammarian, circa 1728

ON MUDD, ORGANIST OF LINCOLN CATHEDRAL, (1662–1663)

PRECENTOR OF LINCOLN CATHEDRAL TO THE DEAN

I wish you would be pleased to send us downe an able and more civill organist.

We dare trust him no more with our organ, but request you (if you can) to help us to another; and with what speed be.

ON 'THE BEGGAR'S OPERA'

DEAN SWIFT (1667–1745)

This comedy likewise exposes, with great justice, that unnatural taste for Italian musick among us, which is wholly unsuitable to our northern climate, and the genius of the people, whereby we are over-run with Italian effeminacy, and Italian nonsense. An old gentleman said to me, that many years ago, when the practice of unnatural vice grew frequent in London, and many were prosecuted for it, he was sure it would be the forerunner of Italian operas and singers; and then we should want nothing but stabbing, or poisoning, to make us perfect Italians.

The Intelligencer, No. 3

COLLEY CIBBER (1671–1757)

The inclination of our people of quality for foreign operas, had now reached the ears of Italy, and the credit of their taste had drawn over from thence, without any more particular invitation, one of their capital singers, the famous Signior Cavaliero Nicolini: from whose arrival, and the impatience of the town to hear him, it was concluded that operas, being now so completely provided, could not fail of success; and that by making Swiney sole director of them, the profits must be an ample compensation for his resignation of the actors. This matter being thus adjusted, by Swiney's acceptance of the opera only to be performed at the Hay-Market House; the actors were all ordered to return to Drury-Lane, there to remain (under the patentees) Her Majesty's only company of comedians.

Plays, and operas, being thus established, upon separate interests, they were now left to make the best of their way into favour by different merits. Although the opera is not a plant of our native growth, nor what our plainer appetites are fond of, and is of so delicate a nature, that without excessive charge it cannot live long among us; especially while the nicest connoisseurs in musick fall into such various heresies in taste, every sect pretending to be the true one; yet, as it is called a theatrical entertainment, and by its alliance, or neutrality has more or less affected our domestick theatre, a short view of its progress may be allowed a place in our history.

After this new regulation, the first opera that appeared was 'Pyrrhus'. Subscriptions at that time were not extended, as of late, to the whole season, but were limited to the first six days only of a new opera. The chief performers, in this, were Nicolini, Valentini, and Mrs. Tofts; and for the inferior parts, the best that were then to be found. Whatever praises may have been given to the most famous voices that have been heard since Nicolini;

upon the whole, I cannot but come into the opinion that still prevails among several persons of condition, who are able to give a reason for their liking, that no singer, since his time, has so justly and gracefully acquitted himself, in whatever character he appeared, as Nicolini. At most, the difference between him and the greatest favourite of the ladies, Farinelli, amounted but to this, that he might sometimes more exquisitely surprise us, but Nicolini (by pleasing the eye as well as the ear) filled us with a more various and rational delight. Whether in this excellence he has since had any competitor, perhaps will be better judged by what the critical censor of Great Britain says of him in his 115th Tatler, viz:

'Nicolini sets off the character he bears in an opera by his action, as much as he does the words of it by his voice; every limb and finger contributes to the part he acts, in so much that a deaf man might go along with him in the sense of it. There is scarce a beautiful posture, in an old statue, which he does not plant himself in, as the different circumstances of the story give occasion for it.—He performs the most ordinary action in a manner suitable to the greatness of his character, and shews the prince even in the giving of a letter or despatching a message, etc.'

His voice at this first time of being among us (for he made us a second visit when it was impaired) had all that strong, clear sweetness of tone, so lately admired in Senesino. A blind man could scarce have distinguished them; but in volibility of throat, the former had much the superiority. This so excellent performer's agreement was eight hundred guineas for the year, which is but an eighth part more than half the sum that has since been given to several that could never totally surpass him; the consequence of which is, that the losses by the operas, for several seasons, to the end of the year 1738, have been so great, that those gentlemen of quality who last undertook the direction of them, found it ridiculous any longer to entertain the publick, at so extravagant an expense, while no one particular person thought himself obliged by it.

Mrs. Tofts, who took her first grounds of musick here in her own country, before the Italian taste had so highly prevailed, was then not an adept in it; yet whatever defect the fashionable skilful might find in her manner, she had in the general sense of her spectators, charms that few of the most learned singers ever arrived at. The beauty of her fine proportioned figure, an exquisitely sweet, silver tone of her voice, with that peculiar rapid swiftness of her throat, were perfections not to be imitated by art or labour. Valentini I have already mentioned, therefore need only say farther of him, that though he was every way inferior to Nicolini, yet as he had the advantage of giving us our first impression of a good opera singer, he had still his admirers, and was of great service in being so skilful a second to his superior.

Three such excellent performers, in the same kind of entertainment at once, England till this time had never seen. Without any further comparison, then, with the much dearer bought who have succeeded them; their novelty, at least, was a charm that drew vast audiences of the fine world after them. Swiney, their sole director, was prosperous, and in one winter a gainer by them of a moderate younger brother's fortune. But as musick by so profuse a dispensation of her beauties, could not always supply our dainty appetites with equal variety, nor for ever please us with the same objects; the opera, after one luxurious season, like the fine wife of a rolling husband, began to lose its charms, and every day discovered to our satiety, imperfections which our former fondness had been blind to.

On Opera, *An Apology for his Life*, 1740

JOSEPH ADDISON (1672–1719)

Spectatum admissi risum teneatis?—HOR.

An Opera may be allowed to be extravagantly lavish in its Decorations, as its only Design is to gratify the Senses and keep up an indolent Attention in the Audience. Common Sense however requires that there should be nothing in the Scenes and Machines which may appear Childish and Absurd. How would the Wits of King Charles's Time have laughed to see Nicolini exposed to a Tempest in Robes of Ermin, and sailing in an open Boat upon a Sea of Paste-Board? What a Field of Raillery would they have been let into had they been entertain'd with painted Dragons spitting Wild-fire, enchanted Chariots drawn up by Flanders Mares, and real Cascades in artificial Land-skips? A little skill in Criticism would inform us, that Shadows and Realities ought not to be mix'd together in the same Piece; and that Scenes, which are designed as the Representations of Nature, should be filled with Resemblances, and not with the Things themselves. If one would represent a wide Champian Country filled with Herds and Flocks, it would be ridiculous to draw the Country only upon the Scenes, and to crowd several Parts of the Stage with Sheep and Oxen. This is joining together Inconsistencies, and making the Decoration partly Real and partly Imaginary. I would recommend what I have said to the Directors, as well as to the Admirers, of our Modern Opera.

As I was walking in the Streets about a Fortnight ago, I saw an ordinary Fellow carrying a Cage full of little Birds upon his Shoulder; and as I was wondering with my self what Use he would put them to, he was met very luckily by an Acquaintance, who had the same Curiosity. Upon his asking him what he had upon his Shoulder, he told him, that he had been buying Sparrows for the Opera. Sparrows for the Opera, says his Friend, licking his lips, what, are they to be roasted? No, no, says the other, they are to enter towards the end of the first Act and to fly about the Stage.

This strange Dialogue awakened my Curiosity so far, that I immediately bought the Opera, by which means I perceived that the Sparrows were to act the part of Singing Birds in a delightful Grove; though upon a nearer Enquiry I found the Sparrows put the same Trick upon the Audience that Sir Martin Mar-all practised upon his Mistress; for, though they flew in Sight, the Musick proceeded from a Consort of Flagellets and Bird-calls which was planted behind the Scenes. At the same time I made this Discovery, I found by the Discourse of the Actors, that there were great Designs on foot for the Improvement of the Opera; that it had been proposed to break down a part of the Wall, and to surprize the Audience with a Party of an hundred Horse, and that there was actually a Project of bringing the New-River into the House, to be employed in Jetteaus and Water-works. This Project, as I have since heard, is postponed till the Summer-Season; when it is thought the Coolness that proceeds from Fountains and Cascades will be more acceptable to People of Quality. In the mean time, to find out a more agreeable Entertainment for the Winter-Season, the Opera of 'Rinaldo' is filled with Thunder and Lightning, Illuminations and Fire-works, which the Audience may look upon without catching Cold, and indeed without much Danger of being burnt; for there are several Engines filled with Water, and ready to play at a Minute's warning, in case any such Accident should happen. However, as I have a very great Friendship for the Owner of this Theater, I hope that he has been wise enough to insure his House before he would let this Opera be acted in it. . . .

But to return to the Sparrows; there have been so many Flights of them let loose in this Opera, that it is feared the House will never get rid of them; and that in other Plays they may make their Entrance in very wrong and improper Scenes, so as to be seen flying in a Lady's Bed-Chamber, or pearching upon a King's Throne; besides the Inconveniences which the Heads of the Audience may sometimes suffer from them. I am credibly informed, that there was once a Design of casting into an Opera the Story of Whittington and his Cat, and that in order to it there had been got together a great Quantity of Mice; but Mr. Rich, the Proprietor of the Play-House, very prudently considered that it would be impossible for the Cat to kill them all, and that consequently the Princes of his Stage might be as much infested with Mice, as the Prince of the Island was before the Cat's Arrival upon it; for which Reason he would not permit it to be Acted in his House. And indeed I cannot blame him; for as he said very well upon that Occasion, I do not hear that any of the Performers in our Opera pretend to equal the famous Pied Piper, who made all the Mice of a great Town in Germany follow his Musick, and by that means cleared the Place of those little Noxious Animals.

Before I dismiss this Paper, I must inform my Reader, that I hear there is a Treaty on foot with London and Wise (who will be appointed Gardeners of the Play-House) to furnish the Opera of Rinaldo and Armida with an Orange-Grove; and that the next time it is acted, the Singing Birds will be personated by Tom-Tits; the Undertakers being resolved to spare neither Pains nor Mony, for the Gratification of the Audience.

Spectator, March 6th, 1711

Equitis quoque jam migravit ab aure voluptas
Omnis ad incertos oculos et gaudia vana.—HOR.

It is my Design in this Paper to deliver down to Posterity a faithful Account of the Italian Opera, and of the gradual Progress which it has made upon the English Stage: for there is no question but our great Grandchildren will be very curious to know the Reason why their Forefathers used to sit together like an Audience of Foreigners in their own Country, and to hear whole Plays acted before them in a Tongue which they did not understand.

'Arsinoe' was the first Opera that gave us a Taste of Italian Musick. The great Success this Opera met with produced some Attempts of forming Pieces upon Italian Plans, which should give a more natural and reasonable Entertainment than what can be met with in the elaborate Trifles of that Nation. This alarmed the Poetasters and Fidlers of the Town, who were used to deal in a more ordinary kind of Ware; and therefore laid down an established Rule, which is received as such to this Day, 'That nothing is capable of being well set to Musick that is not Nonsense.'

This Maxim was no sooner received, but we immediately fell to translating the Italian Operas; and as there was no great Danger of hurting the Sense of the extraordinary Pieces, our Authors would often make Words of their own which were entirely foreign to the Meaning of the Passages they pretended to translate; their chief Care being to make the Numbers of the English Verse answer to those of the Italian, that both of them might go to the same Tune. Thus the famous Song in 'Camilla',

Barbara si t'intendo, etc.
Barbarous Woman, yes, I know your Meaning,

which expresses the Resentments of an angry Lover, was translated into that English Lamentation,

Frail are a Lover's Hopes, etc.

And it was pleasant enough to see the most refined Persons of the British Nation dying away and languishing to Notes that were filled with a Spirit of Rage and Indignation. It happened also very frequently, where the Sense was rightly translated, the necessary Transposition of Words, which were drawn out of the Phrase of one

Tongue that was very natural in the other. I remember an Italian Verse that ran thus Word for Word,

And turned my Rage into Pity;

which the English for Rhime sake translated,

And into Pity turned my Rage.

By this means the soft Notes that were adapted to 'Pity' in the Italian, fell upon the Word 'Rage' in the Original, were made to express Pity in the Translation. It oftentimes happened likewise, that the finest notes in the Air fell upon the most insignificant Words in the Sentence. I have known the word 'And' pursued through the whole Gamut, have been entertained with many a melodious 'The', and have heard the most beautiful Graces, Quavers, and Divisions bestowed upon 'Then', 'For', and 'From'; to the eternal Honour of our English Particles.

The next Step to our Refinement was the introducing of Italian Actors into our Opera; who sung their Parts in their own Language at the same time that our Countrymen performed theirs in our native Tongue. The King or Hero of the Play generally spoke in Italian, and his Slaves answered him in English; the Lover frequently made his Court, and gained the Heart of his Princess, in a Language which she did not understand. One would have thought it very difficult to have carried on Dialogues after this manner, without an Interpreter between the Persons that convers'd together; but this was the State of the English Stage for about three Years.

At length the Audience grew tired of understanding Half the Opera, and therefore to ease themselves intirely of the Fatigue of Thinking, have so ordered it at present that the whole Opera is performed in an unknown Tongue. We no longer understand the Language of our own Stage; insomuch that I have often been afraid when I have seen our Italian Performers chattering in the Vehemence of Action, that they have been calling us Names, and abusing us among themselves; but I hope, since we do put such an entire Confidence in them, they will not talk against us before our Faces, though they may do it with the same Safety as if it were behind our Backs. In the mean time, I cannot forbear thinking how naturally an Historian who writes two or three hundred Years Hence, and does not know the Taste of his wise Forefathers, will make the following Reflection, 'In the Beginning of the Eighteenth Century the Italian Tongue was so well understood in English in England that Operas were acted on the publick Stage in that Language.'

One scarce knows how to be serious in the Confutation of an Absurdity that shews it self at the first Sight. It does not want any great measure of Sense to see the Ridicule of this monstrous Practice; but what makes the more astonishing, it is not the Taste of the Rabble, but of Persons of the greatest Politeness, which has established it.

If the Italians have a Genius for Musick above the English, the English have a Genius for other Performances of a much higher Nature, and capable of giving the mind a much nobler Entertainment. Would one think it was possible (at a time when an Author lived that was able to write the 'Phaedra and Hippolitus') for a People to be so stupidly fond of the Italian Opera, as scarce to give a third Day's Hearing to that admirable Tragedy? Musick is certainly a very agreeable Entertainment, but if it would take the entire Possession of our Ears, if it would make us incapable of hearing Sense, if it would exclude Arts that have a much greater Tendency to the Refinement of Human Nature; I must confess I would allow it no better Quarter than Plato has done, who banishes it out of his Common-Wealth.

At present our Notions of Musick are so very uncertain that we do not know what it is we like; only, in general, we are transported with any thing that is not English; So it be of foreign Growth, let it be Italian, French, or High-Dutch, it is the same thing. In short, our English

Musick is quite rooted out, and nothing yet planted in its stead.

When a Royal Palace is burnt to the Ground; every Man is at liberty to present his Plan for a new one; and though it be but indifferently put together, it may furnish several Hints that may be of use to a good Architect. I shall take the same Liberty in a following Paper, Of giving my Opinion upon the Subject of Musick; which I shall lay down only in a problematical Manner, to be considered by those who are Masters in the Art.

Spectator, March 21st, 1711

From My Own Apartment near Charing-Cross

Honoured Sir,

Having heard that this Nation is a great Encourager of Ingenuity, I have brought with me a Rope-Dancer that was caught in one of the Woods belonging to the Great Mogul. He is by Birth a Monkey; but swings upon a Rope, takes a Pipe of Tobacco, and drinks a Glass of Ale, like any reasonable Creature. He gives great Satisfaction to the Quality; and if they will make a Subscription for him, I will send for a Brother of his out of Holland that is a very good Tumbler; and also for another of the same Family whom I design for my Merry-Andrew as being an excellent Mimick, and the greatest Drole in the Country where he now is. I hope to have this Entertainment in a Readiness for the next Winter; and doubt not but it will please more than the Opera or Puppet Show. I will not say that a Monkey is a better Man than some of the Opera Heroes; but certainly he is a better Representative of a Man, than the most artificial Composition of Wood and Wire. If you will be pleased to give me a good Word in your Paper, you shall be every Night a Spectator at my Show for nothing.

I am etc.

Spectator, April 2nd, 1711

—Serme lingua concinnus utraque
*Soavior, ut cio notasi comminta Falerni est.—*HOR.

There is nothing that has more startled our English Audience than the Italian Recitativo, at its first Entrance upon the Stage. People were wonderfully surprized to hear Generals singing the Word of Command, and Ladies delivering Messages in Musick. Our Countrymen could not forbear laughing when they heard a Lover chanting-out a Billet-doux, and even the Superscription of a Letter set to a Tune. The Famous Blunder in an old Play of 'Enter a King, and two Fidlers solus', was now no longer an Absurdity; when it was impossible for a Hero in a Desart, or a Princess in her Closet, to speak anything unaccompanied with Musical Instruments.

But however this Italian Method of acting in Recitativo might appear at first hearing, I cannot but think it much more just than that which prevailed in the English Opera before this Innovation! The Transition from an Air to Recitative Musick being more natural than the passing from a Song to plain and ordinary Speaking, which was the common Method in Purcell's Operas.

The only Fault I find in our present Practice, is the making use of the Italian Recitativo with English Words.

To go to the bottom of this Matter, I must observe that the Tone or (as the French call it) the Accent of every Nation in their ordinary Speech is altogether different from that of every other people; as we may see even in the Welsh and Scotch, who border so near upon us. By the Tone or Accent, I do not mean the Pronunciation of each particular Word, but the sound of the whole Sentence. Thus it is very common for an English Gentleman when he hears a French Tragedy to complain that the Actors all of them speak in a Tone; and therefore he very wisely prefers his own Country-Men, not considering that a Foreigner complains of the same Tone in an English Actor.

For this reason, the Recitative Musick, in every language, should be as different as the Tone or Accent of each Language; for otherwise, what may properly express a Passion in one Language, will not do it in another. Every one who has been long in Italy knows very well, that the Cadences in the Recitativo bear a remote affinity to the Tone of their Voices in ordinary Conversation; or, to speak more properly, are only the Accents of their Language made more Musical and Tuneful.

Thus the Notes of Interrogation or Admiration in the Italian Musick (if one may so call them) which resemble their Accents in Discourse on such Occasions, are not unlike the ordinary Tones of an English Voice when we are angry; insomuch that I have often seen our Audiences extreamly mistaken as to what has been doing upon the Stage, and expecting to see the Hero knock down his Messenger, when he has been asking him a Question; or fancying that he quarrels with his Friend, when he only bids him 'Good-morow'.

For this reason the Italian Artists cannot agree with our English Musicians in admiring Purcell's Compositions, and thinking his Tunes so wonderfully adapted to his Words; because both Nations do not always express the same Passions by the same Sounds.

I am therefore humbly of Opinion, that an English Composer should not follow the Italian Recitative too servilely, but make use of many gentle Deviations from it, in Compliance with his own Native Language. He may Copy out of it all the lulling Softness and 'Dying Falls' (as Shakespear calls them) but should still remember that he ought to accommodate himself to an English Audience; and by humouring the Tone of our Voices in ordinary Conversation, have the same Regard to the Accent of his own Language, as those Persons had to theirs whom he professes to imitate. It is observed that several of the singing Birds of our own Country learn to sweeten their

Voices and mellow the Harshness of their natural Notes, by practising under those that come from the warmer Climates. In the same manner I would allow the Italian Opera to lend our English Musick, as much as may grace and soften it, but never entirely to annihilate and destroy it. Let the Infusion be as strong as you please, but still let the Subject Matter of it be English.

A Composer should fit his Musick to the Genius of the People, and consider that the Delicacy of Hearing, and Taste of Harmony, has been formed upon those Sounds which every Country abounds with; In short, that Musick is of a Relative Nature, and what is Harmony to one Ear, may be Dissonance to another.

The same Observations which I have made upon the Recitative Part of Musick, may be applied to all our Songs and Airs in general.

Signior Baptist Lully acted like a Man of Sense in this Particular. He found the French Musick extreamly defective and very often barbarous. However, knowing the Genius of the People, the Humour of their Language, and the prejudiced Ears he had to deal with, he did not pretend to extirpate the French Musick and plant the Italian in its stead; but only to Cultivate and Civilise it with innumerable Graces and Modulations which he borrowed from the Italian. By this means the French Musick is now perfect in its kind; and when you say it is not so good as the Italian, you only mean that it does not please you so well, for there is scarce a Frenchman who would not wonder to hear you give the Italian such a Preference. The Musick of the French is indeed very Properly adapted to their Pronunciation and Accent, as their whole Opera wonderfully favours the Genius of such a gay airy People. The Chorus in which that Opera abounds, gives the Parterre frequent opportunities of joining in Concert with the Stage. This Inclination of the Audience to sing along with the Actors, so prevails with them, that I have sometimes known the Performers on the Stage do no more in a

Celebrated Song than the Clerk of a Parish Church, who serves only to raise the Psalm, and is afterwards drown'd in the Musick of the Congregation. Every Actor that comes on the Stage is a Beau. The Queens and Heroines are so Painted that they appear as Ruddy and Cherry-Cheek'd as Milk-maids. The Shepherds are all Embroidered, and acquit themselves in a Ball better than our English Dancing-Masters. I have seen a Couple of Rivers appear in red Stockings; and Alpheus, instead of having his Head covered with Sedge and Bull-Rushes, making Love in a fair full-bottomed Perriwig, and a Plume of Feathers, but with a voice so full of Shakes and Quavers that I should have thought the Murmurs of a Country Brook the much more agreeable Musick.

I remember the last Opera I saw in that merry Nation, was the Rape of Proserpine, where Pluto, to make the more tempting Figure, puts himself in a French Equipage, and brings Ascalaphus along with him as his Valet de Chambre. This is what we call Folly and Impertinence; but what the French look upon as Gay and Polite.

I shall add no more to what I have here offered, than that Musick, Architecture and Painting, as well as Poetry and Oratory, are to deduce their Laws and Rules from the general Sense and Taste of Mankind; and not from the Principles of those Arts themselves; or, in other Words, the Taste is not to conform to the Art, but the Art to the Taste. Musick is not designed to please only Chromatick Ears, but all that are capable of distinguishing harsh from disagreeable Notes. A Man of an Ordinary Ear is a Judge whether a Passion is expressed in proper Sounds, and whether the Melody of those Sounds be more or less pleasing.

Spectator, April 3rd, 1711

Sit mihi fas audita loqui.—Virg.

Last Night, upon my going into a Coffee-house not far from the Hay-Market Theatre, I diverted my self for above half an Hour with overhearing the Discourse of one, who, by the Shabbiness of his Dress, the Extravagance of his Conceptions, and the Hurry of his Speech, I discovered to be of that Species who are generally distinguished by the Title of Projectors. This Gentleman, for I found he was treated as such by his Audience, was entertaining a whole Table of Listners with the Project of an Opera, which he told us had not cost him above two or three Mornings in the Contrivance, and which he was ready to put in Execution, provided he might find his Account in it. He said, that he had observed the great Trouble and Inconvenience which Ladies were at, in travelling up and down to the several Shows that are exhibited in different Quarters of the Town. The dancing Monkies are in one Place; the Puppet Show in another; the Opera in a third; not to mention the Lions, that are almost a whole Day's Journey from the politer Part of the Town. By this means People of Figure are forced to lose half the Winter after their coming to Town, before they have seen all the strange Sights about it. In order to remedy this great Inconvenience, our Projector drew out of his Pocket the Scheme of an Opera entitled 'The Expedition of Alexander the Great'; in which he had disposed all the remarkable Shows about Town, among the Scenes and Decorations of his Piece. The Thought, he confest, was not originally his own, but that he had taken the Hint of it from several Performances which he had seen upon our Stage; In one of which there was a Rary-Show; in another, a Ladder-dance; and in others a Posture-Man, a moving Picture, with many Curiosities of the like Nature.

This 'Expedition of Alexander' opens with his consulting the Oracle at Delphos, in which the dumb Conjurer, who has been visited by so many Persons of Quality of late Years, is to be introduced as telling him his Fortune: At the same time Clench of Barnet is represented in another Corner of the Temple, as ringing the Bells of Delphos, for joy of his Arrival. The Tent of

Darius is to be peopled by the Ingenious Mrs. Salmon, where Alexander is to fall in Love with a Piece of Wax-work, that represents the beautiful Statira. When Alexander comes into that Country, in which Quintus Curtius tells us the Dogs were so exceeding fierce that they would not loose their Hold, though they were cut to pieces Limb by Limb, and that they would hang upon their Prey by their Teeth when they had nothing but a Mouth left, there is to be a Scene of Hockley in the Hole, in which is to be represented all the Diversions of that Place, the Bull-Baiting only excepted, which cannot possibly be exhibited in the Theatre, by reason of the Lowness of the Roof. The several Woods in Asia, which Alexander must be supposed to pass through, will give the Audience a Sight of Monkies dancing upon Ropes, with many other Pleasantries of that ludicrous Species. At the same time, if there chance to be any Strange Animals in Town, whether Birds or Beasts, they may be either let loose among the Woods, or driven across the Stage by some of the Country People of Asia. In the last great Battel, Pinkethman is to personate King Porus upon an Elephant, and is to be encountered by Powell, representing Alexander the Great upon a Dromedary, which nevertheless Mr. Powell is desired to call by the name of Bucephalus. Upon the Close of this great decisive Battel, when the two Kings are thoroughly reconciled, to shew the mutual friendship and good Correspondence that reigns between them, they both of them go together to a Puppet Show, in which the ingenious Mr. Powell, Junior, may have an Opportunity of displaying his whole Art of Machinery, for the Diversion of the two Monarchs. Some at the Table urged, that a Puppet Show was not a suitable Entertainment for Alexander the Great; and that it might be introduced more properly, if we suppose the Conqueror touched upon that Part of India which is said to be inhabited by the Pigmies. But this Objection was looked upon as frivolous and the Proposal immediately over-ruled. Our Projector further added, that after the Reconciliation of the two Kings they might invite one another to Dinner, and either of them entertain his Guest with the German Artist, Mr. Pinketham's Heathen Gods, or any of the like Diversions which shall then chance to be in vogue.

This Project was received with very great Applause by the whole Table. Upon which the Undertaker told us, that he had not yet communicated to us above half his Design; for that Alexander being a Greek, it was his Intention that the whole Opera should be acted in that Language, which was a Tongue he was sure would wonderfully please the Ladies, especially when it was a little raised and rounded by the Ionick Dialect; and could not but be acceptable to the whole Audience, because there are fewer of them who understand Greek than Italian. The only Difficulty that remained, was how to get Performers, unless we could persuade some Gentlemen of the Universities to learn to Sing, in order to qualifie themselves for the Stage; but this Objection soon vanished, when the Projector informed us that the Greeks were at present the only Musicians in the Turkish Empire, and that it would be very easie for our Factory at Smyrna to furnish us every year with a Colony of Musicians, by the Opportunity of the Turkish Fleet; besides, says he, if we want any single Voice for any lower Part in the Opera, Lawrence can learn to speak Greek as well as he does Italian in a Fortnight's time.

The Projector having thus settled Matters, to the good liking of all that heard him, he left his Seat at the Table, and planted himself before the Fire, where I had unluckily taken my Stand for the Convenience of overhearing what he said. Whether he had observed me to be more attentive than ordinary, I cannot tell, but he had not stood by me above a quarter of a Minute, but he turned short upon me on a sudden and catching me by the Button of my Coat, attacked me very abruptly after the following manner: Besides, Sir, I have heard of a very extraordinary Genius for Musick that lives in Switzerland, who has so strong a Spring in his Fingers, that he can make the Board of an Organ sound like a Drum, and if I could but procure a Subscription of about Ten thousand Pound every Winter, I would undertake to fetch him over, and oblige him by Articles to set everything that should be sung upon the English Stage. After this he looked full in my Face, expecting I would make an Answer; when by good Luck, a Gentleman that had entered the Coffee-house since the Projector applied himself to me, hearing him talk of his Swiss Compositions, cry'd out with a kind of laugh, Is our Musick then to receive farther Improvements from Switzerland? This alarmed the Projector, who immediately let go my Button, and turned about to answer him. I took the Opportunity of the Diversion, which seemed to be made in favour of me, and laying down my Penny upon the Bar, retired with some Precipitation.

Spectator, April 5th, 1711

'Mr. Spectator'

I am a Country Clergyman, and hope you will lend me your Assistance in ridiculing some little Indecencies which cannot so properly be exposed from the Pulpit.

A Widow Lady, who straggled this Summer from London into my Parish for the Benefit of the Air, as she says, appears every Sunday at Church with many fashionable extravagancies, to the great Astonishment of my Congregation.

But what gives us the most Offence is her Theatrical manner of singing the Psalms. She introduces above fifty Italian Airs into the Hundredth Psalm, and whilst we begin 'All People' in the old Solemn Tune of our Forefathers, she in quite a different Key runs Divisions on the Vowels, and adorns them with the Graces of Nicolini; if she meets with Eke or Aye, which are frequent in the Metre of Hopkins and Sternhold, we are certain to hear her quavering them half a Minute after us to some sprightly Airs of the Opera.

I am very far from being an Enemy to Church Musick, but I fear this Abuse of it may make my Parish ridiculous, who already look on the Singing Psalms as an Entertainment, and not part of their Devotion: besides, I am apprehensive that the Infection may spread, for Squire Squeekum, who by his Voice seems (if I may use the Expression) to be cut out for an Italian Singer, was last Sunday practising the same Airs.

I know the Lady's Principles, and that she will plead the Toleration, which (as she fancies) allows her Non-Conformity in this Particular; but I beg you to Acquaint her, that Singing the Psalms in a different Tune from the rest of the Congregation, is a sort of Schism not tolerated by that Act.

I am, Sir, Your Very Humble Servant,

R.S.

Spectator, Oct. 25th, 1711

Tartaream intendit vocem, qua protinus omne Contremuit nemus.—VIRG.

I have lately received the following Letter from a Country Gentleman.

'Mr. Spectator',

The Night before I left London I went to see a Play, called 'The Humourous Lieutenant'. Upon the Rising of the Curtain I was very surprized with the great Consort of Cat-Calls which was exhibited that Evening, and began to think with myself that I had made a Mistake, and gone to a Musick Meeting instead of the Play-house. It appeared a little odd to me, to see so many Persons of Quality of both Sexes assembled together at a kind of Catterwawling; for I cannot look upon the Performance to have been any thing better, whatever the Musicians themselves might think of it. As I had no Acquaintance in the House to ask Questions of, and was forced to go out of Town early the next Morning, I could not learn the Secret of this Matter. What I would therefore desire of you is, to give some Account of this strange Instrument, which I found the Company called a Cat-Call; and particularly to let me know whether it be a piece of Musick lately come from Italy. For my own part, to be free with you, I would rather hear an English Fiddle; though I durst not shew my Dislike whilst I was in the Playhouse, it being my Chance to sit the very next Man to one of the Performers.

I am, Sir,

Your most affectionate Friend and Servant,

John Shallow Esq.

In compliance with Squire Shallow's Requests, I design this Paper as a Dissertation upon the Cat-Call. In order to make my self a Master of the Subject, I purchased one the Beginning of last Week, though not without great Difficulty, being informed at two or three Toy-shops that the Players had lately bought them all up. I have since consulted many learned Antiquaries in relation to its Original, and find them very much divided among themselves upon that Particular. A Fellow of the Royal Society, who is my good Friend, and a great Proficient in the Mathematical Part of Musick, concludes from the simplicity of its Make, and the Uniformity of its Sound, that the Cat-Call is older than any of the Inventions of Jubal. He observes very well, that Musical Inventions took their first Rise from the Notes of Birds, and other Melodious Animals; and what, says he, was more natural than for the first Ages of Mankind to imitate the Voice of a Cat that lived under the same Roof with him? He added that the Cat had contributed more to Harmony than any other Animal; as we are not only beholden to her for this Wind Instrument, but for our String-Musick in general.

Another Virtuoso of my Acquaintance will not allow the Cat-Call to be older than Thespis, and is apt to think

C 2

it appeared in the World soon after the Ancient Comedy; for which Reason it has still a Place in our Dramatick Entertainments: Nor must I here omit what a very curious Gentleman who is lately return'd from his Travels, has more than once assured me, namely, that there was lately dug up at Rome the Statue of a Momus, who holds an Instrument in his Right-Hand very much resembling our modern Cat-Call.

There are others who ascribe this Invention to Orpheus, and look upon the Cat-Call to be one of those Instruments which that famous Musician made use of to draw the Beasts about him. It is certain that the Roasting of a Cat does not call together a greater Audience, of that Species, than this Instrument, if dexterously play'd upon in proper Time and Place.

But not withstanding these various and learned Conjectures I cannot forbear thinking that the Cat-Call is originally a Piece of English Musick. Its Resemblance to the Voice of some of our British Songsters, as well as the Use of it, which is peculiar to our Nation, confirms me in this Opinion. It has at least received great Improvements among us, whether we consider the Instrument it self, or those several Quavers and Graces which are thrown into the Playing of it. Every one might be sensible of this, who heard that remarkable over-grown Cat-Call which was placed in the Center of the Pit, and presided over all the rest at the celebrated Performance lately exhibited in Drury-Lane.

Having said thus much concerning the Original of the Cat-Call we are in the next Place to consider the Use of it. The Cat-Call exerts it self to most Advantage in the British Theatre; It very much improves the Sound of Nonsense, and often goes along with the Voice of the Actor who pronounces it, as the Violin or Harpsicord accompanies the Italian Recitativo.

It has often supplied the Place of the ancient Chorus in the Words of Mr. ——, In short, a bad Poet has as great an Antipathy to a Cat-Call as many People have to a real Cat.

Mr. Collier, in his ingenious Essay upon Musick, has the following Passage:

'I believe 'tis possible to invent an Instrument that shall have a quite contrary Effect to those Martial ones now in Use. An Instrument that shall sink the Spirits, and shake the Nerves, and curdle the Blood, and inspire Despair, and Cowardize and Consternation at a surprizing rate. 'Tis probable the Roaring of Lions, the Warbling of Cats and Scritch-Owls, together with a Mixture of the Howling of Dogs, judiciously imitated and compounded, might go a great way in this Invention. Whether such Anti-Musick as this might not be a Service in a Camp, I shall leave the Military Men to consider.'

What this learned Gentleman supposes in Speculation, I have known actually verified in Practice. The Cat-Call has struck a Damp into Generals, and frighted Heroes off the Stage. At the first Sound of it I have seen a Crowned Head Tremble, and a Princess fall into Fits. 'The Humourous Lieutenant' himself could not stand it; nay, I am told that even Almanzor looked like a Mouse, and trembled at the Voice of this terrifying Instrument.

As it is of a Drammatick Nature, and peculiarly appropriated to the Stage, I can by no means approve the Thought of that Angry Lover, who, after an unsuccessful Pursuit of some Years, took Leave of his Mistress in a Serenade of Cat-Calls.

I must conclude this Paper with the Account I have lately received of an ingenious Artist who has long studied this Instrument, and is very well versed in all the Rules of the Drama. He teaches to play on it by Book, and to express by it the whole Art of Criticism. He has his Base and his Treble Cat-Call; the former for Tragedy, the latter for Comedy; only in Tragy-Comedies they may both play together in Consort. He has a particular Squeak to denote the Violation of each of the Unities, and has different Sounds to shew whether he aims at the Poet or the Player. In short he teaches the Smut-note, the Fustian-note, the Stupid-note, and has composed a kind of Air that may serve as an Act-tune to an incorrigible Play, and which takes in the whole Compass of the Cat-Call.

Spectator, April 24th, 1712

I am very sorry to find, by the Opera Bills, for this Day, that we are likely to lose the greatest Performer in Dramatick Musick that is now living; or that perhaps, ever appeared upon a Stage. I need not acquaint my Reader, that I am speaking of Signior Nicolini. The Town is highly obliged to that Excellent Artist for having shewn us the Italian Musick in its Perfection, as well as for that generous Approbation he lately gave to an Opera of our own Country, in which the Composer endeavoured to do Justice to the Beauty of the Words, by following that Noble Example, which has been set him by the greatest Foreign Masters in that Art.

I could heartily wish there was the same Applications and Endeavours to cultivate and improve our Church Musick, as have been lately bestowed on that of the Stage. Our Composers have one very great Incitement to it: They are sure to meet with Excellent Words, and at the same time, a wonderful Variety of them. There is no Passion that is not finely expressed in those parts of the inspired Writing, which are proper for Divine Songs and Anthems.

There is a certain Coldness and Indifference in the Phrases of our European Languages, when they are compared with the Oriental Forms of Speech; and it happens very luckily, that the Hebrew Idioms run into the English Tongue with a particular Grace and Beauty. Our Language has received innumerable Elegancies and Improvements, from that Infusion of Hebraism, which are derived to it out of the Poetical Passages in Holy Writ.

They give a Force and Energy to our Expressions, warm and animate our Language, and convey our Thoughts in more ardent and intense Phrases, than any that are to be met with in our own Tongue. There is something so pathetick in this kind of Diction, that it often sets the Mind in a Flame, and makes our Hearts burn within us. How cold and dead a Prayer appears, that is composed in the most Elegant and Polite Forms of Speech, which are natural to our Tongue, when it is not heightened by that Solemnity of Phrase which may be drawn from the Sacred Writings. It has been said by some of the Ancients, that if the Gods were to talk with Men, they would certainly speak in Plato's Stile; but I think we may say, with Justice, that when Mortals converse with their Creator, they cannot do it in so proper a Stile as in that of the Holy Scriptures. . . .

Since we have therefore such a Treasury of Words, so beautiful in themselves, and so proper for the Airs of Musick, I cannot but wonder that Persons of Distinction should give so little Attention and Encouragement to that kind of Musick which would have its Foundation in Reason, and which would improve our Virtue in proportion as it raised our Delight. The Passions that are excited by ordinary Compositions generally flow from such silly and absurd Occasions, that a Man is ashamed to reflect upon them seriously; but the Fear, the Love, the Sorrow, the Indignation that are awakened in the Mind by Hymns and Anthems, make the Heart better, and proceed from such Causes as are altogether reasonable and praise-worthy. Pleasure and Duty go hand in hand, and the greater our Satisfaction is, the greater is our Religion.

Musick among those who were stiled the chosen People was a Religious Art. The Songs of Sion, which we have reason to believe were in high repute among the Courts of the Eastern Monarchs, were nothing else but Psalms and Pieces of Poetry that adored or celebrated the Supreme Being. The greatest Conqueror in this Holy

Nation, after the manner of the old Grecian Lyricks, did not only compose the Words of his Divine Odes, but generally set them to Musick himself. After which, his Works, tho' they were consecrated to the Tabernackle, became the National Entertainment as well as the Devotion of his People.

The first Original of the Drama was a Religious Worship consisting only of a Chorus, which was nothing else but an Hymn to a Deity. As Luxury and Voluptuousness prevailed over Innocence and Religion, this form of Worship degenerated into Tragedies; in which however the Chorus so far remembered its first Office, as to brand every thing that was vicious, and recommend every thing that was laudable, to intercede with Heaven for the Innocent, and to implore the Vengeance on the Criminal.

Homer and Hesiod intimate to us how this Art should be applied, when they represent the Muses as surrounding Jupiter, and warbling their Hymns about his Throne. I might shew, from innumerable Passages in Ancient Writers, not only that Vocal and Instrumental Musick were made use of in their Religious Worship, but that their most favourable Diversions were filled with Songs and Hymns to their respective Deities. Had we frequent Entertainments of this Nature among us, they would not a little purifie and exalt our Passions, give our Thoughts a proper Turn, and cherish those Divine Impulses in the Soul, which every one feels that has not stifled them by sensual and immoderate Pleasures.

Musick, when thus applied, raises noble Hints in the Mind of the Hearer, and fills it with great Conceptions. It strengthens Devotion, and advances Praise into Rapture. It lengthens out every Act of Worship, and produces more lasting and permanent Impressions in the Mind, than those which accompany any transient Form of Words that are uttered in the ordinary Method of Religious Worship.

Spectator, June 14th, 1712

HENRY GROVE

Oxford, Nov. 22

Sir,

If you would be so kind to me, as to suspend that Satisfaction, which the Learned World must receive in reading one of your Speculations, by publishing this Endeavour, you will very much oblige and improve one who has the boldness to hope, that he may be admitted into the number of your Correspondents.

I have often wondered to hear Men of good Sense and good Nature profess a Dislike to Musick, when, at the same time, they do not scruple to own, that it has the most agreeable and improving Influences over their Minds; It seems to me an unhappy Contradiction, that those Persons should have an indifference for an Art, which raises in them such a Variety of sublime Pleasures ·

However, though some few, by their own or the unreasonable Prejudices of others, may be led into a Distaste for those Musical Societies which are erected meerly for Entertainment, yet sure I may venture to say, that no one can have the least Reason for Disaffection of that solemn kind of Melody which consists of the Praises of our Creator.

You have, I presume, already prevented me in an Argument upon this Occasion (which some Divines have successfully advanced upon a much greater) that Musical Sacrifice and Adoration has claimed a Place in the Laws and Customs of the most different Nations: As the Grecians and Romans of the Prophane, the Jews and Christians of the Sacred World did as unanimously agree in this, as they disagreed in all other Parts of their Economy.

I know there are not wanting some who are of Opinion that the pompous kind of Musick which is in Use in foreign Churches is the most excellent, as it most affects our Senses, But I am swayed by my Judgement to the

Modesty which is observed in the musical Part of our Devotions. Methinks there is something very laudable in the Custom of a Voluntary before the first Lesson; by this we are supposed to be prepared for the Admission of those Divine Truths, which we are shortly to receive. We are then to cast all worldly Regards from off our Hearts, all Tumults within are then becalmed, and there should be nothing near the Soul but Peace and Tranquility. So that in this short Office of Praise, the Man is raised above himself and is almost lost already amidst the Joys of Futurity.

I have heard some nice Observers frequently commend the Policy of our Church in this Particular, that it leads us on by such easie and regular Methods, that we are perfectly deceived into Piety. When the Spirits begin to languish (as they often do) with a constant Series of Petitions, she takes care to allow them a pious Respite, and the sublimest Poetry, softened in the most moving Strains of Musick, can never fail of humbling or exalting the Soul to any Pitch of Devotion. Who can hear the Terrors of the Lord of Hosts described in the most expressive Melody without being awed into a Veneration? Or who can hear the kind and endearing Attributes of a merciful Father, and not be softened into Love towards him?

As the rising and sinking of the Passions, the casting soft or noble Hints into the Soul, is the natural Privilege of Musick, so more particularly of that kind which is employed at the Altar. These Impressions which it leaves upon the Spirits are more deep and lasting as the Grounds from which it receives its Authority are founded more upon Reason. It diffuses a Calmness all around us, it makes us drop all those vain or immodest Thoughts which would be an hindrance to us in the Performance of that great Duty of Thanksgiving, which as we are informed by our Almighty Benefactor, is the most acceptable Return which can be made for those infinite Stores of Blessings which He daily condescends to pour down upon his Creatures. When He makes Use of this pathetical Method of addressing our selves to Him, we can scarce contain from Raptures! The Heart is warmed with a Sublimity of Goodness! We are all Piety and Love!

How do the Blessed Spirits rejoice and wonder to behold unthinking Man prostrating his Soul to his dread Sovereign in such a Warmth of Piety as they themselves might not be ashamed of!

I shall close these Reflections with a Passage taken out of the third Book of Milton's Paradise Lost, where those harmonious Beings are thus nobly described.

> The Crown'd again their Gold'n Harps they took,
> Harps ever tuned, that glittering by their side
> Like Quivers hung, and with Preamble sweet
> Of Charming Symphony they introduce
> The Sacred Song, and waken Raptures high,
> No one exempt, no Voice but well could join
> Melodious part, such Concord is in Heav'n.

Spectator, Dec. 8th, 1714

REV. ARTHUR BEDFORD (?)

The common Notes in our Church Musick are Minims and Semibreves; instead of these we have Crotchets, Quavers, and Semi-Quavers; And as the quicker Notes increase, so the Design of the Composer is that the other may be sung so much the slower, and consequently make the Antient Musick seem dull and heavy, which of itself is of a far different Nature.

Our Antient Church Musick is lost, and that solid grave Harmony fit for a Martyr to delight in, and an Angel to hear, is now chang'd into a Diversion for Atheists and Libertines, and that which Good Men cannot but lament. Everything which is serious, is called Derision, The Old Cow Path, and reputed as dull and heavy.

The Great Abuse of Musick, 1711

STEELE (1672–1729)

Will's Coffee-house, April 18

Letters from the Hay-market informs us, that on Saturday night last the Opera of 'Pyrrhus and Demetrius' was performed with great Applause. This Intelligence is not very acceptable to us Friends of the Theatre; for the Stage being an Entertainment of the Reason, and all the Faculties, this Way of being pleased with the Suspense of them for three Hours together, and being given up to the shallow Satisfaction of the Eyes and Ears only, seems to arise rather from the Degeneracy of our Understanding than an Improvement of our Diversions. That the Understanding has no part in the Pleasure is evident, from what these letters very positively assert, to wit, that a great Part of the Performance was done in Italian: And a great Critic fell into Fits in the Gallery, at seeing, not only Time and Place, but Languages and Nations confused in the most incorrigible Manner. His Spleen is so extremely moved on this Occasion, that he is going to publish a Treatise against Operas, which, he thinks, have already inclined us to Thoughts of Peace, and if tolerated, must infallibly dispirit us from carrying on the War. He has communicated his Scheme to the whole Room, and declared in what Manner Things of this Kind were first introduced. He has upon this Occasion considered the Nature of Sounds in general, and made a very elaborate Digression upon the London Cries, wherein he has shown from Reason and Philosophy, why Oysters are cried, Card-matches sung, and Turneps and all other Vegetables neither cried, sung, nor said, but sold, with an Accent and Tone neither natural to Man or Beast. This Piece seems to be taken from the Model of that excellent Discourse of Mrs. Manly the School-mistress, concerning Samplers. Advices from the Upper End of Piccadilly say, that May-Fair is utterly abolished; and we hear Mr. Pinkethman has removed his ingenious Company of Strollers to Greenwich. But other Letters from Deptford say, the Company is only making hither, and not yet settled; but that several Heathen Gods and Goddesses, which are to descend in Machines, landed at the King's Stairs last Saturday. Venus and Cupid went on Foot from thence to Greenwich; Mars got drunk in the Town, and broke his Landlord's Head, for which he sat in the Stocks the whole Evening; but Mr. Pinkethman giving Security that he should do Nothing this ensuing Summer, he was set at Liberty. The most melancholy part of all was, that Diana was taken in the Act of Fornication with a Boatman, and committed by justice Wrathful, which has, it seems, put a Flop to the Diversions of the Theatre of Blackheath. But there goes down another Diana and a Patient Griffel next Tide from Billingsgate.

Tatler, April 18th, 1709

Will's Coffee-house, May 3rd

... Mr. Durfey generally writes State-plays, and is wonderfully useful to the World in such Representations. The Method is the same that was used by the old Athenians, to laugh out of Countenance, or promote opinions among the People. My Friend has therefore against this Play is acted for his own Benefit, made two Dances, which may be also of an Universal Benefit. In the first, he has represented absolute Power in the Person of a tall Man with an Hat and Feather, who gives his first Minister, that stands just before him, an huge Kick; the Minister gives the Kick to the next before; and so to the end of the Stage. In this Moral and practical Jest, you are made to understand, that there is, in an Absolute Government, no gratification, but giving the Kick received from one above you, to one below you. This is performed to a grave and melancholy Air; but on a sudden the Tune moves quicker, and the whole Company fall into a Circle, and take Hands; and then at a sharp Note, they

move round, and kick as kick can. This latter Performance he makes to be the Representation of a Free State;
where, if you all mind your Steps, you may go round and
round very jollily, with a Motion pleasne to yourselves
and those you dance with: Nay, if you put yourselves
out, at the worst you only kick and are kicked, like
Friends and Equals.

Tatler, May 5th, 1709

From My Own Apartment, Aug. 29th

. . . Five young Ladies, who are of no small Fame for
their great severity of Manners, and exemplary Behaviour, would lately go no where with their Lovers but to
an Organ-loft in a Church; where they had a cold Treat
and some few Opera Songs, to their great Refreshment
and Edification.

Tatler, Aug. 30th, 1709

Bombalio, clangor, stridor, taratantara, murmur.

FARN. Rhet.

Rend with tremendous Sounds your Ears asunder
With Gun, Drum, Trumpet, Blunderbuss, and Thunder.

POPE.

From My Own Apartment, March 31st

I have heard of a very valuable Picture, wherein all the
Painters of the Age in which it was drawn, are represented
sitting together in a Circle, and joining in a Concert of
Musick. Each of them plays upon such a particular
Instrument as is the most suitable to his Character, and
expresses that style and manner of Painting which is
peculiar to him. The famous Cupola-Painter of those
Times to shew the Grandeur and Boldness of his Figures,
hath a Horn-in his Mouth which he seems to wind with
great Strength and Force. On the contrary, an eminent

Artist, who wrought up his Pictures with the greatest Accuracy and gave them all those delicate Touches which are apt to please the nicest Eye, is represented as tuning a Theorbo. The same kind of Humour runs through the whole Piece.

I have often, from this Hint, imagined to myself, that different Talents in Discourse might be shadowed out after the same Manner by different kinds of Musick; and that the several conversable parts of Mankind in this great City, might be cast into proper Characters and Divisions, as they resemble several Instruments that are in use among the Masters of Harmony. Of these therefore in their Order; and first the Drum.

Your Drums are the Blusterers in Conversation, that with a loud Laugh, unnatural Mirth, and a Torrent of Noise, domineer in Public Assemblies; overbear Men of Sense; stun their Companions; and fill the Place they are in with a rattling Sound, that hath seldom any Wit, Humour, or good Breeding in it. The Drum notwithstanding, by this boisterous vivacity, is very proper to impose upon the Ignorant; and in Conversation with Ladies who are not of the finest Taste, often passes for a Man of Mirth and Wit, and for wonderful pleasant Company. I need not observe, that the Emptiness of the Drum very much contributes to its Noise.

The Lute is a Character directly opposite to the Drum, that sounds very finely by it self, in a very small Consort. Its Notes are exquisitely sweet, and very low, easily drowned in a Multitude of Instruments, and even lost among a few, unless you give a particular Attention to it. A Lute is seldom heard in a Company of more than five, whereas a Drum will show itself to Advantage in an Assembly of Five Hundred. The Lutenists therefore are Men of fine Genius, uncommon Reflection, great Affability, and esteemed chiefly by Persons of Good Taste, who are the only proper Judges of so delightful and soft a Melody.

The Trumpet is an Instrument that has in it no Compass of Musick, or Variety of Sound, but is notwithstanding very agreeable, so long as it keeps within its Pitch. It has not above four or five Notes, which are however very pleasing, and capable of exquisite Turns and Modulations. The Gentlemen who fall under this Denomination are your Men of the most fashionable Education, and refined Breeding, who have learned a certain smoothness of Discourse, and Sprightliness of Air, from the polite Company they have kept: but at the same time have shallow Parts, weak Judgements, and a short Reach of Understanding. A Playhouse, a Drawing-room, a Ball, a Visiting-day, or a Ring at Hyde-park, are the few Notes they are Masters of, which they touch upon in all Conversations. The Trumpet, however, is a necessary Instrument about a Court, and a proper Enlivener of a Consort, though of no great Harmony by itself.

Violins are the lively, forward, importunate Wits, that distinguish themselves by the Flourishes of Imagination, Sharpness of Repartee, Glances of Satire, and bear away the upper Part in every Consort. I cannot however but observe, that when a Man is not disposed to hear Musick, there is not a more disagreeable Sound in Harmony than that of the Violin.

There is another musical Instrument, which is more frequent in this Nation than any other; I mean your Bass-Viol, which grumbles in the bottom of the Consort, and with a surly masculine Sound strengthens the Harmony, and tempers the sweetness of the several Instruments that play along with it. The Bass-Viol is an Instrument of a quite different Nature to the Trumpet, and may signify Men of rough Sense, and unpolished Parts; who do not love to hear Themselves talk, but sometimes, break out with an agreeable Bluntness, unexpected Wit, and surly Pleasantries, to the no small Diversion of their Friends and Companions. In short, I look upon every sensible true-born Briton to be naturally a Bass-Viol.

As for your rural Wits, who talk with great Eloquence and Alacrity of Foxes, Hounds, Horses, quickset Hedges, six-bar Gates, double Ditches, and broken Necks, I am in doubt, whether I should give them a Place in the conversable World. However, if they will content themselves with being raised to the Dignity of Hunting-Horns, I shall desire for the Future, that they may be known by that Name.

I must not here omit the Bag-Pipe species, that will entertain you from Morning to Night with the Repetition of a few Notes, which are played over and over, with the perpetual humming of a Drone running underneath them. These are your dull, heavy, tedious Story-tellers, the load and burden of Conversations, that are set up for Men of Importance by knowing secret History, and giving an Account of Transactions, that whether they ever passed in the World or not, doth not signify an Half-Penny to its Instruction, or its Welfare. Some have observed that the Northern Parts of this Island are more particularly fruitful in Bag-Pipes.

There are very few Persons who are Masters in every kind of Conversation, and can talk on all Subjects, that I do not know whether we should make a distinct Species of them: Nevertheless, that my Scheme may not be defective, for the Sake of those Few who are endowed with such extraordinary Talents, I shall allow them to be Harpsichords, a kind of Musick which every one knows is a Consort by itself.

As for your Passing-bells, who look upon Mirth as criminal, and talk of nothing but what is melancholy in itself, and mortifying to Human Nature, I shall not mention them.

I shall likewise pass over in Silence all the Rabble of Mankind, that croud our Streets, Coffee-houses, Feasts, and Public Tables. I cannot call their Discourse Conversation, but rather something that is practised in Imitation of it. For which Reason, if I should describe them by any Musical Instrument, it should be by those modern Inventions of the Bladder and String, Tongs and Key, Marrow-bone and Cleaver.

My Reader will doubtless observe, that I have only touched here upon Male Instruments, having reserved my female Consort to another Occasion. If he has a Mind to know where these several Characters are to be met with, I could direct him to a whole Club of Drums; not to mention another of Bag-Pipes, which I have before given some Account of in my Description of our nightly Meetings in Sheer-Lane. The Lutes may often be met with in couples upon the Banks of a chrystal Stream, or in the Retreats of shady Woods, and flowery Meadows; which for different Reasons are likewise the great Resort of your Hunting-horns. Bass-Viols, are frequently to be found over a Glass of Stale-beer, and a Pipe of Tobacco; whereas those who set up for Violins, seldom fail to make their appearance at Will's once every Evening. You may meet with a Trumpet any where on the other Side of Charing-Cross.

That we may draw something for our Advantage in Life out of the foregoing Discourse, I must intreat my Reader to make a narrow Search into his Life and Conversation, and upon his leaving any Company, to examine himself seriously, whether he has behaved himself in it like a Drum or a Trumpet, a Violin or a Bass-Viol; and accordingly endeavour to mend his Musick for the Future. For my own Part, I must confess, I was a Drum for many Years; nay, and a very noisy one, until having polished myself a little in good Company, I threw as much of the Trumpet into my Conversation, as was possible for a Man of an impetuous Temper, by which Mixture of different Musicks, I look upon myself, during the Course of many Years, to have resembled a Tabor and Pipe. I have since very much endeavoured at the

Sweetness of the Lute; but in spite of all my Resolutions, I must confess, with a great Confusion, that I find myself daily degenerating into a Bag-Pipe; whether it be the Effect of my Old Age or of the Company I keep, I know not. All that I can do, is to keep a Watch over my Conversation, and to silence the Drone as soon as I find it begin to hum in my Discourse, being determined rather to hear the Notes of Others, than to play out of Time, and to incroach upon their Parts in the Consort by a Noise of so tiresome an Instrument.

I shall conclude this Paper with a Letter which I received last Night from a Friend of mine, who knows very well my Notions upon this Subject, and invites me to pass the Evening at his House, with a select Company of Friends, in the following Words:

Dear Isaac,

I intend to have a Consort at my House this Evening, having by great Chance got a Harpsichord, which I am sure will entertain you very agreeably. There will be likewise two Lutes, and a Trumpet: Let me beg of you to put yourself in Tune, and believe me

Your very faithful Servant,
Nicholas Humdrum
Tatler, April 1st, 1710

Facile est inventis addere.
It is easy to improve an Invention.

From My Own Apartment, April 10th

I was last Night in an Assembly of very fine Women: How I came among them is of no great Importance to the Reader. I shall only let him know, that I was betrayed into so good Company by the Device of an old Friend, who had promised to give some of his Female Acquaintance a sight of Mr. Bickerstaff. Upon hearing my Name mentioned, a Lady who sat by me, told me, they had brought together a female Consort for my Entertainment.

You must know, says she, that we all of us look upon ourselves to be musical Instruments, though we do not yet know of what kind; which we hope to learn from you, if you will give us Leave to play before you. This was followed by a general Laugh, which I always look upon as a necessary Flourish in the Opening of a Female Consort. They then struck up together, and played a whole Hour upon two Grounds, viz. the Trial and the Opera. I could not but observe, that several of their Notes were more soft, and several more sharp than any that I heard in a male Consort; though I must confess, there was not any Regard to Time, nor any of those Rests and Pauses which are frequent in the Harmony of the other Sex. Besides that the Musick was generally full, and no particular Instrument permitted to play long by itself.

I seemed so very well pleased with what every one said, and smiled with so much Complaisance at all their pretty Fancies, that though I did not put one Word into their Discourse, I have the Vanity to think, they looked upon me as very agreeable Company. I then told them, that if I were to draw the Picture of so many charming Musicians, it should be like the one I had seen of the Muses, with their several Instruments in their Hands; upon which the Lady Kettle-Drum tossed back her Head, and cried, A very pretty Simile! The Consort again revived; in which, with Nods, Smiles, and Approbations, I bore the Part rather of one who beats the Time, than of a Performer.

I was no sooner retired to my Lodgings, but I ran over in my Thoughts the several Characters of this fair Assembly; which I shall give some Account of, because they are various in their Kind, and may each of them stand as a Sample of a whole Species.

The Person who pleased me most was a Flute, an Instrument, that, without any great Compass, hath something exquisitely sweet and soft in its Sound: It lulls and sooths the Ear, and fills it with such a gentle kind of

Melody, as keeps the Mind awake without startling it, and raises a most agreeable Passion between Transport and Indolence. In short, the Musick of the Flute is the Conversation of a mild and amiable Woman, that has nothing in it very elevated, nor, at the same Time, any thing mean or trivial.

I must here observe, that the Hautboy is the most perfect of the Flute Species, which, with all the Sweetness of the Sound, hath a great Strength and Variety of Notes; though at the same Time I must observe that the Hautboy in one Sex is as fearce as the Harpsichord in the Other.

By the Side of the Flute there sat a Flagelet; for so I must call a certain young Lady, who, fancying herself a Wit, despised the Musick of the Flute as low and insipid, and would be entertaining the Company with tart ill-natured Observations, pert Fancies, and little Turns, which she imagined to be full of Life and Spirit. The Flagelet therefore doth not differ from the Flute so much in the Compass of its Notes, as in the shrillness and sharpness of the Sound. We must however take Notice, that the Flagelets among their own Sex are more valued and esteemed than the Flutes.

There chanced to be a Coquette in the Consort, that, with a great many skittish Notes, affected Squeaks, and studied Inconsistencies, distinguished herself from the rest of the Company. She did not speak a Word during the whole Trial; but I thought she would never have done upon the Opera. One while she would break out upon, 'That hideous King!' then upon 'the charming Black-Moor!' then 'O that dear Lion!' then would hum over two or three Notes; then run to the Window to see what Coach was coming. The Coquette therefore I must distinguish by that musical Instrument which is commonly known by the Name of Kit, that is more jiggish than the Fiddle itself, and never sounds but to a Dance.

The fourth Person who bore a Part in the Conversation was a Prude, who stuck to the Trial, and was silent upon the whole Opera. The Gravity of her Censures, and Composure of her Voice, which were often attended with supercilious Casts of the Eye, and a seeming Contempt for the Lightness of the Conversation, put me in Mind of that ancient, serious, Matron-like Instrument, the Virginal.

I must pass over in Silence a Lancashire Hornpipe, by which I would signify a young Country Lady, who with a great Deal of Mirth and Innocence, diverted the Company very agreeably; and, if I am not mistaken, by that Time the wildness of her Notes is a little softened, and the Redundancy of her Musick restrained by Conversation and good Company, will be improved into one of the most amiable Flutes about the Town. Your Romps and Boarding-school Girls fall likewise under this Denomination.

On the Right Hand of the Hornpipe sat a Welsh Harp, an Instrument which very much delights in the Tunes of old historical ballads, and in celebrating the renowned Actions and Exploits of ancient British Heroes. By this Instrument, I therefore would describe a certain Lady, who is one of those female Historians that upon all occasions enters into Pedigrees and Descents, and finds herself related, by some off-shoot or other, to almost every great Family in England: For which Reason, she jarres and is out of Tune very often in Conversation, for the Company's Want of due Attention and Respect to her.

But the most sonorous part of our Consort was a She-Drum, or, as the Vulgar call it, a Kettle-drum, who accompanied her Discourse with Motions of the Body, tosses of the Head, and brandishes of the Fan. Her Musick was loud, bold, and masculine. Every Thump she gave alarmed the Company, and very often set some body or other in it a-blushing.

The last I shall mention was a certain romantic Instrument called a Dulcimer, who talked of nothing but shady Woods, flowery Meadows, purling Streams, Larks and Nightingales, with all the Beauties of the Spring, and the Pleasures of a Country-life. This Instrument hath a fine melancholy Sweetness in it, and goes very well with the Flute.

I think most of the conversable art of Womankind may be found under one of the foregoing Divisions; but it must be confessed, that the Generality of that Sex, notwithstanding they have naturally a great Genius for being talkative, are not Mistresses of more than one Note; with which, however, by frequent Repetition, they make a greater Sound than those who are possessed of the whole Gamut; as may be observed in your Larums or Householdscolds, and in your Castanets or impertinent Tittle-tattles, who have no other Variety in their Discourse but that of talking slower or faster.

Upon communicating this Scheme of Musick to an old Friend of mine, who was formerly a Man of Gallantry, and a Rover, he told me, that he believed he had been in Love with every Instrument in my Consort. The first that smit him was a Hornpipe, who lived near his Father's House in the Country; but upon his failing to meet her at an Assize, according to appointment, she cast him off. His next Passion was for a Kettle-drum, whom he fell in Love with at a Play; but when he became acquainted with her, not finding the softness of her Sex in her Conversation, he grew cool to her; though at the same time he could not deny but that she behaved herself very much like a Gentlewoman. His third Mistress was a Dulcimer, who he found took great delight in sighing and languishing, but would go no further than the Preface of Matrimony; so that she would never let a Lover have any more of her than her Heart, which after having won, he was forced to leave her, as despairing of any further Success. I must confess, says my Friend, I have often considered her with a great deal of Admiration; and I find her Pleasure is so much in this first step of an Amour, that her life will pass away in Dream, Solitude, and Soliloquy, until her decay of Charms makes her snatch at the worst Man that ever pretended to her. In the next Place, says my Friend, I fell in Love with a Kit, who led me such a Dance through all the Varieties of a familiar, cold, fond, and indifferent Behaviour, that the World began to grow censorious, though without any Cause; for which Reason, to recover our Reputations, we parted by Consent. To mend my Hand, says he, I made my next Application to a Virginal, who gave me great Encouragement, after her cautious Manner, until some malicious Companion told her of my long Passion for the Kit, which made her turn me off as a scandalous Fellow. At length, in Despair, says he, I betook myself to a Welsh Harp, who rejected me with contempt, after having found that my Great Grandmother was a Brewer's Daughter. I found by the Sequel of my Friend's Discourses, that he had never aspired to a Hautboy; that he had been exasperated by a Flagelet; and that, to this very Day, he pines away for a Flute.

Upon the whole, having thoroughly considered how absolutely necessary it is, that two Instruments, which are to play together for Life, should be exactly tuned, and go in perfect Consort with each other; I would propose Matches between the Musick of both Sexes, according to the following Table of Marriage.

1. Drum and Kettle-drum.
2. Lute and Flute.
3. Harpsichord and Hautboy.
4. Violin and Flagelet.
5. Bass-Viol and Kit.
6. Trumpet and Welsh-Harp.
7. Hunting-horn and Hornpipe.
8. Bagpipe and Castanet.
9. Passing-Bell and Virginal.

Tatler, April 11th, 1710

From My Own Apartment, May 1st

I was looking out of the Parlour-Window this Morning, and receiving the Honours which Margery, the Milk-Maid to our Lane, was doing me, by dancing before my Door with the Plate of half her Customers on her Head, when Mr. Clayton, the Author of 'Arsinoe', made me a visit, and desired me to insert the following Advertisement in my ensuing Paper.

'The pastoral Masque, composed by Mr. Clayton, Author of "Arsinoe", will be performed on Wednesday, the third instant, in the great Room at York-Buildings. Tickets may be had at White's Chocolate-house, St. James's Coffee-house in St. James's-street, and Young Man's Coffee-house.

'Note; the Tickets delivered out for the twenty-seventh of April, will be taken then.'

When I granted his Request, I made one to him, which was, that the Performers should put their Instruments in Tune before the Audience came in; for that I thought the Resentment of the Eastern Prince who, according to the old Story, took Tuning for Playing, to be very just and natural. He was so civil, as not only to promise that Favour; but also to assure me, that he would order the Heels of the Performers to be muffled in Cotton, that the Artists in so polite an Age as ours, may not intermix with their Harmony a Custom, which so nearly resembles the stamping Dances of the West-Indians or Hottentots.

Tatler, May 2nd, 1710

My wife is a great Pretender to Musick, and very ignorant of it; but far gone in the Italian Taste. Tom goes to Armstrong, the famous fine Writer of Musick, and desires him to put this Sentence of Tully in the Scale of an Italian Air, and write it out for my Spouse from him '. . . Does he live like a Gentleman who is commanded by a Woman? He to whom she gives Law, grants and denies what she pleases? Who can neither deny her anything she asks, or refuses to do anything she commands.'

To be short, my Wife was extremely pleased with it; said the Italian was the only language for Musick; and admired how wonderfully tender the Sentiment was, and how pretty the Accent is of that Language: with the rest that is said by Rote on that Occasion, Mr. Meggot is sent for to sing this Air, which he performs with mighty Applause; and my Wife is in Ecstasy on the Occasion, and glad to find by my being so much pleased, that I was at last come into the Notion of the Italian; for, said she, it grows upon one when one once comes to know a little of the Language; and pray, Mr. Meggot, sing again those Notes 'Nihil Imperanti negare, nihil recusare'.

Spectator, Nov. 2nd, 1711

Jan. 24th, 1712

'Mr. Spectator'

I am Clerk of the Parish from whence Mrs. Simper sends her Complaint in your Yesterday's 'Spectator'. ... As to herself, I had one Day set the hundredth Psalm, and was singing the first Line in order to put the Congregation into the Tune, she was all the while curtsying to Sir Anthony in so affected and indecent a Manner, that the Indignation I conceived at it made me forget my self so far, as from the Tune of that Psalm to wander into 'Southwell' Tune, and from thence into 'Windsor' Tune, still unable to recover myself till I had with the utmost Confusion set a new one. Nay, I have often seen her rise up and smile, and curtsey to one at the lower End of the Church in the midst of a 'Gloria Patri'; and when I have spoke the Assent to a Prayer with a long 'Amen' uttered with decent Gravity, she has been rowling her Eyes round about in such a manner, as plainly shewed however she was moved, it was not towards an Heavenly Object.

Spectator, Jan. 25th, 1712

ON BACH (1685–1750)

SIR JOHN HAWKINS

This person was celebrated for his skill in the composition of canon, as also for his performance on the organ, especially in the use of the Pedals. Mattheson says that on this instrument he was even superior to Handel.

A General History of the Science and Practice of Music, 1776

DR. CHARLES BURNEY

If Sebastian Bach and his admirable son Emmanuel, instead of being musical directors in commercial cities, had been fortunately employed to compose for the stage and the public of the great Capitals, such as Naples, Paris, or London, and for performances of the first class, they would doubtless have simplified their style more to the level of their judges; the one would have sacrificed all unmeaning art and contrivance and the other been less fantastical and 'recherché', and both, by writing in a style more popular, and generally intelligible and pleasing, would have expended their fame and been indisputably the greatest musicians of the present century.

History of Music, 1776

MUSICAL WORLD

The chorus is accompanied, we believe, by three obligati trumpets, the alto tromba extending to E in alt. This part of course Mr. Harper could not play, nor indeed could anybody, with the instrument now in use in our orchestras. The aria 'Qui sedes' has an obligato accompaniment for the tenoroon or oboe d'amore, an instrument which extended below the Corno Inglese. This Mr. Grattan Cooke attempted on the common oboe, and,

D   D.M.C.

of course, stopped at the very outset of his exertions. The bass solo 'Quoniam tu solus', is accompanied by a horn as next to impracticable, and Mr. Denman was furnished with a fagotti part which appeared greatly incorrect. Of course the selection was slaughtered, with soli players retiring in dismay, and leaving Mr. Knyvett to play their parts on the organ, which he did most manfully, after the fashion of the men of the last generation, 'Solo on the Cornet stop'.

Mass in B minor, 1838

ATHENAEUM

. . . his songs, if we are to judge from the selections of the season, are rather mechanical dialogues for the voice with some instrument of the kind, than such airs of expression as make Handel immortal.

June 2nd, 1838

It will, of course, be a long time before the intricate music of Bach can be properly and effectively executed; and when a thoroughly efficient ensemble is secured, it will be still doubtful whether the 'Passione' according to St Matthew or St John can ever be permanently retained in the oratorio repertoire.

Feb. 18th, 1871

SIR GEORGE MACFARREN

Bach had especially the principles of counterpoint at heart in the development of manifold melodies; but in the entanglement of his melodies there cannot be a question he introduced often such progressions between parts as are acceptable only because they are Bach's, but would be condemned in the writing of any man who placed not side by side with them such incidents of absolute brilliancy as dazzle our senses and make us incapable of perceiving the unbeautiful passages. From time to time, since musical laws were first inaugurated, there has been forbidden the progression of two parts in perfect intervals, one with another, from fifth to fifth, from eighth to eighth, and fourth to fourth. From eighth to eighth one will not find in Bach's music, but fifths and fourths are not of seldom occurrence, and still worse, and still more often, one finds that his parts proceed in seconds or in sevenths, progressions so hideous that the early law givers never deemed necessary to prohibit them, believing, one may conjecture, that nobody could be seduced to write what would be repugnant to himself and to everybody else to hear. Will you think from this that I disparage the master? Will you think from this that I slight the genius of the man who, more than anyone else, proved the capabilities of counterpoint, proved the boundless resources of fundamental harmony? Oh, no! Let me not so misrepresent the feeling that I have at heart. We should do injustice to even this great master if blindly, or may I say deafly, we accepted everything he wrote as a model for our imitation. It is only by dissecting the music and observing what is to be avoided that we may learn what is to be imitated. To reproduce his beauties is beyond our power, to avoid his faults is within the reach of everyone, and we pay him the greatest homage when we distinguish what is excellent from what is inevitable.

From a Paper read to the Royal
Musical Association, March 2nd, 1885

SAMUEL BUTLER

It is imputed to him for righteousness that he goes over the heads of the general public and appeals mainly to musicians. But the greatest men do not go over the heads of the masses, they take them rather by the hand. The true musicians would not snub him so much as a musical critic. His instinct is towards the man in the street rather than the Academy.

Perhaps I say this as being myself a man in the street musically. I do not know, but I know that Bach does not appeal to me and I do appeal from Bach to the man in the street and not to the Academy, because I believe the first of these to be the sounder.

Still, I own Bach does appeal to me sometimes. In my own poor music I have taken passages from him before now, and have my eye on others which I have no doubt will suit me somewhere. Whether Bach would know them again when I have worked my will on them, and much more whether he would own them, I neither know nor care. I take or leave as I choose, and alter or leave untouched as I choose. I prefer my music to be an outgrowth from a germ whose sources I know, rather than a waif and stray which I fancy to be my own child when it was all the time begotten of a barrel organ. It is a wise tune that knows its own father and I like my music to be the legitimate offspring of respectable parents. Roughly, however, as I have said over and over again, if I think something that I know and greatly like in music, no matter whose, is appropriate, I appropriate it. I should say I was under most obligations to Handel, Purcell, and Beethoven.

Note Books

J. A. FULLER-MAITLAND

Bach's position in regard to the fugue is precisely that of Beethoven towards the sonata; that is to say, the form attained, in his hands, to an eloquence, a directness of expression, and a vitality, which gave the crowning touch to the structure upon which so many other hands had laboured. Yet as the student of sonata-form would be required to study a more conventional type of sonata than Beethoven's in order to assimilate the strict rules by which that form is governed, so the laws of fugue can be more clearly deduced from the works of the older, more conventional masters, than from those of Bach, whose wealth of ideas impelled him to frequent departure from the established code, with whom the essential import of the composition was of greater consequence than the manner of its treatment. It is perhaps a logical consequence of the freedom which these illustrious masters introduced into forms that were becoming stereotyped at the time they wrote, that their utterance in these forms should have been in some degree the final expression, as well as the highest, of their possibilities. Here and there, since the time of Bach, a fugue has been produced which strikes us as a spontaneous creation, and there are sonatas of the post-Beethoven period would have a value of their own; but the great majority of modern fugues, and a good many modern sonatas, suggest that the writers are deliberately adopting the costume of an earlier day, that they are in fact posing in fancy dress.

'The Age of Bach and Handel',
Oxford History of Music, Vol. IV, 1902

SIR HUBERT PARRY

... Bach not only took infinite pains to develop his musical insight ... by the close scrutiny to which he subjected the works of other composers; the spirit of adventure was strong in him and impelled him constantly to speculative courses. This is shown in every phase of his work. When the mood was on him, his part-writing is sometimes positively reckless, and the voice parts occasionally are almost unsingable. But yet it is not the clumsiness of the composer who does not know how to write otherwise, but the conviction of one who chooses the more stirring course because that expresses most decisively what is in his mind. His experimental ventures were serviceable in other ways; for, while the mere procedure of contrapuntal art had been thoroughly explored and tested before his time, the various structural types were otherwise, and he was bent on finding as many different schemes as possible wherein to cast the musical impulses which welled up in him. It was for this end that he not only speculated in all kinds of forms such as concertos, suites, variations, sonatas, overtures, sinfonias, chorale preludes, chorale fantasias, but tried how one could be combined with another, and how they could be transferred from the sphere for which they had been devised into new conditions. It was with the view of widening his resources of design that he imported the form of the French and Italian overtures and concertos into the choral movements of his cantatas, that he expanded the form of the chorale preludes and fantasias into immense choruses, adapted the orchestral to a solo instrument, and adorned his instrumental fugues with unfugal episodes annexed from other types of art.

All such novel experiments were tested by his own musical instinct and not by reference to schemes propounded by theorists. He anticipated the fact that form is another word for organisation, and that organisation varies in its relation to the quality of the matter or ideas dealt with and the style adopted. His methods of organisation cover the field from one extreme to another. . . .

His humanity manifested itself in many and various ways. He delighted in frank rhythm. No composer ever attained to anything approaching the spontaneity, freshness, and winsomeness of his dances . . . ; while many of his great choruses and his instrumental fugues are inspired with a force of rhythmic movement which thrills the hearer with a feeling of being swept into space out of the range of common things. But his ample humanity is equally shown in his love of melody. He is wonderful enough in the more conventional and regular forms of tune, but far more so in the deeply expressive rhapsodical melody, the outpouring of copious and genuine feeling, such as is displayed in his ariosos, the slow movements for solo violin, and the slow movement of the Italian concerto. Here again he anticipates the trend of true Teutonic melody, free, unconstrained, welling out untrammelled by convention, the direct emanation of spiritual exaltation.

. . . He realised quite early in his career that mere bald harmony without inner motion is too often dead weight, and that the movement of its components, either by counterpoint or figuration, is necessary to give it full artistic life. And in this sphere the supreme mastery of technical resource which his ceaseless labours produced served him in the greatest stead. His readiness and the absolute ease with which he manipulated large numbers of parts produced texture of a richness which seems almost unapproachable. . . .

Bach's scope was so comprehensive and concentrated that he frequently cumulates several tracts of thought and emotion simultaneously. One of his favourite devices is to throw in an independent comment on the sentiment expressed by the parts which are associated with the words, by characteristic figures in the accompaniment, by counter-subjects, even by references to extraneous chorale tunes. The idea may actually have come to him first in connection with counter-subjects of fugues, which often have a commentary character. But he does not confine himself to combining sentiments in different parts. It is by no means uncommon to find a single part representing several different concepts, or different aspects of the same idea. The figure of two notes given to the pedals in the Chorale prelude 'Durch Adam's Fall' is interpreted by one commentator to be the expression of profound sorrow at the awesome idea of the Fall and its consequences; by another it is held to be one of Bach's quaintly symbolic touches of realistic suggestion. The latter is obviously right, and so, perhaps, is the former; and if it were added that Bach wrote the figure because it was convenient to the pedals, and also because it introduced a characteristic rhythmic element into the movement, and also because the broken character of the passages given to the hands, he would not have half exhausted the multitudinous motives which impelled the composer. The justification of the practice of transferring movements originally written to secular words to works which were to serve for sacred purposes lies in such many-sided implications; for where a single passage or movement represents various combined intentions, different meanings may be specially emphasised.

Johann Sebastian Bach, 1909

W. G. WHITTAKER

No doubt the factors which decided the composition of these (the solo cantatas) were the conditions of his choir and the presence of solo singers of exceptional merit. It is interesting to speculate on the individual singers who served under the master. He utilised everyone's capabilities to the full, rejoicing in the possession of some good vocalist or writing within such restricted limits as would suit a person of truncated range and feeble execution. We can find at various periods clear evidence, for instance, of some bass of wide compass and considerable power, of altos with exceptionally low range or of peculiarly sympathetic quality, of a soprano of brilliant technique, of tenors bordering on the counter-tenor, and of others little higher than baritones. This is one of the difficulties which beset performance; with restricted means one cannot always select soloists who are vocally and temperamentally fitted to the arias and recitatives Bach wrote for particular singers.

Evidence of this nature shatters the fallacy that Bach was a man hopelessly unpractical, and that in his writings, his vocal writings particularly, he consulted only his own ideals of what should be, and not the capabilities of his performers. He was, on the contrary, a working musician who, without sacrificing any ideals, accommodated himself to the forces he had at hand, and to the conditions of performance existing for him. Occasionally, no doubt, he wrote music just for the sheer joy of writing, as if at times he was bound to give out the mighty thoughts that were within him, whatever the medium might be. The B minor Mass, or at any rate, many portions of it, was such a piece of self-expression, possibly never heard complete by the composer. In the case of the violin chaconne and the first movement of the B minor flute sonata, the instrumental medium is hopelessly inadequate for the greatness of the thoughts; but these are exceptions. We know that he wrote mostly chamber music at Cöthen, and mostly church music at Leipzig, that when he went to Hamburg he tried to meet the Northern Organists on their own ground with the Fantasia in G minor, that for the meetings of the Telemann Society he wrote, or arranged from existing violin compositions, concertos for harpsichord and strings etc. And so in the cantatas we find him adapting himself to the material at hand, both instrumental and vocal.

While the performances of that day would not equal in ensemble and nuance the standard we look for now, it is scarcely to be believed that he went on year after year writing music which was beyond the performing capacities of his forces. In fact, we should look at it the other way, and acknowledge that the weekly performances of such music, with all the disadvantages of single parts, hastily written and often incorrectly, with but little time for rehearsal, argues a generally high standard of attainment on the part of his vocalists and instrumentalists, inadequate as they may have been at times.

Bach's Cantatas, 1924

W. J. TURNER

Perfect outward formality, an extreme refinement of manner and exceptional control of gesture—if of the very finest quality—are the result of an extreme sensitiveness to impressions without. Natures of inwardly burning volcanic force do not always possess this sensitiveness to the outer world of sense—at least not habitually and at will. Bach's roughness and uncouthness were due to a lack (as compared with Mozart) of this sensitiveness as closely to the lack of sensitiveness to the medium of sound itself. One cannot imagine Bach being ravished by the mere sounds of notes struck on instruments as Debussy must have been. Bach was comparatively indifferent to tone-colour. We have no piece of evidence about him similar to that which relates that Mozart disliked the sound of trumpets. Bach was emphatically one of those men of extraordinary artistic vitality who do not control but are in the grip of their inspiration . . . no composer benefited more from a prolonged and arduous application to the sheer drudgery of constant composition than did Bach. Yet, in spite of his enormous output, his work lacks variety. Bach is undoubtedly inventive and he can range from profound melancholy to a joyous exuberance which has never been surpassed in music. It is this latter power which makes him most conspicuous. He was also a stayer (the exact antithesis to the short-winded Brahms), even as much of a stayer as Wagner. . . .

In imagination and in originality of thought I think we must put Bach below Beethoven and Wagner, but his wonderful virility and Rabelaisian vitality give him an unique place in the history of music. No composer gives one a greater sense of power, and his limitations are a source of strength—for it is the absence of all appeal to the imagination that enables us to take such pleasure in his workmanship. I am heretic enough to believe that Bach is in no respect a better craftsman than Wagner (I will leave out Mozart, as most critics would grant me that), and in support of this contention I would ask, Where in all Bach's music is to be found an example of technical virtuosity comparable to Wotan's long narrative to Brunhilde in the second act of 'Die Walküre'? There is not a single aria in the whole of Bach's myriad cantatas that has the breadth, the variety, the imagination and the sustained musical flight of that amazing scene. Technically Bach's best arias are wonderful examples of expressive polyphony but they move within narrower limits than Wagner's monologue. Could Bach have written the love scene in the second act of 'Tristan'? Never! Could Wagner have written anything comparable with, anything as thrilling as the great organ Toccata in F? Yes, he did. He did it in the 'Meistersinger' overture. Nevertheless, if we grant that in sensibility—that sensibility which when allied to great intellectual power and vitality produces the finest imagery, whether in poetry or music—Bach was below Beethoven, Mozart, and Wagner, yet he is among the greatest composers by virtue of a sublimity of conception, an intrinsic greatness, almost impossible to define but comparatively easy to feel. Bach was a great artist, not merely a clever musician or a virtuoso of genius, and there are so few of these that we can be tolerant of the enthusiasm of his admirers.

Musical Meanderings, 1928

H. V. JERVIS-READ

One finds it as impossible to allude to texture without alluding to Bach's incomparable resultant perpendicular coherence: his harmony, as it would be to consider fugal construction without his supreme aid; and it is interesting to observe that Bach's instrumental texture shows to its greatest advantage on the organ and not on the piano (for which instrument he did not write: and the texture suffers undoubtedly on this account), when each part is of equal dynamic importance. (It has to be allowed that the organ permits a wider spacing, a bigger disposition of the part-writing than the piano does).

Often a pianist's capabilities and intellectual capacity are assessed from his Bach playing. This is an erroneous convention (most conventions are erroneous), and the error is due to a bad habit, or else to hero-worship. (For unreasoning and unreasonable hero-worship, it is hard to beat a report of a recital I read, at which the pianist had played both Bach's Chromatic Fantasia and Fugue and Glazounov's Prelude and Double Fugue. It was acknowledged that the Glazounov was a fine work finely played. The writer then found it necessary to add that Glazounov cannot compare on any count with Bach, and implied that the acid test of musicianship resides in Bach playing. Honestly, why? Because the writer of the article is better acquainted with Bach than with Glazounov? Is not this sort of thing pompous superciliousness, and a dreary effort at intellectual superiority? And is it not mis-applied hero-worship more suited to the criticaster than to the accomplished critic?).

A good deal is demanded of a pianist playing Bach beyond agile and deft finger-work, but the custom of playing the subject of a fugue 'un peu en dehors' is irritating; and the simplicity of mind: the ingenuousness, which pathetically is at the bottom of this custom, diverting. Paradoxically enough, .it is, too, the quintessence of obscurity; surely the subject should mix on equal terms with its attendant counterpoint, and so merge in the perpendicular coherence: so be sunk in Bach's incomparable harmony.

The Arrant Artist, 1939

ON HANDEL (1685–1759)

LADY A. IRWIN

Last week we had an oratorio composed by Handel out of the story of Borak (sic) and Deborah, the latter of which name it bears. Handel thought, encouraged by the Princess Royal, it had merit enough to deserve a guinea, and for the first time it was performed at that price, exclusive of subscribers' tickets; and there was but 120 people in the House. The subscribers being refused unless they would pay a guinea, they insisting on the rights of their season tickets, forced into the House and carried their point. I was at the entertainment on Tuesday; 'tis excessive noisy, a vast number of instruments and voices who all perform at a time and is in music what I fancy a French ordinary in conversation.

Letter to Lord Carlisle, March 31st, 1733

FRANCIS HARE, BISHOP OF CHICHESTER

London. After the service, there was a large Anthem, the words by the Sub-Dean of Westminster, the music set by Mr. Handel, and is reckoned to be as good a piece as he ever made; it was above fifty minutes in singing.

Letter to his son, Dec. 18th, 1737

HORACE WALPOLE

Handel has set up an Oratorio against the Operas, and succeeds. He has hired all the goddesses from farces and the singers of 'Roast Beef' from between the acts at both theatres, with a man with one note in his voice, and a girl without ever an one; and so they sing, and make brave hallelujahs; and the good company encore the recitative, if it happens to have any cadence like they call a tune.

Letter to Sir Horace Mann, Feb. 24th, 1743

DR. ARBUTHNOT

Inprimis, you are charged with having bewitched us for the space of twenty years past.

Secondly, you have most insolently dared to give us good musick and harmony, when we wanted and desired bad.

Thirdly, you have most feloniously and arrogantly assumed to yourself an uncontrolled property of pleasing us, whether we would or no; and have often been so bold as to charm us when we were positively resolved to be out of humour.

★   ★   ★

Have you taken your degree?
Are you a doctor?
A fine composer, indeed, and not a graduate . . . why, Dr. Pushpin (Pepusch) and Dr. Blue (Greene) laugh at you, and scorn to keep you company.

★   ★   ★

You have made such musick as never man did before you, nor, I believe, never will be thought of again when you are gone . . .

Harmony in an Uproar: a Letter to
Frederick Handel, Esqre., 1754

REVEREND THOMAS MOREL

And now as to Oratorio's: 'There was a time (says Mr. Addison) when it was laid down as a maxim, that nothing was capable of being well set to music that was not nonsense.' And this I think though it might be wrote before Oratorio's were in fashion, supplies an Oratorio-Writer (if he may be called a writer) with some sort of apology; especially if it be considered what alterations he must submit to, if the composer be of an haughty disposition, and has but an imperfect acquaintance with the English language. As to myself, great lover as I am of music, I should never have thought of such an under-taking (in which, for the reasons above, little or no credit is to be gained), had not Mr. Handell applied to me when in Kew, in 1746, and added to his request the honour of a recommendation from Prince Frederick, upon this I thought I could do as well as some who had gone before me and within two or three days carried him the first act of 'Judas Macchabaeus', which he approved of. 'Well,' says he, 'and how are you to go on?' 'Why, we are to suppose an engagement and that the Israelites have conquered and so begin with a chorus as "Fallen is the Foe", or something like it.' 'No. I will have this," cried Handell, and began working it, as it is, upon the Harpsichord. 'Well, go on. I will bring you more to-morrow.' 'No, something now,

"So fall thy foes, O Lord",

that will do', and immediately carried on the composition as we have it in that most admirable chorus. That incomparable Air, 'Wise men, flattering, may deceive us' (which was the last he composed, as 'Sion, now thy head shall rise' was his last chorus) was designed for 'Belshazzar', but that not being performed, he happily flung it into 'Judas Maccabeus'. N.B. The plan of 'Judas Maccabeus' was designed as a compliment to the Duke of Cumberland, upon his returning victorious from Scotland. I had introduced several incidents more apropos, but it was thought they would make it too long and was therefore omitted. The Duke however made me a handsome present by the hands of Mr. Pointz. The success of the Oratorio was very great, and I have often wished, that at first I had asked in jest, for the benefit of the thirtieth night instead of the third. I am sure he would have given it me; on which night there was above £400 in the House. He left me a legacy, however, of £200. The next year he desired another, and I gave him 'Alexander Belus', which follows the history of the fore-going on the 'Maccabeus'. In the first part there is a very pleasing Air, accompanied with the 'Hark, Hark, Hark, he strikes the Golden Lyre'. In the 2nd, two charming duets 'O What Pleasure past expressing' and 'Hail, Wedded Love, mysterious Law'. The 3rd begins with an incomparable Air, in the 'affetuoso' style, intermixed with the chorus Recitative that follows it. And so to the last Air, I cannot help telling you, that, when Mr. Handell first read it, he cried out, 'Damn your Iambics.' 'Don't put yourself in a passion, they are easily Trochees.' 'Trochees? What are Trochees?' 'Why, the very reverse of Iambics by leaving out a syllable in every line, as instead of:

> Convey me to some peacefull shore,
> Lead me to some peacefull shore.'

'This is what I want.' 'I will step into the parlour and alter them immediately.' I went down and returned with them altered in about 3 minutes when he would have them as they were, and had set them, most delightfully accompanied with only a quaver and a rest of 3 quavers.

The next I wrote was 'Theodora' (in 1749) which Mr. Handell himself valued more than any performance of the kind; and when I once asked him, whether he did not look upon the Grand Chorus in the 'Messiah' as his master piece? 'No,' says he, 'I think the chorus at the end of the 2nd part in "Theodora" far beyond it.' 'He saw the lovely youth', etc.

The 2nd night of 'Theodora' was very thin, though Princess Amelia was there. I guessed it a losing night, so did not go to Mr. Handell as usual; but seeing him smile I ventured, 'When will you be there?' 'Next Friday night,' says he, 'and I will play it you.' I told him I had just seen Sir T. Hanket and he desired me to tell you, that if you would have it again, he would engage for all the boxes. 'He is a fool; the Jews will not come to it (as to "Judas") because it is a Christian story; and the Ladies will not come because it is a virtuous one.'

My own favourite is 'Jeptha', which I wrote in 1751 and in the composing of which Mr. Handell fell blind. I had the pleasure to hear it finely performed at Salisbury under Mr. Harris; and in much greater perfection, as to the vocal part, at the Concert in Tottenham Court Road. . . .

To oblige Mr. Smith, Mr. Handell's successor, I wrote 'Nabal' in 1764 and 'Sideon'. The music of both are entirely taken from some old genuine pieces of Mr. Handell. In the latter is an inimitable chorus: 'Gloria

Patri, Gloria Filio', which at first sight I despaired of setting with proper words; but at last struck out 'Glorious Patron, Glorious Hero' etc. which did mighty well.

Letter written in 1764

SIR JOHN HAWKINS

The character of an author is but the necessary result of his works, and as the compositions of Handel are many and various, it is but justice to point out such of them as seem the most likely to be the foundation of his future fame. Many of the excellencies, which as a musician recommended him to the favour and patronage of the public during a residence of fifty years in this country, he might perhaps possess in common with a few of the most eminent of his contemporaries; but, till they were taught the contrary by Handel, none were aware of that dignity and grandeur of sentiment of which music is capable of conveying, or that there is a sublime in music as there is in poetry. This is a discovery which we owe to the genius and inventive faculty of this great man; and there is little reason to doubt that the many examples of this kind with which his works abound, will continue to engage the admiration of judicious hearers as long as the love of harmony shall exist.

A General History of the Science and Practice of Music, 1776

DR. CHARLES BURNEY

Handel despised the pedantry of Pepusch, and Pepusch, in return constantly refused to join in the general chorus of Handel's praise.

In organ-playing and composition, Handel and Sebastian Bach seem not only to have surpassed their contemporaries, but to have established a style for that instrument which is still respected and imitated by the greatest organists in Germany.

Handel was perhaps the only great Fuguist, exempt from pedantry. He seldom treated barren or crude subjects; his themes being almost always natural and pleasing. Sebastian Bach, on the contrary, like Michael Angelo in painting, disdained facility so much, that his genius never stooped to the easy and graceful. I never have seen a fugue by this learned and powerful author upon a motive that is natural and chantant; or even an easy and obvious passage, that is not loaded with crude and difficult accompaniments.

History of Music, 1776

REV. WILLIAM MASON

Mr. Handell has taken more liberty with the words than is usually done. So much indeed as might lead one to conclude that he formed the composition out of his musical commonplace, and adapted the words to airs previously invented; which it is probable enough was the case, not only in this, but in many of his later productions.

'Chandos Anthems' from *Essays, Historical
and Critical, of English Church Music*, 1782

FANNY BURNEY

July 22nd, 1786. Charles Wesley played the organ; and after the service was over he performed six or seven pieces by the King's order. They were all of Handel, and so well suited to the organ, and so well performed on a remarkably good instrument, that it was a great regale to me to hear them. The pleasure I received from the performance led me into being too late for the Queen.

Aug. 6th, 1788. We sat in what are called the Steward's places immediately under their Majesties. The performance was very long, and tolerably tedious, consisting of Handel's gravest pieces and fullest choruses. . . .

My cousins called in the evening and we accompanied

them to the concert, where I was much more pleased than in the morning, but obliged to come away at the end of the first act, as it was already ten o'clock, so late did they begin the performance.

Feb. 2nd, 1789. . . . He (George III) next talked to me a great deal of my dear father, and made a thousand inquiries concerning his 'History of Music'. This brought him to his favourite theme, Handel; and he told me innumerable anecdotes of him, and particularly that celebrated tale of Handel's saying of himself, when a boy, 'While that boy lives, my music will never want a protector.' And this, he said, I might relate to my father.

Then he ran over most of his oratorios, attempting to sing the subjects of several of the airs and choruses, but so dreadfully hoarse that the sound was terrible.

$$\star \qquad \star \qquad \star$$

He now spoke of my father, with still more kindness and told me he ought to have had the post of Master of the Band and not that little poor musician Parsons, who was not fit for it. 'But Lord Salisbury', he cried, 'used your father very ill in that business, and so he did me! However, I have dashed out his name, and I shall put your father's in—as soon as I get loose again!'

May 28th, 1790. The Princess Augusta condescended to bring me a most gracious message from the King, desiring to know if I wished to go to Handel's Commemoration, and if I should like the 'Messiah', or prefer any other day.

With my humble acknowledgements for his goodness, I fixed instantly on the 'Messiah'.

Diary

MARIA EDGEWORTH

May 1st, 1813. . . . The organ began to play an anthem of Handel's while we were in the chapel: I wished for you, my dear Sneyd, particularly at that moment!

Letter to C. S. Edgeworth

GEORGE HOGARTH

Music may sometimes be the handmaid of debauchery;
... Bacchanalian songs and glees may heighten the riot
of a dissolute party; but that man must be profligate
beyond conception whose mind can entertain gross
propensities while the words of inspiration, clothed with
the sounds of Handel, are in his ears.

Musical History, 1835

EDWARD FITZGERALD

... and now Sunday is over: I have been to church: I
have dined at Portland Place: and now I come home to
my lodgings: light my pipe: and will whisper something
over to Italy. You talk of your Naples: and that one
cannot understand Theocritus without having been on
these shores. I tell you, you can't understand Macready
without coming to London and seeing his revival of Acis
and Galatea. You enter Drury Lane at a quarter to seven;
the pit is already nearly full: but you find a seat, and a
very pleasant one. Box doors open and shut: ladies take
off their shawls and seat themselves: gentlemen twist their
side curls: the musicians come up from under the stage
one by one: 'tis just upon seven. Macready is very
punctual: Mr. T. Cooke is in his place with his marshall's
baton in his hand: he lifts it up: and off they set with
Handel's noble overture....

The choruses were well sung, well acted, well dressed,
and well grouped; and the whole thing creditable and
pleasant. Do you know the music? It is of Handel's best:
and as classical as any man who wore a full bottomed wig
could write. I think Handel never gets out of his wig:
that is, out of his age: his Hallelujah chorus is a chorus
not of angels, but of well-fed earthly choristers, ranged
tier above tier in a Gothic Cathedral, with princes for
audience and their military trumpets flourishing over the
full volume of the organ. Handel's gods are like Homer's,

and his sublime never reaches beyond the region of the clouds. Therefore I think that his great marches, triumphal pieces, and coronation anthems are his finest works. There is a little bit of Auber's at the end of the Bayadiere when the God resumes his divinity and retires into the sky which has more of pure light and mystical solemnity than anything I know of Handel's: but then this is only a scrap: and Auber could not breathe in that atmosphere long: whereas old Handel's coursers, with necks with thunder clothed and long resounding pace, never tire.

Letter to F. Tennyson, Feb. 6th, 1842

I play of evenings some of Handel's great choruses which are the bravest music after all. I delight in Handel's Allegro and Penseroso. Do you know the fine pompous joyous chorus of 'These pleasures, Mirth, if thou canst give', etc.? Handel certainly does in music what old Bacon desires in his Essay on Masques, 'Let the songs be loud and cheerful, not puling', etc. One might think the Water Music was written from this text.

Letter to F. Tennyson, Feb. 24th, 1844

Concerning the bagwigs of composers. Handel's was not a bagwig, which was simply so named from the little stuffed black silk watch-pocket that hung down behind the back of the wearer. Such were Haydn's and Mozart's —much less influential on the character: much less ostentatious in themselves: not towering so high, nor rolling down in following curls so low as to overlay the nature of the brain within. But Handel wore the Sir Godfrey Kneller wig: greatest of wigs: one of which some great General of the day used to take off his head after the fatigue of the battle, and hand over to his valet to have the bullets combed out of it. Such a wig was a fugue in itself. I don't understand your theory about trumpets, which have always been so little spiritual in use, that they have been the provocatives and celebrators of physical force from the beginning of the world. 'Power', whether spiritual or physical, is the meaning of the trumpet: and so well used, as you say, by Handel in his approaches to the Deity. The fugue in the overture to the Messiah expresses perhaps the thorny wandering ways of the world before the one in the wilderness, and before 'Comfort ye, my people', etc.

Letter to F. Tennyson, June 12th, 1845

SAMUEL BUTLER

Handel's Jig in the ninth 'Suite de Piéces', in G minor, is very fine but it is perhaps a little long. Probably Handel was in a hurry, for it takes much more time to get a thing short than to leave it a little long.

On Brevity

I

If you tie Handel's hands by debarring him from the rendering of human emotion, and if you set Bach's free by giving him no human emotion to render—if, in fact, you rob Handel of his opportunities and Bach of his difficulties—the two men can fight after a fashion, but Handel will even so come off victorious. Otherwise it is absurd to let Bach compete at all. Nevertheless the cultured vulgar have at all times preferred gymnastics and display to reticence and the healthy, graceful, normal movements of a man of birth and education, and Bach is esteemed a more profound musician than Handel in virtue of his frequent and more involved complexity of construction. In reality Handel was profound enough to eschew such wildernesses of counterpoint as Bach instinctively resorted to, but he knew also that public opinion would be sure to place Bach on a level with himself, if not above him, and this probably made him look askance at Bach. At any rate he twice went to Germany without being at any pains to meet him, and once, if not twice, refused Bach's invitation.

II

Rockstro says that Handel keeps much more closely to the old Palestrina rules of counterpoint than Bach does, and that when Handel takes a licence it is a good bold one taken rarely, whereas Bach is niggling away with small licences from first to last.

On Handel and Bach

I only ever met one American who seemed to like and understand Handel. How far he did so in reality I do not know, but, *inter alia*, he said that Handel 'struck ile with the Messiah', and that 'it panned out well, the Messiah did'.

On a Yankee Handelian

It takes as great a composer as Handel—or rather it would take as great a composer if he could be found—to be able to be as easily and triumphantly commonplace as Handel often is, just as it takes—or rather would take—as great a composer as Handel to write another Hallelujah chorus. It is only the man who can do the latter who can do the former as Handel has done it. Handel is so great and so simple that no one but a professional musician is unable to understand him.

On Handel's Commonplaces

The falling shower in the air 'As cheers the sun' in Joshua is, I think, the finest description of a warm sunny refreshing rain that I have ever come across and one of the most wonderfully descriptive pieces of music that even Handel ever did.

On Handel's 'Shower of Rain'
Note Books

ERNEST WALKER

The history of art can hardly show a parallel to the enormous influence which Handel exercised over English music for well-nigh a century after his death; even yet the composer's name is a sort of national fetish with thousands of people who could not for their lives see any difference of quality between the best and the worst things in 'The Messiah', or 'Israel in Egypt'. 'The Messiah' is, indeed, still a part of the average Englishman's religion, and he criticizes its music no more than he criticizes its words; and though it is true that now almost all Handel's other large works are, as wholes, but seldom performed, yet many extracts from them still display their popular halo almost untarnished by lapse of time and changes of fashion. Handel himself . . . took originally to oratorio-writing simply as an experiment towards recapturing the favour of his patrons among the gentry and nobility who had grown tired of Italian opera; but the experiment, risky as it was, secured alike the virtual extinction of original English music for more than a hundred years, and the artistic canonisation of the experimenter. No other musical work in the history of the world has won the kind of homage which in England has fallen to the lot of 'The Messiah'; and none, in spite of its genius, has had a more crushing influence on national artistic individuality.

Yet, passionate as has been the English worship of Handel, we have treated our idol very badly; no other composer who ever lived has had to suffer a tithe of the indignities that we have heaped, and still heap, on his head. The score of 'The Messiah' is full of careful directions that at least ninety-nine per cent of our performances complacently and totally ignore, and only a handful of organists have any notion of even the proper chords of the Dead March in 'Saul'; singers with famous names distort his rhythm out of all recognition, and insert top notes that would have driven him wild, and comparatively few people seem to think that it matters in the very least degree whatever. Until quite recent times, hardly any pianoforte arrangement of his music was in existence which did not blandly ignore and neglect most of the details of his part-writing, and indeed insert chords the like of which neither he nor his contemporaries ever wrote; and the most vilely ignorant 'traditions' of all kinds have sprung up round wellnigh every page of his works. No doubt of late years a very considerable cleansing process has been set on foot—though there is still a vast amount more to be done; but the curious thing is that this uprising of a proper respect for the intentions of a great composer coincides with a very sharply marked decline of his reputation among such musical circles as artistically count for anything.

Of course, it is merely an inevitable reaction against a century's tyranny, and in many cases (as always happens), the reaction has no doubt gone considerably too far. Still, there is really no denying the truths which lie at the bottom of the revolt of the last twenty years or so; to any one who has once shaken himself free from the old fetters, Handel's faults lie on the surface plainly enough. Any one can see the acres of complacent commonplaces, devoid alike of invention and workmanship; ... Indeed, no other composer can even attempt to rival Handel in his power of intensely irritating those who have the strongest and sanest admiration for his genius; no one, it is true, is always at his best, but the pity is that Handel is so very often at his worst.

We can indeed no longer speak of his music, even at its highest, as the supreme crown of the art; the day for that sort of adoration is gone for ever, and we can now see that, secure as is his place among the immortals, he is far from being one of their kings. He was at once too careless and too practical; he lacked the steady self-criticism which rejects inadequate material and when the material is adequate, looks to its polished presentation, and at the same time he kept an unnecessarily steady finger on the pulse of his visible public, and, so far as a man of genius could, wrote for the taste of the moment in the spirit of the mere impresario. Though it is true that in the process he never sacrificed personal self-respect, he took up oratorio, as indeed he took up everything else, because he thought it would pay. His sadly unenterprising contemporary at Leipzig—a mere 'musical director in a commercial city', as the fashionable Dr. Burney sneers— had to wait for something like a century and a half before his supremacy had any chance of being realised; but now the judgements are reversed, and the old idol, hurled down somewhat indignantly from the impossible position that he formerly occupied, is in danger of being relegated to the rubbish-heap. But it would be a million pities if 'The Messiah' were to disappear into the limbo of those artistic works for which the relatively unmusical public retains a superstitious reverence long after the musicians themselves have come to a final, and on the whole—at any rate in comparison—an adverse judgement.

After all, a great man is to be judged ultimately by his greatness; there are, for example, writers who are among the glories of European literature in virtue of a golden handful rescued from a mass of forgotten rubbish. And the student of Handel's oratorios lives in a state of continual exultant surprise. He may, for example, be examining the recitatives, and deploring the almost entire absence of the living spirit that breathes through those of Purcell and Bach, when suddenly he comes across wonderful pages like 'Deeper and deeper still' in 'Jeptha' or 'Thy rebuke hath broken his heart' in 'The Messiah'; he may be wading through the instrumental movements —the purely perfunctory overtures, and the interludes (the Battle Symphonies and the rest) that say remarkably little or indeed nothing—and his attention is suddenly caught by a miraculously impressive thing like the Dead March in 'Saul', or one or two other numbers in 'Judas Maccabeus' or 'Samson' that are similarly oases in a dreary desert. In gratitude for the gift of magnificent music like 'The people shall hear'—full of the thrill that only the immortal things possess—we may well be content to forget the dullness of most of the surrounding pages of 'Israel in Egypt'; and the great movements of 'The Messiah' more than cover a multitude of sins.

A History of Music in England, 1907

ON DR. MAURICE GREENE (1694 or 9–1755)

SIR JOHN HAWKINS

Notwithstanding that he was an excellent organist, and not only perfectly understood the nature of the instrument, but was a great master of fugue, he affected in his voluntaries that kind of practice on single stops, the cornet and the vox-humana for instance, which puts the instrument almost on a level with the harpsichord; a voluntary of this kind being in fact little more than a solo for a single instrument, with the accompaniment of a bass; and in this view Greene may be looked as the father of modern organists. This kind of performance, as it is calculated to catch the ears of the vulgar, who are ever more delighted with melody or what is called air, than harmony, was beneath one, whose abilities were such, that Mattheson, a man but little disposed to flattery, and who was himself one of the first organists in Europe, has not scrupled to rank him among the best of his time.

A General History of the Science and Practice of Music, 1776

J. A. FULLER-MAITLAND

The one English composer of the period who undoubtedly deserves the honour of being mentioned in the same breath with the great masters of the continent is Dr. Maurice Greene, a man who, in more favourable surroundings, would have attained an European celebrity. With more individuality than any of his English contemporaries, he possessed a true and practical admiration for the style of the older church composers, and contrived to solve the problem of combining it with the more modern modes of expression with more success than might have been expected. Such a combination, to our ears, cannot fail to convey some hint of incongruity, and Greene's very eclecticism may have been a subsidiary reason for the brevity of his fame.

'The Age of Bach and Handel',
Oxford History of Music, Vol. IV, 1902

The Eighteenth Century

The Italians exalt music; the French enliven it; the Germans strive after it; and the English pay for it well. The Italians serve music; the French make it into a companion; the Germans anatomize it, and the English compel it to serve them.

MATTHESON, *Neu-eröffnete Orchester* 1713

WHAT IS A MASTER OF MUSICK?

WILLIAM TANSUR (1706–1783)

Musick, the Subject of this Discourse, is a Science of Sound; or an Art that Teaches how to bring all Sounds to the Ear, whether Grave or Acute; and consists of three Parts, i.e. Tune, Time, and Concord.

★ ★ ★

Many years have I laboured in this Divine Science, under the Denomination of a Master of Musick, and have been acknowledged as such by my Pupils; when, alas, I knew, and acknowledged at the same Time, that I fell a great Way short of it.

Any Person that is qualified for such a Title must not only be a Grammarian, but also a Master of Letters and Languages, in order to unfold what is lock'd up in the Closets of the Learned—He must be an Arithmetitian and able to explain Numbers, and even the Misteries of Algebra; and also a Geometrician, to evince in great Variety, the Original of Intervals, Consonant and Disonant; by the Mechanical Division of a Monochord— He must be a Poet, to conform his Thoughts and Words to the Laws of precise Numbers; and Distinguish the Euphony of Vowels and Syllables, &c. He must be a Mechanick, in order to know the exquisite Structure of all Instruments, Wind, Stringed, or Pulsatile. A Mettalist, to explore or find out the different Contemperations of Grave and Acute Toned Metals, for casting Bells for Chimes, &c. He must be an Anatomist, to shew the manner of the sense of Hearing—An Harmonian to lay down the Demonstrative Rules for Composing, &c., and he must be so far a Magician, as to excite Wonder, by bringing into Practice all the admirable Secrets of Musick; Such as Sympathetic and Antipathetic between Consonant and Discord; Together with the artifice of Tubes, for the strengthening and continuing of weak Remote

Sounds, and melorating those which are Strong, &c.—
But stop here, What a Field of Learning must I pass
through to be justly called Master of Musick?—A Title
that no one could ever justly claim, yet attain to.

Preface to *A New Musical Grammar, or*
The Harmonical Spectator, 1746

CHARLES AVISON (*circa* 1710–1770)

The Hautboy will best express the Cantabile, or
singing Style, and may be used in all Movements whatever under this Denomination; especially those Movements which tend to the Gay and Cheerful. In Compositions for the German Flute, is required the same Method
of proceeding by conjoint Degrees, or any such other
natural Intervals, as, with the Nature of its Tone, will
best express the languishing, or melancholy Style. With
both these Instruments, the running into extreme Keys,
the Use of the Staccato, or distinct Separation of Notes;
and all irregular Leaps, or broken and uneven Intervals
must be avoided; for which Reason alone, these Instruments ought never to be employ'd in the Ripieno Parts
of Concertos for Violins, but in such Pieces only as are
composed for them; and these, perhaps, would be most
agreeably introduced as principal Instruments in some
intervening Movements in the Concerto, which might
not only give a pleasing variety, but shew their different
Expressions to the greatest Advantage.

'Elementary Orchestration', *Essay on*
Musical Expression, 1752

REV. WILLIAM MASON (1724–1797)

It is somewhat singular that Italian music, adapted to
English words, as it has been by Aldrich from Palestrina,
and Carissimi (and by Nalson from Fiocco) should produce so good an effect; it is still more singular that the
very ingenious Mr. Garth, of Durham, should have been

able to adapt the music of fifty Psalms in succession, which Benedetto Marcello originally composed for a poetical version in Italian. . . . It is not easy to account for the phenomenon; for, though we are able frequently to perceive that these transmutations have been for the worse (which, besides other reasons, the different degrees of softness in the two languages must necessarily occasion), yet still these attempts must be allowed to have been attended with greater success than might in any reason have been expected, in so much that we may venture to assert that the English Cathedrals have gained some of their best Anthems from this kind of naturalisation, as it may be called, of Italian masters.

'On Adaptations', from *Essays, Historical and Critical, on English Church Music*, 1782

ON HAYDN (1732–1809)

DR. CHARLES BURNEY

I am now happily arrived at that part of my narrative where it is necessary to speak of HAYDN! The admirable and matchless HAYDN! From whose productions I have received more pleasure late in my life, when tired of most other Music, than I ever received in the most ignorant and rapturous part of my youth, when every thing was new, and the disposition to be pleased undiminished by criticism or satiety.

. . . he is now as much respected by professors for his science as invention. Indeed his compositions are in general so new to the player and hearer, that they are equally unable, at first, to keep pace with his inspiration. But it may be laid down as an axiom in Music, that whatever is EASY is OLD, and what the hand, eye, and ear are accustomed to and, on the contrary, what is NEW is of course DIFFICULT, and not only scholars but professors have it to learn. The first exclamation of an embarrassed

E   D.M.C.

performer and a bewildered hearer is, that the Music is very ODD, or very COMICAL; but the queerness and comicality cease, when by frequent repetition, the performer and hearer are at their ease. There is a general cheerfulness and good humour in Haydn's allegros, which exhilarate every hearer. But his adagios are often so sublime in ideas and the harmony in which they are clad, that though played by inarticulate instruments, they have a more pathetic effect on my feelings, than the first opera air united with the most exquisite poetry. He has likewise movements that are sportive, 'folatres', and even grotesque, for the sake of variety; but they are only the 'entre-mets' or rather 'intermezzi', between the serious business of his other movements.

History of Music, 1776

Haydn! Great Sovereign of the tuneful art!
Thy works alone supply an ample chart
Of all the mountains, seas, and fertile plains
Within the compass of its wide domains.
Is there an Artist of the present day
Untaught by thee to think as well as play?
Whose head thy science has not well supplied?
Whose hand thy labours have not fortified?

Old rules, geographic soon were out of date,
When the terrestrial sphere was found oblate:
When wise Copernicus the orbs arranged,
The system of Astronomy was chang'd:
And new laws of harmony are found,
No treatise, code, or theory by pedants vain,
Thy bold, creative genius can restrain.
Imagination, which like garden bird,
Was long forbid the skies, by rules absurd,
Has now broke loose—now takes her airy flight
To explore new worlds, and regions of delight.

Thy style has gain'd disciples, converts, friends,
As far as Music's thrilling power extends.
Nor has great Newton more to satisfaction
Demonstrated the influence of attraction.
And though to Italy of right belong
The indisputed sov'reignty of Song,
Yet ev'ry nation of the earth must now
To Germany pre-eminence allow
For instrumental powers, unknown before
Thy happy flights had taught her sons to soar.

Welcome, great master! to our favour'd isle,
Already partial to thy name and style;
Long may thy fountain of invention run
In streams as rapid as it first begun;
While skill for each fantastic whim provides,
And certain science ev'ry current guides!
Oh, may thy days, from human suff'rings free,
Be blest with glory and felicity,
With full fruition, in a distant hour,
Of all thy magic and creative power!
Blest in thyself, with rectitude of mind,
And blessing, with thy talents, all mankind.

Verses on the Arrival of the Great
Musician Haydn in England, 1789

MONTHLY MAGAZINE

Were it necessary to bring farther illustrations of the superior powers of the new music, compared with that of the ancients, we might attempt a description of the Chaos which opens the work . . .

It commences with all the known instruments, displayed in 23 distinct parts. After these are amalgamated in one tremendous note, a slight motion is made perceptible in the lower parts of the band, to represent the rude masses of nature in a state of chaos. Amidst this turbid modulation, the bassoon is the first that makes an effort to rise and extricate itself from the cumbrous mass. The sort of motion with which it ascends, communicates a like disposition to the surrounding materials, but which is stifled by the falling of the double basses, and the contra fagotto.

In this mingled confusion, the clarionet struggles with more success, and the ethereal flutes escape into air. A disposition verging to order is seen and felt, and every resolution would intimate shape and adjustment, but not a concord ensues! After the volcanic eruption of the clarini and tromboni, some arrangement is promised; a perception follows of the discordant sounds, and leaves a misty effect that happily expresses the 'Spirit of God moving upon the face of the waters'. At the fiat 'Let there be light!' the instruments are unmuted, and the audience is lost in the refulgence of the harmony.

On 'The Representation of Chaos'
from *The Creation*, 1811

W. GARDINER

The manner in which Haydn has employed the wind instruments, opens a field for experiment in the musical art which may not be exhausted for ages. He was the first who discovered that each instrument has a peculiar faculty, and who appointed to each its proper office. He has not only drawn from the several instruments their peculiar language, but has grouped them into classes, for purposes entirely new. Turn to the trio in the Creation, 'On thee each living soul awaits'. The Symphony opens with a flute, two clarionets, two bassoons, and two horns, mingling in a melody, so full and delicious, as to produce that sated effect which the words demand.

'O Lord, on thee they beg their meat;
Thou openest thy hand,
And sated all they are.'

The violins, violoncellos, and double basses, follow in

a separate band, and gradually sink into the depths of the darkest melody, to express,

> 'But as to them thy face is hid.'

This strain is awfully sublime. At the words, 'With sudden terror they are struck,' we feel a paralytic sensation, never before produced by the power of sound. It is a palsied and shivering effect, which is brought about by a singular junction of time and accent.

> 'Thou takest their breath away;
> They vanish into dust;'

is so forcible and commanding, that we begin to doubt whether it is the sound of strings that we have heard. At the passage,

> 'Life with vigour fresh returns'

all contrariness is banished, and the different bands coalesce with a smoothness which produces 'new force and new delight'. All these novelties result from that knowledge of the characteristic powers of the several instruments which Haydn was the first to discover.

A Life of Haydn, 1817

THOMAS BUSBY

Great as was Haydn's native wealth, far from always depending on his own stock, he frequently fed, or manured his imagination with the floating riches of other times and other countries. . . .

. . . powerful and commanding as was the genius of Haydn in the province of instrumental composition, splendid and original as were his conceptions,—grand and varied as the effect he uniformly produces,—nature had not crowned her gifts with that exalted, glowing, and intense feeling, which, not satisfied with sounds alone, pants for the riches of applied sentiment, and seeks them in the treasury of the poetic muse. He was not a great vocal composer. . . .

It was received, says a writer, who tells us he was present, with the most rapturous applause; and I can easily believe him; because the audience were unacquainted with the sublime loftiness, and profound contrivance of Handel, and went ... with ears and minds prepared to be enchanted. But what are the real and prominent features of this composition? A series of attempted imitations of many things inimitable by music, the sudden creation of light happily expressed by an unexpected burst of sound, airs not abundantly beautiful, or original, smothered with ingenious accompaniments, and choruses in which the composer toils under his incumbent weight, labours in fugue, copies with a faint pencil the clear lustre of a glorious prototype, and supplies the absence of true taste and dignity, with the congregated powers of a complicated band. My respect for the great talents of Haydn obliges me to be sorry that his judgement did not forbid his compromising himself in Oratorio composition. But it should be the first policy of so great an artist NEVER to be seen failing; never to let it appear that he CAN fail.

'The Creation', *History of Music*, 1819

WILLIAM BINGLEY

His transcendent genius soon enabled him to soar high above all his competitors; and, as envy seldom fails to pursue merit, the German masters became so jealous of his rising fame, that they entered into a kind of combination in order to decry his compositions. Some went so far as even to write pamphlets against his works, complaining of them as wild, flighty, and trifling; and as tending to introduce new musical doctrines, which till then had been totally unknown in that country. The only notice that Haydn deigned to take of the scurrility and abuse which was thus heaped upon him, was to publish lessons written in imitation of the several styles of his adversaries.

In these their peculiarities were so closely copied, and their extraneous passages so inimitably burlesqued, that they all felt keenly the poignancy of his musical wit, and were silent.

It has often been asserted that the compositions of Haydn are very unequal; that some are replete with elegance and scientific knowledge, whilst others are extravagant to excess. . . .

The national music of the Germans is by nature rough, bold, and grand; and although they do not possess the softness of the Italians, yet it must be confessed that in instrumental music, and particularly in that for wind instruments, they have excelled all other nations. The refinement of their music was reserved for Haydn to accomplish; and this he has done, in a very ample manner, by originality, novelty, and beautiful air, in which he has greatly excelled all his predecessors.

Musical Biography, 1834

SIR HUBERT PARRY

Haydn . . . without being dependent on Mozart or copying his manner, only came to his finest achievements after Mozart's career was over. Then in the year 1791 began the wonderful series of symphonies which he wrote at the invitation of the violinist and concert-manager Salomon for performance in London. These are as much the crown of his fame as the Prague and Vienna symphonies are of Mozart's. The crudity of his earlier orchestral writing has entirely disappeared; and though he never succeeds in getting such a perfectly mellow equal tone as Mozart's, he treats all his instruments with absolute freedom and fitness. The old traditions some-times peep out again in rather long solos for wind instruments, and long passages for small groups of instruments in contrast to the 'tuttis'; but everything is highly characteristic, clear, definite, and mature. On the whole, the treatment inclines to be a little more polyphonic than Mozart's; which accounts for the sound of the instruments not assimilating in the mass of tone quite so well. It was not natural for Mozart to think of the harmonies which supported the melodies in terms of neatly contrived figures of accompaniment, where Haydn, with Teutonic impulse, would incline to think of his mass of tone as divided into various melodic lines. But the shades of difference are so delicate, and each composer is so far alternately harmonic and contrapuntal in turn, that it would be unwise to lay too much stress on this point. Mozart achieves a degree of beauty in his slow movements to which Haydn does not attain; but in the solid 'Allegros' Haydn is more genuinely vigorous than Mozart. In the Minuet movements—which form an important addition to their scheme—it is difficult to award the palm. Mozart's are certainly the most popular, but Haydn's dance tunes have some of the ring that comes of his lineage; which indeed is apparent through almost all his work. Even to the last there is a flavour of rusticity about it. His humour and his merriment are those of the simple honest peasant, while Mozart's is the wit of a man of the world.

Evolution of the Art of Music, 1893

JAMES BOSWELL (1740–1795)

'There is nothing, I think, in which the power of art is shewn so much as in playing on the fiddle. In all other things we can do something at first. Any man will forge a bar of iron, if you give him a box, though a clumsy one; but give him a fiddle and a fiddle-stick and he can do nothing.' ...

In the evening, our gentleman-farmer, and two others, entertained themselves and the company with a great number of tunes on the fiddle. Johnson desired to have

'Let ambition fire thy mind' played over again, and appeared to give patient attention to it; though he owned to me that he was very insensible to the power of music. I told him that it affected me to such a degree, as often to agitate my nerves painfully, producing in my mind alternate sensations of pathetic dejection, so that I was ready to shed tears; and of daring resolutions, so that I was inclined to rush into the thickest part of the battle. 'Sir,' (said he) 'I should never hear it, if it made me such a fool.'

Much of the effect of musick, I am satisfied, is owing to association of ideas. That air, which instantly and irresistably excites in the Swiss, when in a foreign land, the 'maladie du pais', has, I am told, no intrinsick power of sound. And I know from my own experience, that Scotch Reels, though brisk, make me melancholy, because I used to hear them in my early years, at a time when Mr. Pitt called for soldiers 'from the mountains of the north', and numbers of the brave Highlanders were going abroad, never to return. Whereas the airs in 'The Beggar's Opera', many of which are very soft, never fail to render me gay, because they are associated with the warm sensations and high spirits of London. This evening, while some of the tunes of ordinary compositions were played with no great skill, my frame was agitated, and I was conscious of a generous attachment to Dr. Johnson, as my preceptor and friend, mixed with an affectionate regret that he was an old man, whom I should probably lose in a short time. . . .

Mr. Langton and he having gone to see a Freemason's funeral procession, when they were at Rochester, and some solemn musick being played on French-Horns, he said, 'This is the first time that I have ever been affected by musical sounds:' adding, 'that the impression made upon him was of a melancholy kind.' Mr. Langton saying, that this effect was a fine one. JOHNSON 'Yes, if it softens the mind so as to prepare it for the reception of salutary feelings, it may be good. But inasmuch as it is melancholy *per se*, it is bad.

Life of Dr. Johnson, 1791

ON CLEMENTI (1746 or 52–1832)

HARMONICON

Edited by WILLIAM AYRTON

At seeing Mr. Clementi preside over this concert, and in witnessing the performance of his new Symphony, under his own direction, we felt an indescribable pleasure, which we know will, through the medium of this work, be communicated to many, in all parts of the world. It is now between fifty and sixty years since this very celebrated composer's second opera appeared, and immediately stamped him as a man of the highest genius. It continues to this hour admired by all who know how to estimate fine music—music that time cannot obliterate, though fashion may, for a moment, neglect. During the long period that has elapsed, almost as many of his works have appeared, as years have rolled away; and to see their author still fresh—and to hear that his talent yet retains all its youthful verdure—is not merely gratifying to his personal friends, and to those who admire him as a musician; but it encourages human nature, and invigorates those hopes which, without the occasional occurrence of such an instance, the casualties of life are too apt to depress, if not utterly extinguish.

May, 1823

We had the pleasure to see the venerable but still vigorous Clementi conduct this concert. How this justly-celebrated composer must have enjoyed the symphonies! How he must have laughed in his sleeve at the vocal music placed before him! But he is a philosopher . . . .

June, 1825

ON MOZART (1756–1791)

HON. DAINES BARRINGTON

If I was to send you a well-attested account of a boy seven feet in height when he was not more than eight years of age . . .

. . . I said to the boy, that I should be glad to hear an extemporary Love Song . . . .

The boy on this (who continued to sit at his harpsichord) looked back with much archness, and immediately began five or six lines of a jargon recitative proper to introduce a Love Song.

He then played a Symphony which might correspond with an air complimentary to the single word 'Affetto'.

It had a first and second part, which together with the symphonies, was of the length that opera songs generally last: if the extemporary composition was not amazingly capital, yet it was really above mediocrity, and shewed most extremely readiness of invention.

Finding that he was in humour, and as it were inspired, I then desired him to compose a Song of Rage . . . .

The boy again looked back with much archness and began five or six lines of a jargon proper to precede a Song of Rage.

This lasted also about the same time with the Song of Love, and in the middle of it, he had worked himself up to such a pitch, that he bent his head like a person possessed, rising sometimes in his chair.

The word he pitched upon for this second extemporary composition was 'Perfido'.

After this, he played a difficult lesson, which he had finished a day or two before: his execution was amazing, considering that his little fingers could scarcely reach a fifth on the keyboard.

His astonishing readiness, however, did not arise merely from great practice: he had a thorough knowledge of the fundamental principle of composition, as upon producing a treble, he immediately wrote a bass under it, which, when tried, had a very good effect.

He was also a great master of modulation, and his transitions from one key to another were excessively natural and judicious; he practised in this manner for a considerable time with an handkerchief over the keys of the harpsichord.

... I have been informed by two or three able musicians, when (John Christian) Bach the celebrated composer had begun a fugue, and left off abruptly, that little Mozart hath immediately taken it up, and worked it after a most masterly manner.

'Account of a very Remarkable Musician', Paper in the Philosophical Transactions of the Royal Society, 1770

W. GARDINER

This great work is a solemn mass in D minor for the burial of the dead, hung round with the funereal pomp and imagery which the forebodings of the author inspired. At its opening, the ear is accosted by the mournful notes of the Corno di Bassetto, mingling with the bassoons in a strain of bewailing harmony, which streams with impressive effect amidst the short sorrowful notes of the accompanying orchestra.

The 'Dies Irae' follows in a movement full of terror and dismay. The 'Tuba Mirum', is opened by the sonorous tromboni, to awaken the sleeping dead. Every one acquainted with the powers of this instrument acknowledges the superiority of its tones for the expression of this sublime idea.

'Rex tremendae Majestatis', is a magnificent display of regal grandeur, of which none but Mozart would have dared to sketch the outline. It is followed by the beautiful movement 'Recordare', which supplicates in the softest inflexions. The persuasive tone of the Corno di Bassetto is again introduced with unexampled effect.

It is too evident where the pen of our author was arrested; and this wonderful performance is very absurdly finished by repeating some of the early parts of the work to words of a very contrary import. The 'Lux aeterna', is a subject worthy of the pen of Beethoven, and it is to be hoped he will yet finish this magnificent work, in a style worthy of its great projector.

A note in *A Life of Mozart*, 1817

THOMAS BUSBY

Mozart with a genius not less vigorous than that of Haydn, possessed an imagination more versatile, and nerves more tremulous... In vocal composition, especially the drammatical, the composer of 'The Creation' cannot vie with him; and, perhaps, only years were wanting to the life of the latter to render him, at least, as splendid, and quite as voluminous a symphonist. His felicity in the use of wind instruments is so well known, that it would be superfluous to insist upon the unrivalled art he uniformly displays in their management. His accompaniments derive from his peculiar skill, a charm that no other resource of his genius could have supplied. But with Mozart, it was a NATURAL resource. The breathing sweetness of the flute, pouring reediness of the hautboy, and mellow murmuring of the bassoon, accorded with the passive delicacy of his nerves, and lively tenderness of his sensations. When we consider how much, we are surprised to observe how variously he wrote. His vocal compositions are scarcely more different from his instrumental than from each other. The diversity, is as conspicuous as the beauty, of his melodies, and his imagination can scarcely be said to have ever failed.

History of Music, 1819

That portion of Mozart's Requiem was given, afforded an almost new and most glorious specimen of science and of art. The effect of the serpent in the bass solo 'Tuba Mirum' was superlatively awful, and in the 'Benedictus' the vocalists and the orchestra seemed to rival each other. Nothing more exquisite was ever heard.

Vol. III, 1821

MICHAEL KELLY

He favoured the company by performing fantasias and capriccios on the pianoforte. His feeling, the rapidity of his fingers, the great execution and strength of his left hand particularly, and the apparent inspiration of his modulations, astounded me. . . .

He was a remarkably small man, very thin and pale, with a profusion of fine fair hair, of which he was rather vain. He gave me a cordial invitation to his house, of which I availed myself, and passed a great part of my time there. He always received me with kindness and hospitality. . . .

He gave Sunday concerts at which I never was missing. He was kind-hearted, and always ready to oblige, but so very particular when he played, that if the slightest noise were made he instantly left off. He one day made me sit down to the piano, and gave credit to my first master, who had taught me to place my hand well on the instrument. He conferred on me what I considered a high compliment. I had composed a little melody to Metastasio's canzonetta. 'Graze agl' inganni tuoi', which was a great favourite wherever I sang it. It was very simple, but had the good fortune to please Mozart. He took it, and composed variations upon it, which were truly beautiful and had the further kindness and condescension to play them wherever he had an opportunity.

Encouraged by his flattering approbation, I attempted several little airs, which I showed him, and which he kindly approved of, so much indeed, that I determined to devote myself to the study of counterpoint, and consulted with him, by whom I ought to be instructed. He said, 'My good lad, you ask my advice, and I will give it you candidly; had you studied composition when you were at Naples, and when your mind was not devoted to other pursuits, you would perhaps have done wisely; but now that your profession of the stage must, and ought, to occupy all your attention, it would be an unwise measure to enter into a dry study. You may take my word for it. Nature has made you a melodist, and you would only disturb and perplex yourself. Reflect, "a little knowledge is a dangerous thing"; should there be errors in what you write, you will find hundreds of musicians, in all parts of the world, capable of correcting them, therefore do not disturb your natural gift. Melody is the essence of music,' continued he; 'I compare a good melodist to a fine racer, and counterpointists to hack post-horses; therefore, be advised, let well alone and remember the old Italian proverb, "Chi sa piu, meno sa" (Who knows most, knows least).' The opinion of this great man made on me a lasting impression.

My friend Attwood (a worthy man and an ornament to the musical world) was Mozart's favourite scholar, and it gives me great pleasure to record what Mozart said to me about him; his words were: 'Attwood is a young man for whom I have a sincere affection and esteem; he conducts himself with great propriety, and I feel much pleasure in telling you that he partakes more of my style than any scholar I ever had, and I predict that he will prove a sound musician.' Mozart was very liberal in giving praise to those who deserved it; but felt a thorough contempt for insolent mediocrity.

Reminiscences, 1826

EDWARD FITZGERALD

The finale of C minor is very noble. I heard it twice at Jullien's. On the whole I like to hear Mozart better;

Beethoven is gloomy. Besides incontestably Mozart is the purest musician; Beethoven would have been Poet or Painter as well, for he had a deep Soul and Imagination. I do not think it is reported that he showed any very early predeliction for Music: Mozart, we know, did. They say Holmes has published a very good life of M. Only think of the poor fellow not being able to sell his music latterly, getting out of fashion, so taking to drink .˙. . and enact Harlequin at Masquerades! When I heard Handel's Alexander's Feast at Norwich this Autumn I wondered; but when directly afterward they played Mozart's G minor Symphony, it seemed as if I had passed out of a land of savages into sweet civilised Life.

Letter to F. Tennyson, after Sept. 1845

As to Mozart, he was a musical Genius, more wonderful than all. I was astonished at the Don Giovanni lately. It is certainly the Greatest Opera in the world.

Letter to F. Tennyson, June 12th, 1845

And to London have I been since my last Letter: and have seen the Old Masters; and finished them off by such a Symphony as was worthy of the best of them, two Acts of Mozart's 'Cosi'. You wrote me that you had 'assisted' at that also: the Singing, as you know, was inferior: but the Music itself! Between the Acts a Man sang a song of Verdi's: which was a strange Contrast, to be sure: one of Verdi's heavy Airs, however: for he has a true Genius of his own, though not Mozart's. Well: I did not like even Mozart's two Bravuras for the Ladies: a bad Despina for one: but the rest was fit for—Raffaelle, whose Christ in the Garden I had been looking at a little before.

Letter to W. F. Pollock, March ? 1873

SAMUEL BUTLER

Jones and I went last Friday to Don Giovanni . . . It bored us both . . . . We admit the beauty of many of the beginnings of the airs, but this beauty is not maintained, in every case the air tails off into something that is much too near being tiresome. The plot, of course, is stupid to a degree, but plot has very little to do with it; what can be more uninteresting than the plot of many of Handel's oratorios? We both believe the scheme of Italian opera to be a bad one; we think that music should never be combined with acting to a greater extent than is done, we will say, in the Mikado; and that the oratorio form is far more satisfactory than opera; and we agreed that we had neither of us ever yet been to an opera (I mean a Grand Opera) without being bored by it. I am not sorry to remember that Handel never abandoned oratorio after he had once fairly taken to it.

'At the Opera', *Note Books*

We went last night to the Philharmonic concert and sat in the shilling orchestra just behind the drums, so that we could see and hear what each instrument was doing. The concert began with Mozart's G minor Symphony. We liked this fairly well, especially the last movement, but we found all the movements too long and, speaking for myself, if I had a tame orchestra for which I might write programmes, I should probably put it down once or twice again, not from any spontaneous wish to hear more of it but as a matter of duty that I might judge it with fuller comprehension—still, if each movement had been half as long I should probably have felt cordially enough towards it, except of course in so far as that the spirit of the music is alien to that of the early Italian school with which alone I am in genuine sympathy and of which Handel is the climax.

Note Books

W. S. ROCKSTRO

... some ... have so artfully concealed the constructional points which Mozart never cared to disguise, that incautious students have sometimes failed to discern in them the veritable 'pillars of the house', and have accused

Mozart of poverty of style, because he left them boldly exposed to view, as a great Architect delights to expose the piers upon which the tower of his Cathedral depends for its support. But, woe to the neophyte who mistakes the true office of those supposed 'weak points' in Mozart's most perfect designs! Who, seeking to construct the ornament, instead of ornamenting the construction, builds an edifice which must necessarily crumble beneath his feet.

History of Music, 1886

JOHN RUSKIN

And yonder musician who used the greatest power which (in the art he knew) the Father of spirits ever yet breathed into the clay of this world;—who used it, I say, to follow and fit with perfect sounds the words of the 'Zauberflöte' and of 'Don Giovanni'—foolishest and most monstrous of conceivable human words and subjects of thought—for the future 'amusement' of his race! No such spectacle of unconscious (and in that unconsciousness all the more fearful) moral degradation of the highest faculty to the lowest purpose can be found in history. But Mozart is nevertheless a nobler creature than the horse at the siding; nor would it be the least nearer the purpose of his Maker that he, and all his frivolous audiences, should evade the degradation of the profitless piping, only by living, like horses, in daily physical labour for daily bread.

Time and Tide, V, §§ 20, 21, 'Man and Beast'

SIR HUBERT PARRY

Mozart ... began writing symphonies as well as operas at the age of eight, and some of his early work is skilful, neat, and artistic. But it was not till after his experiences at Mannheim in 1777 and 1778, so often alluded to, that his full powers in the line of instrumental music were called into play. The musical traditions at Mannheim were at that time probably the best in Europe, and their effect upon Mozart was immediate and salutary. For when he moved on to Paris in 1778, in company with some of the Mannheim instrumentalists, he wrote, for performance there, the first of his symphonies, which occupies an important place in musical history. For artistic delicacy in detail, general interest, skilful use of orchestral resources, variety in quality and force of tone, no symphony had ever yet appeared which in any way approached to its standard. But even this by no means represents his highest achievement in the symphonic line. The symphony written for Prague in 1786 is a still further advance, and throws the Parisian one into the shade in every respect. The general quality of the musical thoughts is finer, richer, and more interesting; while the purely orchestral effects, especially in the slow movement, are among the most successful things of the kind he ever achieved. And finally the three great symphonies which he wrote in Vienna in 1788 represent the highest level in idea and style and in every distinguished quality of art he ever attained to. They are the crown of his life's work; for in them he more nearly escapes the traditional formulas of the Italian opera than in any other form of instrumental art except the quartets; and their general standard of treatment and thought is nobler and more genuinely vigorous than that of any other of his works except the Requiem. In management of orchestral effect these latter symphonies must have been a revelation compared with the standard of the works of his contemporaries and predecessors. His treatment of design had also become much more free and interesting. The introduction of short subtle excursions out of his principal keys in unexpected directions; the variations introduced into his subjects on repetition, by altering the scoring and the actual melodic and harmonic details, and many other devices which infuse new interest into the obviousness of familiar procedure, show a much greater concentration of artistic faculty than had been usual with him. The general treatment is harmonic, but of more expressive character than in his operas; and though the designs are often helped out by conventional formulas which were the common property of all composers in those days, the general mastery of design is almost perfect.

The Evolution of the Art of Music, 1893

E. J. DENT

There is no doubt that it is Wagner and Verdi who have taught us to appreciate the real value of Mozart as a dramatic composer; it is in the spirit of Verdi that Mozart must be sung; it is in the spirit of Wagner that he must be played and put on the stage. Verdi more than any other composer will teach us modern musicians the intellectual beauty of pure singing, especially in his middle period ('Un ballo in maschera', 'Aida', and the Requiem) during which his marvellous command of harmony helps us to understand the logic of that earlier language which we to our shame have now almost completely forgotten. The Verdi of 'Otello' and 'Falstaff' has also his lessons to teach us; but they are lessons which we shall not be capable of understanding until we have saturated our minds with the style which preceded them. From Wagner we must learn to grasp the conception of an opera as a musical whole—orchestra, voices and stage effects all combining to form one immense and uninterrupted symphony, in which every detail has to be fitted in exactly at its proper place and time. And it is therefore eminently desirable that Mozart's operas should take their place in this country as works which are accessible to all lovers of music and drama by means of frequent performances in our own language, because it is from Mozart more than any other composer that we can learn in the easiest way to understand operatic ideals at their best. Mozart will furnish us with a permanent standard for opera, just as Beethoven does for the Symphony and Handel for the oratorio, even though all three belong to an age that is far remote from our own. It is indeed this very remoteness that gives the standard its permanence, for we have now reached a stage when no composer in his senses would try to write an opera in the style of Mozart, any more than he would write a symphony in the manner of Beethoven or a Handelian oratorio; these standards are safe against unintelligent copying, while to those who will study them patiently and intelligently they will yield up their real secrets, the principles of musical reasoning on which their construction is based.

. . . The first duty of a composer of opera is to make us feel throughout his work that music is the normal language of all the characters on the stage; his next and equally important duty is to make his opera a consistent organic musical whole from beginning to end. It is in these respects that Mozart's genius is most strikingly apparent. He has no need for the tricks of the second-rate composer—for 'local colour', for sudden 'tremolos', for harsh successions of inconsequent chords, for declamatory and descriptive effects; in a word, for any of those methods by which music leaves off being music and pretends to be something else. Such things always impress a moderately cultivated audience, and distract attention from the fact that the opera as a whole may have no logical musical unity. Indeed, no small success has sometimes been made by operas which have made use of various types of psychological and associational appeal without the presentation of a single really musical and original thought. Such works, however, belong to the domain not of art but of commerce.

Moreover, composers possessed of a higher artistic standard have often failed to produce good work simply from not knowing what they were really aiming at. What they have in practice aimed at has been the external imitation of those effects which they have seen to be conspicuously successful in Wagner or Verdi, but they have not always been able to grasp the scheme of an opera as a whole, and so have not understood what Wagner or Verdi were aiming at themselves. Hence comes uncertainty of intention, which is more fatal in opera than in any other branch of music. If a composer does not know himself what he means, he certainly cannot expect an unsophisticated audience to discover it. It must, moreover, be understood that what Wagner and Verdi aimed at in the past is not necessarily a suitable aim in all its details for our musical dramatists of the present day; nevertheless, a careful study of their aims will certainly be fruitful in the discovery of sound principles, on which the methods of our modern technique may be grafted. And by way of preliminary to the investigation of these composers and their ideals, there can be no better study, for composers, singers, librettists and audiences alike— and we may add that no study can be more delightful as well as profitable—than the operas of Mozart.

Mozart's Operas, 1913

SIR GEORGE DYSON

... rare is the composer of high rank whose intuitions are of such a nature that no kind of formal rigidity appears to disconcert him. Mozart is, in music, a supreme, if not a unique, example of this complete and effortless accord between inspiration and form. He could and did accept apparently without suspicion of discomfort, the conventional formulae which he found to hand, and he invested everything he touched with an atmosphere and resiliency that has been, and is likely for long to be, without parallel. His imagination appears to play unrestrained within the narrowest limits. He is never mechanical, yet every creative impulse seems but to render still more perfect the balance of his formal models. Fashions of design were to him not obstacles but opportunities. They became in his hands the most innocent and engaging companions. That there should be anything in the nature of a technical problem seems hardly to have entered his head. He assimilated in infancy certain well-defined forms. Thenceforth whatever he had to say, lyric or dramatic, grave or gay, sacred or secular, seemed to fit into a few precise patterns as a hand fits into a glove. Something has already been said of the factor of range in expression. Mozart did not as a rule attempt those long flights which have often challenged and defeated men of very great gifts. But it is none the less a source of perennial wonder to the student to see how Mozart, in what may be imaginatively a most fluid or dramatic situation, will suggest characters, illustrate moods, accompany any and every variety of action, and at the same time preserve not only an extreme purity of melodic or harmonic diction, but with it an undisguised technical formality which is as precise and regular as it is unfailingly alive.

The New Music, 1924

SAMUEL WESLEY (1766–1837)

DR. CHARLES BURNEY

. . . Samuel Westley (*sic*) before he could write was a composer and mentally set the airs of several oratorios, which he retained in memory till he was eight years old, and then wrote them down.

Philosophical Transactions of the
Royal Society, 1779

ON BEETHOVEN (1770–1827)

HARMONICON

Edited by WILLIAM AYRTON

The overture to the opera of 'Fidelio' is a very eccentric composition, full of genius, and never fails to please the cognoscenti.

April, 1823

. . . a specimen of Beethoven's wildest and most original flights; his mind must have been full of uncommon imagery when he wrote it. It always brings to our view Blake's illustrations of Blair's poem, 'The Grave'; or some of Fuselli's designs from 'Paradise Lost'. But it will ever please those who have acquired a taste for the highest branches of instrumental music.

The 'Overture *Coriolan*', April, 1823

Opinions are much divided concerning the merits of the Pastoral Symphony of Beethoven, though very few venture to deny that it is much too long. The andante alone is upwards of a quarter of an hour in performance, and being a series of repetitions, might be subjected to abridgement without any violation of justice, either to the composer or his hearers. In saying this, we do not mean to undervalue the work, but range ourselves on the side of those who think it abounds in traits of singular genius, and in beautiful effects; though we certainly never heard it through, without rejoicing, on account of its prolixity, at its termination.

June, 1823

The pastoral symphony of Beethoven has many excellent points in it, undeniably; there is enough in it to set up two or three second-rate composers: but the subjects are much too spun out—it is an interminable piece. The andante would please if about two-thirds of it were omitted: as it stands, it is upwards of a quarter of an hour in duration, and sheds its narcotic influence over the audience before it is half finished. In other parts of this Symphony also, there is a great deal of false taste unworthy of such a composer.

April, 1824

. . . we shall anticipate in part our regular criticism on it, by observing that it manifests many brilliant traits of Beethoven's vast genius; that it embodies enough of original matter, of beautiful effects, and skilful contrivances, to form an admirable Symphony of ordinary duration but that, unfortunately, the author has spun it out to so unusual a length, that he has 'drawn out the thread of his verbosity finer than the staple of his argument', and what would have been delightful had it been contained within moderate limits, he has rendered wearying by expansion and diluted his subjects till they become weak and vapid. When we add that the time which it is calculated this composition will take in performance, cannot be much less than an hour and twenty minutes, our readers, though they have not heard it, may almost judge for themselves of its inadequacy to fix the attention of any audience, or to produce such an effect as the admirers of Beethoven must earnestly wish.

'Ninth Symphony', March, 1825

The new Symphony of Beethoven, composed for and purchased at a liberal price by the Philharmonic Society was now publicly produced. In the present Symphony we discover no diminution of Beethoven's creative talent; it exhibits many perfectly new traits, and in its technical formation shows amazing ingenuity and unabated vigour of mind. But with all its merits which it unquestionably possesses it is at least twice as long as it should be; it repeats itself and the subjects in consequence become weak by reiteration. The last movement, a chorus, is heterogeneous and though there is much vocal beauty in parts of it, yet it does not, and no habit will ever make it, mix up with the first three movements. This chorus is a hymn of joy commencing with a recitative and relieved by soli passages. What relation it bears to the Symphony we could not make out; and here, as well as in other parts, the want of intelligible design is too apparent ... The most original feature in this Symphony is the Minuet (*sic*), and the most singular part, the succeeding Trio—striking because in duple time, for which we are not acquainted with anything in the shape of a precedent. We were also much pleased by a very noble march which is introduced. In quitting the present subject we must express our hope that this new work of the great Beethoven may be put into a produceable form. The Symphony will then be heard with unmixed pleasure and the reputation of its author will, if possible, be further augmented.

'Ninth Symphony', April, 1825

Altogether it seems to have been intended as a kind of enigma—we had almost said a hoax.

'Pastoral Symphony', July, 1825

Beethoven's Symphony (in D) abounds in all the varieties of this composer's rich fancy: the expression and energy of the opening adagio—the brilliancy and vigour of the following allegro—the exquisite beauty of the larghetto, which is quite vocal in its expression—the playfulness, and unexpected modulation of the scherzo, with the delicious beauty of the succeeding trio—and the spirit, almost intoxicating, of the finale—these altogether leave one in a state of excitation which the repose of a full half hour would hardly subdue. In such cases it is to be wished that a short interval were granted for the gradual subsidence of the exalted and almost overwrought spirits; if a few minutes only were allowed, the mind would be better prepared for what succeeds, than it usually is when hurried to attend to something which, though perhaps differing in character, demands nearly the same attention.

June, 1826

QUARTERLY MUSICAL MAGAZINE

In closing the history of so great a life, we are naturally led to remark on the attributes of one who has for so long a time held the first place in a peculiar branch of art. Little however remains to be added, for conspicuous characters are always the objects of such continual discussion, that the theme is frequently exhausted before their lives are ended, and so it is with Beethoven. Born with an energy of mind that taught him to despise the rules by which common intellects are guided, by the fearlessness of genius he accomplished effects that others would have shrunk from attempting; the same forces of character which, when applied to the everyday occurrences of life, prompted him to hold the established forms of society in contempt, and to chafe like a fiery steed at the curb and the rein, made him irritable, gloomy, and eccentric; but his moral character was unimpeachable. Beethoven was great in every thing; as a composer his beauties and his faults were alike in extremes, and it is to be regretted that his defects are so dazzling, and sanctioned by such a name as to mislead many. He has not been such a benefactor to art as either Haydn or Mozart, because he has made no splendid inventions like the former, nor did he possess the fertility of the latter, but his dauntless mind has ventured further than either in the untried regions of harmony. It remains for time to prove if in these researches he has collected materials sufficiently solid to build a fame that shall endure like his great predecessors, unrivalled and unshaken.

Vol. IX, 1827

The Heroic Symphony contains much to admire, past all doubt, but it is difficult to keep up admiration of this kind during three long quarters of an hour. It is infinitely too lengthy. The 'marcia funebre' in C minor is exceedingly beautiful, but the whole of what may be termed the coda, which constitutes three-fourths of it, should be omitted. Sacrificing a part to save the whole is prudent in all cases, and if this symphony is not by some means abridged, it will soon fall into disuse.

April, 1829

We shall certainly never become reconciled to either the first or last movements of this, both being full of asperities and almost unbearably whimsical.

'Seventh Symphony', May, 1829

We have exhausted the language of praise in speaking of the best symphonies of Beethoven.

June, 1829

Beethoven has put forth no strength in his violin concerto; it is a 'fiddling' affair, and might have been written by any third or fourth rate composer.

'Violin Concerto', May, 1832

MUSICAL WORLD

Beethoven also mystified his passages by a new treatment of the resolution of discords, which can only be described in words by the term, 'resolution by ellipsis', or the omission of the chord upon which the discordant notes should descend. ... Many of his passages also appear confused and unintelligible, by a singular freedom in the use of diatonic discords or discords of transition; many instances appear of passages by contrary motion, each carrying their harmonies with them. In the obstinate manner in which he drives one passage through and against another, he has no equal, except Sebastian Bach and our own illustrious countryman Samuel Wesley. Lastly, he produces the most mysterious effects, by the use of the 'point d'orgue' and its inversions.

March, 1836

EDWARD FITZGERALD

Beethoven has been too analytical and erudite: but his inspiration is nevertheless true. I have just read his Life by Moscheles: well worth reading. He shewed no very decided preference for music when a child, though he was the son of a composer: and I think that he was, strictly speaking, more of a thinker than a musician. A great genius he was, somehow. He was very fond of reading: Plutarch and Shakespeare his great favourites. He tried to think in music, almost to reason in music; whereas perhaps we should be contented with feeling in it. It can never speak very definitely. . . .

Beethoven's Sonata, Op. 14, is meant to express the discord and gradual atonement of two lovers, or a man and his wife: and he was disgusted that every one did not see what was meant: in truth, it expresses resistance gradually overcome—Dobson shaving with a blunt razor, for instance. Music is so far the most universal language, that any one piece in a particular strain symbolises all the analogous phenomena spiritual or material —if you can talk of spiritual phenomena. The Eroica symphony describes the battle of the passions as well as of armed men. This is long and muddy discourse: . . .

Letter to F. Tennyson, March 31st, 1842

Ah, I should like to hear Fidelio again, often as I have heard it. I do not find so much 'Melody' in it as you do: understanding by Melody that which asserts itself independently of Harmony, as Mozart's Airs do. I miss it especially in Leonora's Hope song. But, what with the story itself, and the Passion and Power of the Music it is set to, the Opera is one of those that one can hear repeated as often as any.

If any one ever would take a good suggestion from me, you might suggest to Mr. Sullivan, or some competent Musician, to adapt that Epilogue part of Tennyson's King Arthur, beginning—

> 'And so to bed: where yet in sleep I seem'd
> To sail with Arthur', etc.

down to
> 'And war shall be no more—'

To adapt this, I say, to the Music of that grand last Scene in Fidelio: Sullivan & Co. supplying the introductory Recitative; beginning dreamily, and increasing, crescendo, up to where the Poet begins to 'feel the truth and stir of Day'; till Beethoven's pompous March should begin, and the Chorus, with 'Arthur is come' etc.; the chief Voices raising the words aloft (as they do in Fidelio), and the Chorus thundering in upon them. It is very grand in Fidelio; and I am persuaded might have a grand effect in this Poem. But no one will do it, of course; especially in these Days when War is so far from being no more!

Letter to W. F. Pollock, Dec. 24th, 1871

SAMUEL BUTLER

Then came a terribly long-winded recitative by Beethoven and an air with a good deal of 'Che faro' in it. I do not mind this and if it had been 'Che faro' absolutely I should, I daresay, have liked it better. I never want to hear it again and my orchestra should never play it.

Beethoven's Concerto for violin and orchestra (op. 61) which followed was longer and more tedious still. I have not a single good word for it. If the subject of the last movement was the tune of one of Arthur Roberts' comic songs, or of any music-hall song, it would do very nicely and I daresay we should often hum it. I do not mean at the opening of the movement but about half-way through, where the character is just that of a common music-hall song and, so far, good.

Note Books

LIEUT. H. W. L. HIME, ROYAL ARTILLERY

The five movements of Beethoven's Trio, Op. 97, are the five acts of a tragedy, of the meaning of which there can be no doubt, as the composer himself explained it shortly before his death. In one of his sublimest moods, Beethoven took for his subject the overthrow of a virtuous man by adverse Fate.

The first of the five movements is an Allegro, joyous but subdued,—Job feasting with his sons, but ever mindful to sanctify himself when the days of feasting are over. We are carried down a smooth gay stream of harmony, and the sounds we hear are those of sober joy, not riotous mirth. Following the Allegro comes the Scherzo, gayer and more sparkling still, where all goes 'merry as a marriage bell', and the melody bounds forward, 'like childhood, laughing as it goes.' Suddenly a deep sound strikes like a rising knell, and the Trio, into which the Scherzo glides like a murmuring rivulet merging into some hoarse torrent, mutters indistinct warning of approaching calamity. The warning is disregarded—it was but the wind soughing through the leaves, the waves breaking on the shore. On with the dance! The feast is renewed, the Scherzo is repeated.

'But hark! that heavy sound breaks in once more,
And nearer, clearer, deadlier than before.'

The Ides of March approach—again we hear the Trio—and the notes of the violoncello, sinking lower and deeper, 'with hollow harmony, dark and profound,' presage a woe that is to come quickly.

At length the supreme hour arises, and the unequal struggle is over. Unrelenting Fate overtakes the virtuous and the just, angels waft the spotless soul of a hero where the wicked cease from troubling and the weary are at rest, and his dirge is sung in strains of heavenly music. Whether we regard the melody of this movement in itself, or the wondrous skill with which the melody is varied and transformed, the Andante remains for ever a surpassing triumph of genius. Like fitful gusts of wind this burst of lamentation rises and falls, passes from us and returns again, swells and dies away. We sit, we must sit motionless and silent before this grief, for it is very great.

> 'Art and eloquence,
> And all the shows of the world, are frail and vain
> To weep a loss that turns their lights to shade.
> It is a woe "too deep for tears" when all
> Is reft at once, when some surpassing spirit
> Whose light adorned the world around it, leaves
> Those who remain behind, not sobs or groans,
> The passionate tumult of a clinging hope—
> But pale despair and cold tranquility,
> Nature's vast frame, the web of human things,
> Birth and the grave, that are not as they were.'

But let the dead bury their dead. Be he peer or peasant, the world rolls on oblivious of the individual, and Nature, though she regards the All, disregards the One—

> 'So careful of the type she seems,
> So careless of the single life.'

And so, by a daring stroke, Beethoven makes an abrupt transition from the key of D natural to the key of B flat, and transmutes the Andante into a trivial, commonplace air, the humdrum of everyday life, the song of the un-concerned traveller, as he passes by the house where the master lies dead, and within is mourning. If Time brought to the making of man a gift of tears, Grief bore a glass that ran. We must forget our grief, we must betake ourselves to the ordinary duties of life, and remand our sorrows—

> 'To memories darkest hold,
> If not to be forgotten—not at once—
> Not all forgotten.'

Yet who can

> '. . . minister to a mind diseased;
> Pluck from the memory a rooted sorrow;
> Raze out the written troubles of the brain;
> And, with some sweet oblivious antidote,
> Cleanse the stuffed bosom of that perilous stuff,
> Which weighs upon the heart?'

In Heaven which is our home, all tears shall be wiped away from our eyes, and there shall be no more death, neither sorrow nor crying. But in this life of error, ignorance, and strife, Duty cannot always overcome Love; tears will gush forth betimes; and our secret grief may rise in the silence of the night from the grave in which we have buried it, deep, deep. These things being so, Beethoven's great Tragedy fitly ends in a despairing Presto movement, that cries with a great and exceeding bitter cry

> 'O for the touch of a vanished hand,
> And the sound of a voice that is still.'
>
> *Monthly Musical Record*, Oct., 1871

SIR GEORGE GROVE

. . . I would call attention, though with reluctance, to a singular feature in this great work—namely, to the occur-rence more than once during the working-out of the first movement of a vacillation or hesitancy in expression of which I know no trace in any of the other Symphonies, but which can but be recognised here by a loyal hearer; where the notes of Flutes and Oboes seem to tremble and falter as if they were the utterance of human lips, the organs of an oppressed human heart. These places need not be specified, they cannot but strike the sympathetic listener, and will almost suggest, if it be not disrespectful to entertain such a thought, that the great Beethoven was, with all his experience, too much overpowered by his feelings to find adequate expression for them. These tokens of human weakness may be safely left to the affectionate sympathy of the friends and admirers of this great poet.

On the Ninth Symphony, first movement,
Beethoven and His Nine Symphonies, 1896

These works he did as no one ever did, and probably no one ever will. But of orchestral music he wrote no more after the Ninth Symphony. Music will advance in richness, scope, and difficulty; but such music as Beethoven's great instrumental works, in which thought, emotion, melody, and romance combine with extraordinary judgement and common sense, and a truly wonderful industry, to make a perfect whole, can hardly any more be written. The time for such an event, such a concurrence of the man and the circumstances, will not arrive. There can never be a second Beethoven or a second Shakespeare. However much orchestras may improve and execution increase, Beethoven's Symphonies will always remain at the head of music as Shakespeare's plays are at the head of the literature of the modern world—

Age cannot wither them, nor custom stale
Their infinite variety.

Beethoven and His Nine Symphonies, 1896

SIR W. H. HADOW

At the beginning of the eighteenth century the level of skill in string playing was still very low: Corelli was regarded as the climax of sheer difficulty, and the few comparative virtuosi required for their display the position of first violin or violoncello. It is indeed probable that these alone were at all clearly heard. The ears of the patron were not yet attuned to nice distinctions, and so long as there was a recognisable tune at the top and a solid bass at the bottom it did not seem to matter much what happened between them. Bach, no doubt, would have entirely altered the course of events, but it must be remembered that by the end of the century not a page of Bach's concerted music had been published, and the general standard of the age may almost be illustrated by a rejoinder of the child Mozart, who when warned by his father not to come and spoil the quartet-party, replied with weeping tears, 'But, papa, one doesn't need to have learned the violin in order to play a second-violin part.' From the beginning of the Viennese period there was unquestionably a great improvement; both Haydn and Mozart himself advanced nearer and nearer to the ideal of a 'quatuor dialogue'; but it is no disrespect to their genius to say that they never wholly attained to it. And of this we may, if we will, find a crucial instance. Haydn's latest quartets were written during the same years as Beethoven's earliest. For melody, for purity, for transparence of style, Haydn's are in their kind unsurpassed: in balance of instruments they seem to belong to an earlier generation than Beethoven. The first violin parts are always brilliant and characteristic, the cello parts very often; the intervening voices, though far removed from the supers and chorus singers of the earlier days, are too frequently contented with the role of the hero's friend or the heroine's confidante. But in Beethoven's Op. 18 the balance is perfect, the interest is distributed with an entirely even hand. He has, indeed, less virtuosity than Haydn, though he demands more concentrated intelligence; the steady light which illumines his work is diffused over the whole canvas. And part of the reason may well be that he had at his disposal a complete group of executive artists such as were not gathered together even at Eisenstadt.

Of his constructive power there is little need here to speak: the subject has been abundantly discussed in text-books and critical essays. The two focal points are: one, that he had the greatest constructive genius of any musician who ever lived—perhaps of any artist except Shakespeare; the other, that entered into the full inheritance of Mozart and Haydn, that he could assume in his hearers a general acquaintance with the forms of the sonata movements, and could therefore treat them with a freedom which would have been impossible to his predecessors. The result is that in all six quartets there is not an otiose or superfluous bar. The themes may differ in value . . . but the interweaving of this texture is as perfect as human art can achieve. In later life he touches deeper issues: he never wrote with a more complete mastery of his resources.

Beethoven's Op. 18 Quartets, 1926

SIR JOHN B. MCEWEN

Naturally, Beethoven's first works, based as they were on the example of his predecessors, approximate to that example both in manner and intention; but even in these first works there are indications eloquent of a new outlook and objective. With regard to the technical processes of composition, Beethoven's attitude was fundamentally different from that of his predecessors, and this difference is illustrated both in his methods and in the results of these methods. He seems always to have composed with difficulty—not because he was less able to manipulate structure and design than the older musicians, but because he could not regard design as an end in itself. His methods were laborious, because he was unable to content himself with the unessential and the insignificant, and the search for the right and final expression of his thought did not proceed too easily. Lacking neither fluency nor facility, wisely he distrusted both.

As time went on he became more concerned with the effort after significant expression rather than purely sensuous appeal and formal symmetry; and an interesting indication of this personal attitude towards his artistic work, is the frequent association of this work with ideas other than musical. . . .

To the idiom which he inherited from the eighteenth century—the principles of design on which was created a self-sufficient instrumental style—he added the expressive methods of the older polyphony. As Bach based his work on the polyphonic idiom tempered by the frequent and systematic employment of the newer principles, so Beethoven, starting from the homophonic standpoint, developed his final style by uniting to these newer principles the methods of the older school. Both effected a union between the two styles, but they started from opposite poles; and while Bach consistently throughout his career is mainly polyphonic in method, Beethoven equally consistently adhered to the principles of design which had been perfected under the homophonic system. Even in his latest works the rhythmically balanced structure, built up and buttressed by key relationship and contrast, persists; but while symmetry remains, squareness is eliminated; and the texture becomes more highly organised and more expressively polyphonic.

In practically every one of his last great instrumental works the two methods are either united or stand side by side. Movements like the opening movement of the Sonata in A flat, Op. 110, which combines the noble symmetry and exquisite proportions of a Greek vase with the expressive significance of a Shakespeare sonnet, and which conforms in every way to the standardised outlines of sonata form, occur in the same work as movements which—like the finale of the same sonata—are built up on the principles of expressive vocal polyphony. The fugue—that apotheosis of polyphonic method—or the fugal principle, is illustrated in practically all the larger works from Op. 106 onwards. Several, such as the pianoforte sonatas, Op. 106 and Op. 110; the quartets, Op. 130 and Op. 131, contain fully developed examples in this form. The finale of the Choral Symphony illustrates the same point, and the great Mass in D openly acknowledges it as the basis of vocal composition.

Limitations of space preclude the detailed consideration of many interesting technical features in the latest works of the Master. Such things as his disregard of the practical limitations of both voices and instruments; the stability and continuity of his harmonic sense, which, apart from its polyphonic enlargement, underwent no essential change from first to last; his obvious but tentative endeavours to attain conditions of greater rhythmic freedom and fluidity—to mention only a few of these technical features—could each be illustrated and discussed at length. Perhaps that characteristic of his last style, which, next to his reversion to the methods of polyphony, is most striking and apparent, is the effort to connect up the different movements of a work either by mood or by treatment so as to produce a united and organic whole.

'The Significance of Beethoven's Third Period,' *Music and Letters*, April 1927

SIR WALTER SCOTT (1771–1832)

It is only by long practice that I have acquired the power of selecting or distinguishing melodies; and although now few things delight or affect me more than a simple tune sung with feeling, yet I am sensible that even this pitch of musical taste has only been gained by attention and habit, and, as it were, by my feeling of the words being associated with the tune. I have, therefore, been usually unsuccessful in composing words to a tune, although my friend, Dr. Clarke, and other musical composers, have sometimes been able to make a happy union between their music and my poetry.

Autobiography

SAMUEL TAYLOR COLERIDGE

(1772–1834)

Some music is above me; most music is beneath me. I like Beethoven and Mozart—or else some of the aerial compositions of the elder Italians, as Palestrina and Carissimi—And I love Purcell.

The best sort of music is what it should be—sacred; the next best, the military, has fallen to the lot of the Devil.

Good music never tires, nor sends me to sleep. I feel physically refreshed and strengthened by it, as Milton says he did.

Table Talk, July 6th, 1833

CHARLES LAMB (1775–1834)

I have no ear.

Mistake me not, reader—nor imagine that I am by nature destitute of those exterior twin appendages, hanging ornaments, and (architecturally speaking) handsome volutes to the human capital. Better my mother had never borne me.—I am, I think, rather delicately than copiously provided with those conduits; and I feel no disposition to envy the mule for his plenty, or the mole for her exactness, in those ingenious labyrinthine inlets—those indispensable side-intelligencers.

Neither have I incurred, or done anything to incur, with Defoe, that hideous disfigurement, which constrained him to draw upon assurance—to feel 'quite unabashed', and at ease upon that article. I was never, thank my stars, in the pillory; nor, if I read them aright, is it within the compass of my destiny, that I ever should be.

When therefore I say that I have no ear, you will understand me to mean—for music. To say that this heart never melted at the concord of sweet sounds, would be a foul self-libel. 'Water parted from the sea' never fails to move it strangely. So does 'In infancy'. But they were used to be sung at her harpsichord (the old-fashioned instrument in vogue those days) by a gentle-woman—the gentlest, sure, that ever merited the appellation—the sweetest—why should I hesitate to name Mrs. S——, once the blooming Fanny Weatheral of the Temple—who had the power to thrill the soul of Elia, small imp as he was, even in his long coats; and to make him glow, tremble, and blush with a passion, that not faintly indicated the day-spring of that absorbing sentiment which was afterwards destined to overwhelm and subdue his nature quite for Alice W——n.

I even think that sentimentally I am disposed to harmony. But organically I am incapable of a tune. I have been practising 'God save the King' all my life; whistling and humming of it over to myself in solitary corners; and am not yet arrived, they tell me, within many quavers of it. Yet hath the loyalty of Elia never been impeached.

I am not without suspicion, that I have an undeveloped faculty of music within me. For thrumming in my wild way, on my friend A.'s piano the other morning, while he was engaged in an adjoining Parlour,—on his return he was pleased to say 'He thought it could not be the maid!' On his first surprise at hearing the keys touched in somewhat an airy and masterful way, not dreaming of me, his suspicions had lighted on Jenny. But a grace, snatched from a superior refinement, soon convinced him that some being—technically perhaps deficient, but higher informed from a principle common to all the fine arts—had swayed the keys to a mood which Jenny, with all her (less cultivated) enthusiasm, could never have elicited from them. I mention this as a proof of my friend's penetration, and not with any view of disparaging Jenny.

Scientifically I could never be made to understand (yet have I taken some pains) what a note in music is; or how one note should differ from another. Much less in voices can I distinguish a soprano from a tenor. Only sometimes the thorough-bass I contrive to guess at, from its being supereminently harsh and disagreeable. I tremble, however, for my misapplication of the simplest terms of that which I disclaim. While I profess my ignorance, I scarce know what to say I am ignorant of. I hate, perhaps, by misnomers. 'Sostenuto' and 'adagio' stand in the like relation of obscurity to me; and Sol, Fa, Mi, Re, is as conjuring as 'Baralipton'.

It is hard to stand alone in an age like this—(constituted to the quick and critical perception of all harmonious combinations, I verily believe, beyond all preceding ages, since Jubal stumbled upon the gamut) to remain, as it were, singly unimpressible to the magic influence of an art, which is said to have such an especial stroke at soothing, elevating, and refining the passions.—Yet, rather than break the candid current of my confessions, I must avow to you that I have received a great deal more pain than pleasure from this so cried-up faculty.

I am constitutionally susceptible of noises. A carpenter's hammer, in a warm summer noon, will fret me into more than midsummer madness. But those unconnected, unset sounds, are nothing to the measured malice of music. The ear is passive to those single strokes; willingly enduring stripes while it hath no task to carry out. To music it cannot be passive. It will strive—mine at least will—spite of its inaptitude, to thrid the maze; like

F2   D.M.C.

an unskilled eye painfully poring upon hieroglyphics. I have sat through an Italian Opera till, for sheer pain, and inexplicable anguish, I have rushed out into the noisiest places of the crowded streets, to solace myself with sounds, which I was not obliged to follow, and get rid of the distracting torment of endless, fruitless, barren attention! I take refuge in the unpretending assemblage of honest common life sounds;—and the purgatory of the Enraged Musician becomes my paradise.

I have sat at an Oratorio (that profanation of the purposes of the cheerful playhouse) watching the faces of the auditory in the pit (what a contrast to Hogarth's Laughing Audience!) immoveable, or affecting some faint emotion—till (as some have said, that our occupations in the next world will be but a shadow of what delighted us in this) I have imagined myself in some cold Theatre in Hades, where some of the forms of the earthly one should be kept up, with none of the enjoyment; or like that

> . . . Party in a parlour
> All silent, and all DAMNED.

Above all, those insufferable concertos and pieces of music, as they are called, so plague and embitter my apprehension.—Words are something; but to be exposed to an endless battery of mere sounds; to be long dying; to lie stretched upon a rack of roses; to pile honey upon sugar, and sugar upon honey, to an interminable tedious sweetness; to fill up sound with feeling, and strain ideas to keep pace with it; to gaze upon empty frames, and be forced to make the pictures for yourself; to read a book, all stops, and be obliged to supply the verbal matter to invent extempore tragedies to answer to the vague gestures of an inexplicable rambling mime—these are faint shadows of what I have undergone from a series of the ablest executed pieces of this empty instrumental music.

I deny not, that in the opening of a concert, I have experienced something vastly lulling and agreeable:—

afterwards followeth the languor and the oppression.—
Like that disappointing book in Patmos; or, like the
comings on of melancholy, described by Burton, doth
music make her first insinuating approaches: 'Most pleasant
it is to such as are melancholy given, to walk alone in some
solitary grove, betwixt wood and water, by some brook
side, and to meditate upon some delightsome and
pleasant subject, which shall affect him more "amabilis
insania" and "Mentis gratissimus error". A most incomparable delight to build castles in the air, to go smiling to
themselves, acting an infinite variety of parts, which they
suppose, and strongly imagine, they act, or that they see
done.—So delightsome these toys at first, they could
spend whole days and nights without sleep, even whole
years in such contemplations, and fantastical meditations,
which are like so many dreams, and will hardly be drawn
from them—winding and unwinding themselves as so
many clocks, and still pleasing their humours, until at
last the SCENE TURNS UPON A SUDDEN, and they being now
habited to such meditations and solitary places, can
endure no ceremony, can think of nothing but harsh and
distasteful subjects. Fear, sorrow, suspicion, "subrusticus
pudor", discontent, cares, and weariness of life, surprise
them on a sudden, and they can think of nothing else:
continually suspecting, no sooner are their eyes open, but
this infernal plague of melancholy seizeth on them, and
terrifies their souls, representing some dismal object to
their minds; which now, by no means, no labour, no
persuasions, they can avoid, they cannot be rid of, they
cannot resist.'

Something like this 'SCENE TURNING' I have experienced
at the evening parties, at the house of my good Catholic
friend Nov—; who, by the aid of a capital organ, himself
the most finished of players, converts his drawing-room
into a chapel, his week-days into Sundays, and these
latter into minor heavens.

When my friend commences upon one of those solemn

anthems, which peradventure struck upon my heedless
ear, rambling in the side aisles of the dim Abbey, some
five-and-thirty years since, waking a new sense and
putting a soul of old religion into my young apprehension
—(whether it be that, in which the Psalmist, weary of the
persecution of bad men, wisheth to himself dove's wings
—or that other which, with a like measure of sobriety
and pathos, inquireth by what means the young man shall
best cleanse his mind)—a holy calm pervadeth me.—I
am for the time

> . . . rapt above earth,
> And possess joys not promised at my birth.

But when this master of the spell, not content to have
laid a soul prostrate, goes on, in his power, to inflict more
bliss than lies in her capacity to receive—impatient to
overcome her 'earthly' with his 'heavenly',—still pouring
in, for protracted hours, fresh waves and fresh from the
sea of sound, or from that inexhausted German ocean,
above which, in triumphant progress, dolphin-seated,
ride those Arions, Haydn and Mozart, with their attendant Tritons, Bach, Beethoven, and a countless tribe,
whom to attempt to reckon up would but plunge me
again in the deeps,—I stagger under the weight of harmony, reeling to and fro at my wits' end; clouds as of
frankincense, oppress me—priests, altars, censers, dazzle
before me—the genius of his religion hath me in her toils
—a shadowy triple tiara invests the brow of my friend,
late so naked, so ingenuous—he is a Pope,—and by him
sits, like as in the anomaly of dreams, a she-Pope too,—
tri-coronated like himself!—I am converted, and yet a
Protestant;—at once 'malleus hereticorum', and myself
grand heresiarch: or three heresies centre in my person:—
I am Marcion, Ebion, and Cerinthus—Gog and Magog—
what not?—till the coming in of the friendly supper-tray
dissipates the figment, and a draught of true Lutheran
beer (in which chiefly my friend shows himself no bigot)

at once reconciles me to the rationalities of a purer faith; and restores to me the genuine unterrifying aspects of my pleasant-countenanced host and hostess.

A Chapter on Ears, *Essays of Elia*

Some cry up Haydn, some Mozart,
Just as the whim bites; for my part
I do not care a farthing candle
For either of them, or for Handel,—
Cannot a man live free and easy
Without admiring Pergolesi?
Or through the world with comfort go
That never heard of Dr. Blow?
So help me, God, I hardly have;
And yet I eat, and drink, and shave,
Like other people, if you watch it,
And know no more of Stave or Crotchet
Than did the primitive Peruvians;
Or those old ante-queer Diluvians
That lived in the unwashed world with Tubal,
Before that dirty blacksmith Jubal
By stroke on anvil, or by summ'at
Found out, to his great surprise, the gamut.
I care no more for Cimarosa
Than he did for Salvator Rosa,
Being no painter; and bad luck
Be mine if I can bear that Gluck!
Old Tycho Brahe, and modern Herschel
Had something in 'em; but who's Purcell?
The devil, with his foot so cloven,
For aught I care may take Beethoven,
And, if the bargain does not suit,
I'll throw Weber in to boot.
There's not the splitting of a splinter
To choose 'twixt him last named, and Winter.
Of Dr. Pepusch old queen Dido
Knew just as much, God knows, as I do.

I would not go for miles to visit
Sebastian Bach (or Batch, which is it?)
No more I would for Bononcini.
As for Novello and Rossini,
I shall not say a word to grieve 'em,
Because they're living; so I leave 'em.

Free Thoughts on Several Eminent Composers

MARY LAMB (1785–1847)

The reason why my brother's so severe,
Vincentio, is—my brother has no ear;
And Caradori her mellifluous throat
Might stretch in vain to make him learn a note.
Of common tunes he knows not anything,
Nor 'Rule, Britannia' from 'God save the King'.
He rail at Handel! He the gamut quiz!
I'll lay my life he knows not what it is.
His spite at music is a pretty whim—
He loves it not because it loves not him.

Written in Vincent Novello's Album

ON DR. WILLIAM CROTCH (1775–1847)

AUTHOR UNKNOWN

A boy, son to a carpenter, of only two and three quarter years old, from hearing his father play upon an organ which he is making, has discovered such musical powers as are scarcely credible. He plays a variety of tunes, and has from memory repeated fragments of several Voluntaries which he heard Mr. Garland the organist play at the Cathedral. He has likewise accompanied a person who played upon a Flute not only with a treble, but has formed a base of his own, which to common hearers, seemed harmonious. If any person plays false, it throws him into a passion directly, and though his little fingers can only reach a sixth, he often attempts to play chords. He does not seem a remarkable clever child in any other respect, but his whole soul is absorbed in music.

From a letter to Dr. Charles Burney, *Philosophical Transactions of the Royal Society*, 1779

WILLIAM HAZLITT (1778–1830)

The Opera is a fine thing: the only question is, whether it is not too fine. It is the most fascinating, and at the same time the most tantalising, of all places. It is not the TOO LITTLE, but the TOO MUCH, that offends us. Every object is there collected, and displayed in ostentatious profusion, that can strike the senses or dazzle the imagination; music, dancing, painting, poetry, architecture, the blaze of beauty, 'the glass of fashion, and the mould of form'; and yet one is not satisfied—for the multitude and variety of objects distract the attention and by flattering us with a vain show of the highest gratification of every faculty and wish, leave us at last in a state of listlessness, disappointment, and ennui. The powers of the mind are exhausted, without being invigorated; our expectations are excited, not satisfied; and we are at some loss to distinguish an excess of irritation from the height of enjoyment. To sit at the Opera for a whole evening is like undergoing the process of animal magnetism for the same length of time. It is an illusion and a mockery, where the mind is made 'the fool of the senses', and cheated of itself; where pleasure after pleasure courts us, as in a fairy palace where the Graces and the Muses, weaving in a gay, fantastic round with one another, still turn from our pursuit; where art, like an enchantress with a thousand faces, still allures our giddy admiration, shifts her mask, and again eludes us. The Opera, in short, proceeds upon a false estimate of taste and morals; it supposes that the capacity for enjoyment may be multiplied with the objects calculated to afford it. It is a species of intellectual prostitution; for we can no more receive pleasure from all our faculties at once than we can be in love with a number of mistresses at the same time. Though we have different senses, we have but one heart; and, if we attempt to force it into the service of them all at once, it must grow restive or torpid, hardened or enervated. The spectator may say to the sister-arts of Painting, Poetry, and Music, as they advance to him in a 'pas-de-trois' at the Opera: 'How happy could I be with either, were t'other dear charmer away'; but while 'they all tease him together', the heart gives a satisfactory answer to none of them; is ashamed of its want of resources to supply the repeated calls upon its sensibility, seeks relief from the importunity of endless excitement in fastidious apathy or affected levity; and in the midst of luxury, pomp, vanity, indolence, and dissipation, feels only the hollow, aching void within, the irksome craving of unsatisfied desire, because more pleasures are placed within its reach than it is capable of enjoying, and the interference of one object with another ends in a double disappointment. Such is the best account I can give of the nature of the Opera,—of the contradiction between our expectations of pleasure and our uneasiness there,—of our very jealousy of the flattering appeals which are made to our senses, our passions, and our vanity, on all sides—of the little relish we acquire for it, and the distaste it gives us for other things. Any one of the sources of amusement to be found there would be enough to occupy and keep the attention alive; the 'tout ensemble' fatigues and oppresses it. One may be stifled to death with roses. A headache may be produced by a profusion of sweet smells or of sweet sounds; but we do not like the headache the more on that account. Nor are we reconciled to it, even at the Opera.

What makes the difference between an opera of

Mozart's and the singing of a thrush confined in a wooden cage at the corner of the street? The one is nature, and the other is art: the one is paid for, and the other is not. Madame Fodor sang the air of 'Vedrai Carino' in 'Don Giovanni' so divinely, because she was hired to sing it; she sang it to please the audience, not herself, and did not always like to be encored in it; but the thrush that awakes us at daybreak with its song, does not sing because it is paid to sing, or to please others, or to be admired or criticized. It sings because it is happy: it pours the thrilling sounds from its throat, to relieve the over-flowings of its own heart—the liquid notes come from, and go to the heart, dropping balm into it, as the gushing spring of joy comes pure and fresh to the longing sense, free from art and affectation; the same that rises over vernal groves, mingled with the breath of morning, and the perfumes of the wild hyacinth; it waits for no audience, it wants no rehearsing, and still—

'Hymns its good God, and carols sweet of love.'

This is the great difference between nature and art, that the one is what the other seems to be, and gives all the pleasure it expresses, because it feels it itself. Madame Fodor sang as a musical instrument may be made to play a tune, and perhaps with no more real delight; but it is not so with the linnet or the thrush, that sings because God pleases, and pours out its little soul in pleasure. This is the reason why its singing is (so far) so much better than melody or harmony, than bass or treble, than the Italian or the German school, than quavers or crotchets, or half-notes, or canzonets or quartetts, or anything in the world but truth and nature!

The Opera is the most artificial of all things. It is not only art, but ostentatious, unambiguous, exclusive art. It does not subsist as an imitation of nature, but in contempt of it; and, instead of seconding, its object is to pervert and sophisticate all our natural impressions of things. When the Opera first made its appearance in this country, there were strong prejudices entertained against it, and it was ridiculed as a species of the mock-heroic. The prejudices have worn out with time, and the ridicule has ceased; but the grounds for both remain the same in the nature of the thing itself. At the theatre we see and hear what has been said, thought, and done by various people elsewhere; at the Opera we see and hear what was never said, thought, or done any where but at the Opera. Not only is all communication with nature cut off, but every appeal to the imagination is sheathed and softened in the melting medium of Siren sounds. The ear is cloyed and glutted with warbled ecstasies or agonies; while every avenue to terror and pity is carefully stopped up and guarded by song and recitative. Music is not made the vehicle of poetry, but poetry of music; the very meaning of the words is lost or refined away in the effeminacy of a foreign language. A grand serious Opera is a tragedy wrapped up in soothing airs, to suit the tender feelings of the nurselings of fortune—where tortured victims swoon on beds of roses, and the pangs of despair sink in tremulous accents into downy repose. Just so much of human misery is given as is proper to lull those who are exempted from it into a deeper sense of their own security: just enough of the picture of human life is shewn to relieve their languor without disturbing their indifference;—it is calculated not to excite their sympathy, but 'with some sweet, oblivious antidote', to pamper their sleek and sordid apathy. In a word, the whole business of the Opera is to stifle emotion in its birth, and to intercept every feeling in its progress to the heart. Every impression that, left to itself, might sink deep into the mind, and wake it to real sympathy, is overtaken and baffled by means of some other impression, plays round the surface of the imagination, trembles into airy sound, or expires in an empty pageant. In the grand carnival of the senses the pulse of life is suspended, the link which binds us to

humanity is broken; the soul is fretted by the sense of
excessive softness into a feverish hectic dream; truth
becomes a fable; good and evil matters of perfect indifference, except as they can be made subservient to our
selfish gratification; and there is hardly a vice for which
the mind is not thus gradually prepared, no virtue of
which it is not rendered incapable!

On 'The Opera', *Essays*

ON SPOHR (1784–1859)

HARMONICON

Edited by WILLIAM AYRTON

Among the living composers of orchestral music,
Spohr stands very high; his science, his knowledge of the
powers of various instruments, his elegant taste and
indefatigable industry in revising his compositions, and
in giving the highest finish to them, altogether impart a
charm to his productions, which, if it be not felt, and
admitted by the multitude, is enjoyed and acknowledged
by connoisseurs; and the grand test of his intrinsic merit
is, that the more he is heard, the more he is admired. His
works certainly are much elaborated, and it requires no
slight knowledge of the art to be enabled to appreciate
them. This is particularly the case with the Symphony
(in D) performed at the fourth concert, which does not
unfold all its beauties to the uninstructed hearer but to
skilful judges—or, at least, to the majority of them—it
affords a highly intellectual pleasure.

May, 1824

GEORGE HOGARTH

... his oratorio of 'The Last Judgement' is not surpassed in the sublimity of many of its parts, by anything
that has appeared since the days of Handel. Though it

never descends from the solemnity which belongs to the subject, yet it possesses great variety of expression—passing from the most awful and terrible effects to strains of the deepest pathos and melancholy.

Musical History, 1835

ON WEBER (1786–1826)

HARMONICON

Edited by WILLIAM AYRTON

The most interesting feature in this concert was M. von Weber, the conductor of it. . . . His two overtures were performed, we need scarcely say, with more than common vigour and exactness, and he confessed the admirable manner in which they were executed. . . . The overture to 'Euryanthe' is not so well-known as 'Freischutz'; a few think it equal to the former: in some respects we even grant that it is superior: it is more the fruit of thought: has more of fugal point, and is more elaborately worked up: but it has less the appearance of having been struck out at a heat; is less the effect of inspiration than the other. We, however, do not wish to detract one iota from the praise that is due to it, for seldom such a work is produced.

May, 1826

SAMUEL LANGFORD

The centenary of Weber's death has come round when the immediate use and culture of Weber's music have almost dwindled away to nothing. . . . This is not to say that Weber and the music of Weber are done with. But it may be said of him more surely than of any other composer in the first rank that he died too soon. There was a completion about the work of Mozart, and even about that of Schubert, who died earlier. But Weber had as definite ideas as Wagner upon what he intended to do for dramatic music. It was Kind, the librettist of 'Der Freischutz', and not Wagner, who formulated the doctrine about the union of arts in dramatic music. The contemporaries of Weber charged him with the banality of writing music avowedly for the masses. He was, if not by base intention, yet by the blessing of nature, exceedingly successful in his appeal to the populace. Readers of Heine will remember how he tells that he was once so persecuted by the popularity of a melody from 'Der Freischutz' that, after having fled from one place to another to get out of its way, he took refuge in a droshky, only to find the driver went on whistling it insistently.

The truth is that Weber, in an entirely pious way, had attempted to express in his music the folk-feeling of the German people. This he had so felicitously combined with the expression of his own nature that no one could separate the one thing from the other. And the personal traits of Weber's music were of a unique kind. No one before him had such a wild-springing yet natural melody. No one had endowed music with so much colour, had been able to paint a picture so instantaneously, or to give to the picture so much of magic, rapture, and life. His imagination dwelt in a land, as Wagner said, half-way between the theatre and fairy-land. No one before him, or even since him, has been able to endow the ornamentation of music with so much natural emphasis and life. But while 'Der Freischutz' had all these virtues, it was not in itself sufficient for the composer's aims and genius, and Weber, who was less strong than Wagner in the critical and poetic side of dramatic genius, fell a victim, in his later works, to the feebleness of the librettist. As Goethe says, this want of critical power must be reckoned a defect, for genius should know how to guard itself against such vain labour. And if Weber was unable, in his too short span of life, to redeem his work from this failure on the dramatic side, another, a stronger than he, was to come, in Richard Wagner, who would make so wholesale a pillage of his musical virtues that men would almost forget to whom they originally belonged. A Frenchman may criticize Weber, and an Englishman may admire him, but only a German may love him, said Wagner, in his oration by Weber's final grave at Dresden. It was a very incomplete acknowledgement of his own vast indebtedness to his forerunner.

Musical Criticisms, 1926

ON BISHOP (1786–1855)

GEORGE HOGARTH

The name of Bishop will always hold a high place in the history of English music; but his permanent fame will rest on his earlier works,—on 'The Maniac', 'The Knight of Snowdon', 'The Virgin of the Sun', 'The Miller and His Men', and 'The Slave'. In these admirable operas we find pure, expressive, and forcible English melody, combined with a depth and solidity of the German School. They contain many scenes and concerted movements worthy of Mozart; and their rich and varied, yet chaste and unobtrusive orchestral accompaniments, are very thinly scattered. In truth, he did injustice to his own fame by the excessive haste and rapidity with which he wrote. Holding the situation of composer and director of the music in Covent Garden Theatre, he seems to have considered it his first duty to supply, as far as he could, the insatiable demand for novelty; and, for a succession of years, he produced five, six, seven, and eight musical pieces annually. Having thus tasked himself to write unceasingly, regardless of the will of Minerva, and without considering whether or not he was in the vein, it is not surprising that he should have filled his scores with crudities and common-places, alike unsatisfactory to the learned and unlearned. He thus lowered the character of English music, more especially when contrasted with the works of Mozart, Rossini, Weber, Winter, Paer, and other foreign masters, with which the public was daily becoming better and better acquainted. Still, however, his early and classical works are a sufficient basis for a high and lasting reputation; and if the rich scores of the older English music are ever again resorted to these works will not be overlooked.

Musical History, 1835

ON CZERNY (1791–1856)

HARMONICON

Edited by WILLIAM AYRTON

The 'Fantasia' . . . is the production of a young Hungarian, the pupil of Beethoven, and reported to be one of the most brilliant pianoforte players in Europe. We cannot say much in favour of this specimen of his composition, which is nothing but an air with variations, though a mere (*sic*) dignified name has been given to it, and is destitute of both taste and sentiment: it has an assemblage of difficult passages that have no motive, but to show the agility of human fingers, and might be played as well by means of mechanism, as by the most intellectual performer that ever lived. It also seemed interminable, and occupied, not the attention, but the time of the audience more than twenty minutes. Music will never rise to its proper place among the fine arts, till its professors in their compositions and performance, address themselves to the hearts of their auditors, and abandon all attempts to please by exciting a little momentary surprise.

'Fantasia for Piano and Orchestra', May, 1823

ON MEYERBEER (1791–1864)

EDWARD FITZGERALD

I also went once to the pit of the Covent Garden Italian Opera, to hear Meyerbeer's 'Huguenots', of which I had only heard bits on the Pianoforte. But the first Act was so noisy, and ugly, that I came away, unable to wait for the better part, that, I am told, follows. Meyerbeer is a man of Genius: and works up dramatic Music: but he has scarce any melody, and is rather grotesque and noisy than really powerful. I think this is the fault of modern music; people cannot believe that Mozart is powerful because he is so beautiful: in the same way as it requires a very practised eye (more than I possess) to recognise the consummate power predominating in the tranquil beauty of Greek Sculpture. I think Beethoven is rather spasmodically, than sustainedly, grand.

Letter to F. Tennyson, June 8th, 1852

MONTHLY MUSICAL RECORD

The score of this remarkable work which has always appeared to us to be brimful of experiments in orchestration, resulting in most telling and novel effects, is on this account one of special interest to musical students. It is further remarkable for its dramatic character, the general cleverness of its construction and the boldness displayed in certain harmonic transitions. That a work so generally pleasing and so strikingly effective should not have been more frequently brought forward seems surprising.

'Overture to *Struensee*', Jan., 1877

SIR CHARLES VILLIERS STANFORD

. . . a composer . . . clever to his finger-tips, opportunist of the deepest dye, cultivated, ambitious, and a master of his craft; a composer with great conceptions to his credit, who, nevertheless has never gained the respect of great musicians, because he never hesitated to sacrifice principle to gain success. . . . An early visit to Italy, then under the thrall of Rossini, had appealed to the young man's innate desire for popularity at all costs, and resulted in Weber's historical words; 'My heart bleeds to see a German composer of creative power stoop to become an imitator in order to win favour with the crowd.' The rift was complete, and Meyerbeer betook himself to Paris, where he went to work as assiduously in assimilating French methods as he had those of Italy a few years before. He secured in Scribe the best librettist of the day, and in association with him wrote a series of works for the Grand Opera, 'Robert le Diable', 'Les Huguenots', 'Le Prophète', 'L'Africaine', and for the Opera Comique 'L'Etoile du Nord' and 'Dinorah'. These operas all still exist, and most of them show little signs of wearing out their powers of attraction: but they are one and all an amazing conglomeration of fine music, trivial detail, masterly orchestration, and a striving, (so obvious as to be often silly) after effect. The great duet in the 'Huguenots' (Act IV) could scarcely be bettered, but it shines out all the more because of its tawdry surroundings. Vulgarity hobnobs with nobility on equal terms everywhere. The listener is never sure that a great artistic moment will not be wrecked by some futile concession to the high notes and florid embellishments of a prima donna. In the case of Rossini this was part of his nature and came to him with the native air he breathed; in that of Meyerbeer it was a concoction made to order. The Italian carried conviction, the German Hebrew did not. It is not a little characteristic that Meyerbeer contrived to rule over two such vitally different kingdoms as the Hof-Oper in Berlin and the Grand Opera in Paris, and remain acceptable to both. Such adaptability is a little too artificial to give grounds for admiration; but to a man who could be at once so grandiose and so finicking nothing was impossible. It is difficult to imagine how the composer of the Cathedral Scene in the 'Prophète' could condescend to sit next the chief of the claque at the final rehearsal, and alter passages to suit his cue for applause, or to wander about the back of the stage to hear what the scene shifters said about his music. And yet for all his disregard of high ideals, and lack of self-sacrifice in the nobler interests of his art, Meyerbeer did a great work in developing the constructive side of opera, and showing how great effects of climax can be attained. It is to his credit that, though he could be trivial, he never would consent to be ugly. His worst characters are never delineated by uncouth or unmusicianly means. He had a certain sense of humanity which makes such figures as Marcel, Fides, and Raoul de Nangis stand out as creations in musico-dramatic literature. He advanced orchestration, he knew to a nicety the limitations and capabilities of the voice, and he was not afraid of a big tune, even although it was not always a distinguished one. Upon the German school he had very little influence, upon the French a very considerable one, though his Parisian contemporaries and successors seem to have seen through his artificialities enough to steer fairly clear of them, aided therein by their own innate patriotism.

A History of Music, 1916

ON ROSSINI (1792–1868)

QUARTERLY MUSICAL MAGAZINE

Mr. Bishop has rejected Rossini's Overture and substituted one of his own.

'Barber of Seville', Vol. II, 1820

GEORGE HOGARTH

If Rossini's singers have only lungs strong enough to make themselves heard through the noise of the orchestra, they are as free from restraint as their predecessors were a century ago .... Forced to contend incessantly with such a mass of sound, the females are compelled to scream, and the males to shout; and the incorrect and slovenly harmony which they are accustomed to hear from the orchestra renders them by no means fastidious as to the purity of the irroulades and embellishments. Rossini's scores are full of gross violations of the most established laws of harmony which some people defend by saying that they are not perceptible to the ear. But take one of these passages, and play it on the pianoforte, and its deformity will at once be apparent, though in the theatre the false harmony may be covered by the confusion of many loud instruments. Is such harmony justifiable, because it is tolerated only when the ear is unable to discover of what it consists? Had such things been ever admitted by Haydn or Mozart, they would have been perceived at once by the pellucid clearness of the score; but are impurities less offensive in themselves, because the stream which contains them is turbid?

Musical History, 1835

LEIGH HUNT

We fear it is a little out of the scientific pale to think Rossini a man of genius; but we confess, with all our preference for such writers as Mozart, with whom, indeed, he is not to be compared, we do hold that opinion of the lively Italian. There is genius of many kinds, and of kinds very remote from one another, even in rank. The greatest genius is so great a thing that another may be infinitely less, and yet of the stock. Now Rossini, in music, is the genius of sheer animal spirits. It is a species as inferior to that of Mozart, as the cleverness of a smart boy is to that of a man of sentiment; but it is genius nevertheless. It is rare, effective, and a part of the possessor's character:—we mean, that like all persons who really effect anything beyond the common, it belongs and is peculiar to him, like the invisible genius that was supposed of old to wait upon individuals. This is what genius means; and Rossini undoubtedly has one. 'He hath a devil', as Cowlet's friend used to cry out when he read Virgil; and a merry devil it is, and graceful withal. It is a pity he has written so many commonplaces, so many bars full of mere chatter, and overtures so full of cant and puffing. But this exuberance appears to be a constituent part of him. It is the hey-day in his blood; and perhaps we could no more have the good things without it than some men of wit can talk well without a bottle of wine and in the midst of a great deal of nonsense. Now and then he gives us something worthy of the most popular names of his country . . . 'Di piacer' is full of smiling delight and anticipation, as the words imply. Sometimes he is not deficient even in tenderness, as in one or two airs in his 'Othello'; but it is his liveliest operas, such as 'Il Barbiere di Siviglia' and the 'Italiana in Algieri' that he shines. His mobs make some of the pleasantest riots conceivable; his more gentlemanly proceedings, his bows and compliments, are full of address and even elegance, and he is a prodigious hand at a piece of pretension or foppery. Not to see into his merit in these cases, surely implies only, that there is a want of animal spirits on the part of the observer.

Going to the Play Again

FRANCIS TOYE

Generally speaking . . . Rossini never dogmatised; his approach to music was instinctive rather than intellectual. This is shown in his famous saying that there are only two kinds of music, the good and the bad; or that other, less known, where he states that every kind of music is good except the boring kind. These are scarcely the utterances of a man who attached any value to aesthetic theories as such . . . .

As regards Rossini's technical ability there can scarcely be two opinions. No man not a consummate technician could·have written 'William Tell', while the wonderful ensembles in the earlier operas suffice by themselves to attest his mastery. These ensembles lack as a rule the power of characterisation later attained by Verdi, but as examples of skill and effectiveness in vocal part writing, they are supreme. . . .

His excellence in orchestration, too, has not, I think, been sufficiently emphasised. None of his Italian contemporaries, not even Verdi till the 'Ballo in Maschera' period, scored as well as he did. It has been said, indeed, that, with his retirement in 1829, Italian writing for the orchestra took a definite step backward. All through the Rossini operas we find instruments treated with great skill, with an unerring instinct for their potentialities of expression. The Overtures, in particular, deserve the highest praise in this respect. . . . Everything 'comes off' as well to-day as ever it did. Nobody who has heard them played by a Toscanini or a Beecham is likely to stand in need of conversion on that score. As a matter of fact, these Overtures are little masterpieces from every point of view. In them we find displayed to the best advantage that rhythm in which Rossini so excelled and to which he attached so much importance, saying that in it resided all the power and expressiveness of music. The subject-material itself is nearly always excellent and highly individual; the form is as clear as the treatment.

Rossini: A Study in Tragi-Comedy, 1934

•

ON CIPRIANI POTTER (1792–1881)

QUARTERLY MUSICAL MAGAZINE

Mr. Potter, being an Englishman, so much the more valuable should his work be in the estimation of his countrymen.

Vol. VIII, 1826

HARMONICON

Edited by WILLIAM AYRTON

... it not only shows the thorough knowledge of harmony—of the characters of the different instruments, and of their combined use in the orchestra, that he has always evinced, but it displays invention, the want of which is so oppressively felt in nineteen out of twenty of those things called 'new', that are annually brought forward, in various shapes, and immediately consigned to oblivion. The present work is in the usual number of movements; the Minuet and Trio have the most novelty; herein are some unexpected, excellent effects. There are likewise passages of considerable originality in both the first and last movements, but the finale would be improved by abridgement. The whole met with great applause.

'Symphony', June, 1826

J. W. DAVISON

The directors (of the Philharmonic Society) appear to have been seized with a sudden fit of patriotism. The appearance of an English Symphony, or in other words a symphony written by an English Composer used to be a rare event at the Philharmonic; but now in the course of three concerts, we have had no less than two, at the 7th and 8th concerts, also by English musicians. What was said of the symphony of Mr. Lucas may, in great measure, be applied to that of Mr. Potter, which was composed nearly as long ago as the other, expressly for the Philharmonic Society. It is the work of an admirable musician, one who has studied the greatest models 'con amore' .... Herr Wagner directed the performance with evident goodwill; and though the last movement was somewhat of a scramble, and the scherzo (the weakest part) a little obscure, all the rest went well. There was very great applause at the end, which was not only fair, considering the merits of the symphony, but due to its author on account of the important influence he has exercised for many years on the progress of English music, and on the education of English musicians as principal professor of composition in the Royal Academy of Music.

The Times, May 29th, 1855

W. H. GLOVER

We know not whether Mr. Potter's symphony be a recent production, for, unhappily, its being still in MS. proves nothing to the purpose; but that it is an extremely clever and musicianly work, fully worthy the long-established reputation of Mr. Potter, one of our best native performers, there can be no doubt whatever. It is constructed on the plan followed more or less by all the great symphonists from Haydn (who was its inventor) downwards, and deserves to hold an honourable position amongst other conscientious and skilful compositions of the classical school to which it belongs. Mr. Potter's work was, on the whole, very ably performed, under the direction of Herr Wagner, and frequently elicited applause of the warmest kind.

Morning Post, May 29th, 1855

SIR GEORGE MACFARREN

Mr. Potter's retirement from the profession releases me from the reserve that would be decorous with regard to one working among us.

Programme Note, Royal Philharmonic
Society, May 3rd, 1869

MUSICAL TIMES

The revival of Mr. Cipriani Potter's Symphony in D should not be regarded as a mere compliment to its accomplished composer. Such genuine, healthy music as this has a right to its place in the programmes of an Institution professedly formed to encourage and exhibit talent wherever it can be found; and we trust that the ice being fairly broken, whether the 'music of the future' be accepted or not in the present day, such works as Mr. Potter's may, at all events, not be branded as 'music of the Past'.

June, 1869

ON SCHUBERT (1797–1828)

J. W. DAVISON

A deep shade of suspicion, we regret to say, is beginning to be cast over the authenticity of posthumous compositions. The defunct popular composer not only becomes immortal in the poetical sense, but, by a curious felicity which publishers can best explain, actually goes on composing after he is dead. All Paris has been in a state of amazement at the posthumous diligence of the song-writer F. Schubert, who, while one would think his ashes repose in peace at Vienna, is still making eternal new songs and putting drawing-rooms in commotion.

Musical World, 1839

The ideas throughout it are all of a minute character and the instrumentation is of a piece with the ideas. There is no breadth, there is no grandeur, there is no dignity in either; clearness and contrast and beautiful finish are always apparent, but the orchestra, though loud, is never massive and sonorous, and the music, though always correct, is never serious or imposing.

'Symphony in C', *Musical World*, 1859

SIR GEORGE MACFARREN

Ill trained, nay, all but uneducated in the mechanism of composition, he had such an affluence of ideas as has enriched few of the greatest masters, but he failed in technical skill for their development, and still more for their condensation. Hence it is that many of his larger works, in instrumental music particularly, are prolix from a very excess of beauty. Such vague diffuseness of plan, such redundancy of excellent material, as dissipate the interest and mar the effect of other of his productions, appear not in the (present) unfinished or rather unended work, which is thus, so far as it extends, more nearly assimilated to the greatest masterpieces of its class than any production of Schubert that it has been my fortune to hear; the more delight we receive, therefore, from the fragment that has reached us, the more we must deplore the unrelated accident which rent in twain the artist's purpose and frustated what promised to be by many degrees the best of his works.

'Unfinished Symphony', Programme Note,
Royal Philharmonic Society, April 19th, 1869

MONTHLY MUSICAL RECORD

Notwithstanding its great length, there is no other work of the kind that we can name which more thoroughly rivets the attention or is productive of more pleasurable emotion to the listener. One listens to it throughout without the slightest sense of fatigue; its effect, indeed, is invigorating.

'Symphony in C', Jan., 1875
•

SAMUEL BUTLER

Then came Schubert's 'Erl König' which, I daresay, is very fine but with which I have absolutely nothing in common.

Note Books

W. S. ROCKSTRO

... all he wrote was beautiful. His Songs are known to everyone; and, undoubtedly, his genius shines more

G   D.M.C.

brightly in these than in any of his other compositions. It is true that the effect of direct inspiration is equally evident in his Symphonies and other longer works; but, in these, the most reverent of critics cannot blind his eyes to the results of an imperfect musical education. Where learning is indispensable, Schubert does not show himself at his best.

History of Music, 1886

MUSICAL TIMES

. . . at the close of the first movement the principal horn called out to one of the first violins, 'Tom, have you been able to discover a tune yet?' 'I have not,' was Tom's reply.

Account of an early rehearsal of
the Symphony in C, Feb., 1897

SIR W. H. HADOW

Schubert . . . stands at the parting of the ways. The direct inheritor of Mozart and Beethoven, he belongs by birth, by training, by all the forces of condition and circumstance, to the great school of musical art which they established. In the peculiar quality of his imagination, in his warmth, his vividness, and we may add in his impatience of formal restraint, he points forward to the generation that should rebel against all formality, and bid the inspiration of music be wholly imaginative. Yet there can be no doubt to which of the two periods he belongs. Schumann uses colour for its emotional suggestion, Schubert for its inherent loveliness; Berlioz attempts to make the symphony articulate, Schubert will not allow it to be descriptive; Liszt accentuates rhythm, because of its nervous force and stimulus, Schubert because it enhances the contour of his line. Possessing in full measure all the artistic gifts which we commonly associate with the mid-century, he devoted them, at their highest, to the loftier ideals of its beginning. Like Mozart, whose influence upon his work is noticeable to the very end, he meant his music to be independent of all adventitious aid or interpretation, he never assigned to any composition a picturesque or poetic title, he never gave any indication of specific or content. It is true that he did little to extend or deepen the great symphonic forms; and that in some respects he may even have prepared for their disintegration. Nevertheless his strength lay not in revolt against a method but in loyalty to a principle. The laws of his kingdom were the laws of pure beauty, and in their service he found at once his inspiration and his reward . . .

His Lyric gift was from the first wonderfully mature. Before he was twenty years old he had written nearly all the finest of his songs from Goethe, a collection which by itself would be sufficient to win his immortality. But as in his instrumental music the approach of manhood brought him a firmer hand, so in song it enriched him with an even deeper and more intimate expression. In the earlier compositions we have an extremely vivid illustration of the poet's theme—Gretchen at her spinning wheel, the father and child galloping through the haunted night, restless love beneath the pelting of the pitiless storm—and the same power of pictorial suggestion is apparent in the great mythic odes . . . with which he was at this time much occupied. The later work penetrates more closely, as it were, in his actual person. In the 'Schöne Müllerin' (1823), the songs from Scott and Shakespeare (1825–7), the 'Winterreise' (1827) and the 'Schwanengesang' (1828), the fusion between the two arts is complete: they are no longer two but one, a single indivisible utterance of lyric thought. No songs of Schumann and Heine, of Brahms and Tieck, have attained to a more perfect and indissoluble unity.

'The Viennese Period', *Oxford History of Music*, Vol. V, 1904

ERIC BLOM

The signs of strong personality in an artist's work, though they may be but vaguely apprehended by the bulk of his admirers, appear rarely quite impenetrable to the observer versed in the chemistry of art, for they may as a rule be traced ultimately to purely technical procedures. They may be so recondite as to be inexplicable to the artist himself and only with difficulty accessible to the analytical mind projected upon them subsequently to the procedure of creation. But Schubert is the most transparent of composers. His style bears a hall-mark that is combined with the most elementary musicianship; who was asked to name the chief outward distinction of his writing, would surely, without hesitation, refer to his free and frequent interchange of the major and minor modes. It is a device as conspicuous and familiar as Rembrandt's chiaroscuro, though no such convenient tag has as yet been found for it. If such a descriptive label were really needed for what must be called a mannerism, but a mannerism used again and again in its primeval innocence to serve the ends of genius, there could be no objection to our talking about Schubert's chiaroscuro.

The trick of distributing harmonic light and shade in this way is not a subtle one: it verges upon the commonplace in its obviousness. It was not even a new one in Schubert's time; but it is this very simplicity that lies in the inmost kernel of Schubert's art which makes him of all the great masters the most accessible. He, less than any of them, causes the untutored music lover to shy at the the forbidding classicality which is unfortunately thrust posthumously upon those most qualified to give universal delight. He lightly accepted the handiest and most ancient means of producing a commonly understood musical effect: his reward for not being over-fastidious is a measure of freedom from the unhappy exclusiveness of the great that is enjoyed by no other musical classic— perhaps by no classic of any sort.

The wonder is that, for all his simple way of helping himself to what came but too readily to his hand, he does not offend any musician who keeps his mind reasonably free from prejudice. That his casualness did not prevent him from producing superb art with surprising frequency is due to an extraordinary fund of instinctive good sense which he had to set against it. Though the practice of mixing major and minor is nearly as old as the civilised music we know, his way of carrying it out is as startlingly and unaccountably different as his music altogether was from that of his predecessors. In fact, it brings us as near as anything may to discovering the secret of the newness of Schubert's music. The novelty of his use of transitions from major to minor, and more especially from minor to major, is in part technical, as may be judged from the decisive steps and short cuts they enabled him to make in modulation; but it is a literary—and often literal—employment that gives the device the character of a new departure, of a heading at full tilt towards romanticism, with its striving to convert what had once served purely musical ends into a kind of hyper-flexible vocabulary for the expression of poetical ideas in a way that was at once more vague and more clearly illuminating than mere words.

'His Favourite Device', *Music and Letters*, Oct. 1928

The Nineteenth Century

The concert season of the year 1837 is not worth mentioning.
Equally dull was the opera season . . . .

REV. JOHN EDMUND COX,
Musical Recollections of the
last Half-Century, 1872

ON BERLIOZ (1803–1869)

REV. JOHN EDMUND COX

Of M. Berlioz' 'Benvenuto Cellini' and Spohr's 'Jessonda' ... it may suffice to say, that neither the one nor the other warranted the enormous expense bestowed —or rather wasted—in mounting them. As works of art there could be no comparison between them, the one being as lusciously melodious, although ponderous in method, and full of the mannerisms of the great German composer's peculiar style, as the other was deficient in that quality, and overloaded with eccentricities that savoured more of trick and charlatanism than of anything resembling genius.

Musical Recollections of the last
Half-Century, 1872

W. S. ROCKSTRO

... the very quality on which his own greatness chiefly depends, the strong originality of his conceptions, which lead him into paths absolutely untrodden until he opened a way through them for himself, the exceedingly independence (*sic*) of thought which persistently ignored the existence of all laws and methods and systems whatsoever, tended more than any other circumstance to prevent him from leaving a lasting impression upon Dramatic or Instrumental Music.

History of Music, 1886

FRANCIS HUEFFER

Never having seen one of his operas on the stage, I am loth to give a definite opinion on the point; but, as far as one can judge by pianoforte arrangements, it seems to me Berlioz did not possess dramatic genius in the proper sense of the word. His nature was too lyrical, too ex-

G2   D.M.C.

pansive for that; he lacked the crispness of touch, the succinctness of utterance, the concentration of impulse, which go to the making of a great writer of the stage, apart from which he had no definite and consistent idea of the musico-dramatic form. Much as he despised the fireworks and the meaningless conventionalities of the Italian and light French schools, he employs the same conventionalities in 'Benvenuto Cellini', in 'Beatrice et Benedict', and even in 'Les Troyens', without hesitation and in close and startling juxtaposition with poetic beauties of a very high order. And it is not, perhaps, matter for much regret that the recent Berlioz revivals in France and England have not led to the mounting of a single one of his operas, although Mr. Rosa at one time announced 'Benvenuto' at Her Majesty's Theatre, and had even a statue of Perseus cast for the purpose. I do not mean to deny that an intelligent and artistically-minded manager might and should have made a trial; but I greatly doubt whether such a trial would have redounded much to the credit of Berlioz . . .

Liszt, although less endowed with the creative musical gift than Berlioz, felt the necessity of making form and substance agree with each other much more strongly, and in consequence, gave to music what Berlioz never gave it, a most important addition to its structural apparatus—the Symphonic Poem. Berlioz, much more revolutionary in his tendency than Liszt, was much less independent of established formulas, for the reason that he did not allow the law of nature to guide him to freedom. The equation between matter and manner is in his work a question of chance, not of choice. In 'Romeo and Juliet', that divinest of elegies, the 'Scène d'Amour', is followed later on by a wretched operatic Finale, evidently inspired by the 'Bénédiction des Poignards' in the 'Huguenots', and not even a good specimen of its meretricious kind. To Berlioz, in short, Music owes an infinite debt of gratitude. He is virtually the creator of the modern orchestra; he has infused a spirit of poetry into music; he has, in fact, written some of the finest music ever written. He has converted platitude by his teaching and example; he has, in fact, made a great many things possible, but he has not established a new starting-point for other artists to rise from and continue the work. Perhaps a play upon words may best explain the difference: Berlioz was a reformer, but not a re-former.

Half a Century of Music in England 1837–1887, 1889

SAMUEL BUTLER

And finally there was a tiresome characteristic overture by Berlioz, which, if Jones could by any possibility have written anything so dreary, I should certainly have begged him not to publish.

Note Books

W. J. TURNER

For me Berlioz has a high seat in the great hierarchy of music. I admit him to a place near Beethoven and Mozart in my affections, and it is my sober opinion that he of all other musicians is the only one to equal them in original genius. It is a striking example of the day's perversities of taste to value the music of Bach so much more highly than the music of Berlioz, and this perversity, like most perversities of judgement, is due to an intellectual misconception which dominates the minds of the intelligentsia to-day and spreads from them by the power of snobbishness to the general public.

It is true that in the 'Lacrymosa' Berlioz turns a phrase that might have come out of an Italian opera; it is true that his Mass calls for sixteen kettledrums; it is true that he asks for four brass bands to be played north, south, east, and west of the general body of the chorus and orchestra. All these things in the hands of any one but Berlioz would have resulted in incredible vulgarity, but

Berlioz could not be vulgar; he was as far above our vulgar uses as the sun is above cooking our dinners, and we have proof of this when any other man attempts to use the resources that Berlioz has put into our hands.

Musical Meanderings, 1928

TOM S. WOOTTON

Musical people generally seem to lose their sense of proportion in the face of Berlioz' music, and the reason for this must be sought in his baffling originality. If one would understand him—and he would repay any earnest attempt one hundredfold—one must disabuse one's mind of much that has been written about his music, a great deal of which is mere repetition of what was brought against him in his lifetime, and which, though possibly more or less justified by the current ideas of that day, now seems old-fashioned in the light of the experimentalism of modern music. Parenthetically, I would observe that one thing that bewilders a listener to the French master's works is the difficulty of dating him. Even if the hearer *knows* that the March to Execution was composed less than a score of years after Haydn's death, his ears give him the lie. On the other hand it is obviously unfair to Berlioz to treat him as in some respects a comparatively modern composer. His musical career had ended before Wagner's later works were performed.

Berlioz is an isolated figure, and we must judge him as such, without reference to any other composer.

The Heritage of Music, Vol. II, 1933

J. H. ELLIOT

One thing may be stated with confidence: it is impossible to sum up Hector Berlioz in a single phrase. There is not one Berlioz—there are half a dozen; and they are as different from one another as they are different from all other composers. . . . Berlioz remains the most baffling phenomenon in musical history. He had tremendous genius, but no power—or no desire—to concentrate it into one channel: he allowed it to spread itself in all directions. He was an admirably acute critic, yet he lacked the power to separate the sublime from the ridiculous in his early work and the inspired from the commonplace in his later achievements. His technical skill was immense, yet he could lapse into amazing crudities. He gibed at pedantry, yet rarely lost an opportunity of drawing attention to his own mechanical ingenuities; he points out in his very scores where such and such a theme is united with another, as though fearful lest the reader should miss the point, and even reassures orchestral performers concerning the capacity of their instruments to fulfil his demands. Of Berlioz' masterly orchestration and his remarkable rhythmic inventions, together with the extraordinary subtlety of his phrase markings, it is unnecessary to speak: these are commonplaces of historical knowledge, and their importance has long been recognised.

We come back to the old problem: was Berlioz a great composer or an adventurer in music? He was both. He was a great genius, and he wrote great music—but his work is littered with the crude, the humdrum and the grotesque. Flowers and weeds grow side by side in an immense garden laid out on no definable plan. Berlioz' best is wonderful; his worst is appalling—and the twain, with the degrees between them, are inextricably confused together. It is impossible briefly to describe Berlioz in a way that will satisfy a music lover who is prepared neither to fall blindly before a god, in spite of clay feet of alarming prominence, nor to reject wholesale by ignoring equally outstanding features which are exquisite in their beauty. Hector Berlioz is a strange figure—'a pathetic monument of incompleteness', as Ernest Newman has called him. One can no more define him adequately in a few terse words than one can give in a sentence a complete and accurate description of the English climate. He was a genius without discipline, an enigma without a solution. He defies the first law of Heaven, which is order: he will not fit into any category; no compartment of the logical mind is plastic enough to contain a complete impression of him. To him can be applied, with equal truth and equal untruth, a string of epithets, each different from and contradictory to its predecessor; but none will dispose of him. One can only admire his virtues which were legion, and deplore his vices, which were innumerable. He remains himself—Hector Berlioz, the unique.

Berlioz, 1938

ON BALFE (1808–1870)

EDWARD FITZGERALD

There is a dreadful vulgar ballad, composed by Mr. Balfe and sung with most unbounded applause by Miss Rainforth

'I dreamt that I dwelt in marble halls'

which is sung and organed at every corner in London. I think you may imagine what kind of flowing 6/8 time of the last imbecility it is. The words are written by Mr. Bunn! 'Arcades ambo.'

Letter to F. Tennyson, Oct. 10th, 1844

MUSICAL TIMES

In order to establish some kind of connection between the fireworks and the design of the Festival, one of the set pieces presented a lyre, surrounded by flags and laurel leaves, the name Balfe being conspicuous in fiery letters. The attendance was so large that the foundation of a scholarship at the Royal Academy of Music in memory of the composer—which was announced as the principal object of the meeting—may be considered as secure.

'A Balfe Festival', Sept. 1876

ON MENDELSSOHN (1809–1847)

HARMONICON

Edited by WILLIAM AYRTON

Fertility of invention and novelty of effect, are what first strike the hearers of M. Mendelssohn's Symphony; but at the same time, the melodiousness of his subjects, the vigour with which these are supported, the gracefulness of the slow movement, the playfulness of some parts, and the energy of others, are all felt; though from a first hearing, and without some previous knowledge of the score, it were in vain to attempt any analysis of the work which we can now only describe in general terms, but hope ere long to be able to enter into its details.

'Symphony in C minor', June 1829

So far as music is capable of imitating, the composer has succeeded in his design; the images impressed on his mind he certainly excited, in a general way, on ours: we may even be said to have heard the sound of the winds and waves, for music is capable of imitating these in a direct manner: and, by means of association, we fancied an all-pervading gloom. . . . Whatever a vivid imagination could suggest, and great musical knowledge supply, has contributed to this, the latest work of M. Mendelssohn, one of the finest and most original geniuses of the age; and it will be but an act of justice to him, and a great boon to the frequenters of these Concerts (the Philharmonic) to repeat the present composition before the conclusion of the season. Works such as this are like 'Angel's visits' and should be made the most of.

'The Isles of Fingal', June 1832

He is a composer who spurns at imitation, for he is original almost to overflowing and to the very last note of a piece is inexhaustible in new effects ... the close arrives, which is all calmness—a pianissimo! Such an ending is without example and exceedingly delightful it was admitted to be by universal consent.

'Piano Concerto in G minor', June 1832

GEORGE HOGARTH

Another piece ... is a fine specimen of the descriptive powers of music; but its difficulty and peculiarity of style have prevented it from being so popular as it will one day become.

'The Isles of Fingal'
Musical History, 1835

H. F. CHORLEY

For his oratorio, it would be difficult for us to say too much in its praise—simple, massive, every note of it full of expression, written in the spirit of the great ancients, but not according to their letter. We should be disposed unhesitatingly, to rank it next to the immortal works of Handel, being persuaded that every subsequent hearing must bring its truth increasingly home to every listener. It includes no difficulties crowded together for the production of great effects, the resource of second-best genius ... The airs are as easy as they must be delightful to sing; and the orchestra, though, when it is required, as rich and figurative as a master's hand, guided by a master's mind, can make it, is kept in its proper place—that is, working together with the vocal parts, neither predominating over them, nor lagging behind.

'St. Paul', *Athenaeum*, 1837

Such a Hymn of Praise ought to be an outpouring of thanksgiving, which acknowledging a blessing vouchsafed, is cheerful, but not proud, thus distinct from triumph glorying over an achieved conquest. And this, if impression answer intention, and we have at all comprehended his purpose, Mendelssohn has fully accomplished. There is joy with understanding everywhere evident in the brighter portions of his works, while even in the glances thrown upon the distress and deep affliction gone by—such acknowledgment being indispensable to gratitude's full exercise—the presence of hope and comfort is manifest. The sorrow is not felt to be careless, the shadow of death not displayed as a pall of final sepulture, but as a veil which the Highest has decreed SHALL pass. This general idea has been wrought out by the musician with the happiest skill. From the first bold and exulting phrase of the Symphonic portion of the work, to the last chord of the final fugue, where all the intertwined vocal and instrumental parts return to the same grand and final unison, the prevailing spirit is illustrated with a delightful variety of resource. Witness in the second instrumental movement the major chords of the wind instruments to relieve the minor strings: witness that exquisite duet with its supporting chorus, 'I waited for the Lord'; the subsequent chorus in D major, 'The night is departing'; and the chorale at first harmonised in four parts, and then given in unison by the entire mass of voices, the orchestra maintaining on its repetition, a rich but not distracting accompaniment. More closely to analyse this hymn would require more space than we can command, even were it possible to do so on the strength of a single hearing. We must return, however, for one moment to specify the duet for two soprani already mentioned, as one of the most legitimately engaging movements which modern art has produced, nor can the whole work be left without repeating that, whether as regards poetry of conception or skill of execution, it is worthy of the composer of the conversion scene in 'St. Paul'.

'Lobgesang', *Athenaeum*, 1840

... a vigorous and fanciful invention pervaded it from the first bar to the last, wrought out with that happy and natural ease to which second-rate hands can never attain. The orchestra was not forced to uses for which it was never intended; there was no torturing of simple thoughts, in the vain hope of passing them as profound; no mystery work, to make empty heads shake solemnly, and convulse confused minds with factitious enthusiasm; but healthy nerve, with no lack of such picturesque beauty and poetic colour as characterise the newer style of composition.

'Scotch Symphony', *Athenaeum*, 1842

That Mendelssohn possessed a natural vein of such rich, flowing melody, as Mozart and Beethoven commanded cannot be claimed for him. Yet as a melodist he has been misunderstood and undervalued in no common degree— the fate, by the way, of every new composer who is more than a melodist. Those who have passed hasty judgment on him as 'dry' have done so rather on the strength of some one work which does not suit their humour than on the bulk of his writings. Further, to every man's definition of melody, there goes more of temperament, association, and extraneous sympathy than professors or amateurs will willingly admit.

Modern German Music:
Recollections and Criticisms, 1862

EDWARD FITZGERALD (1809–1883)

I draw a very little, and think of music as I walk in the fields: but have no piano in this part of the world... I hear there is a fine new Symphony by Mendelssohn, who is by far our best writer now, and in some measure combines Beethoven and Handel. I grow every day more and more to love only the old God save the King style: the common chords, those truisms of music, like other truisms so little understood in the full. Just look at the mechanism of Robin Adair.

Letter to F. Tennyson, Aug. 16th, 1842

I went to hear Mendelssohn's Elijah last spring: and found it wasn't worth the trouble. Though very good music it is not original: Haydn much better. I think the day of Oratorios is gone, like the day for painting Holy Families, etc. But we cannot get tired of what has been done in Oratorios more than we can get tired of Raffaelle. Mendelssohn is really original and beautiful in romantic music: witness his Midsummer Night's Dream, and Fingal's Cave.

Letter to F. Tennyson, May 4th, 1848

Mendelssohn's things are mostly tiresome to me.

Letter to F. Tennyson, Dec. 27th, 1853

SIR GEORGE MACFARREN

The fact that Mendelssohn spent more than twelve years upon the composition of his great Symphony in A minor, is no proof of his inability to produce rapidly when occasion demanded it.

'Serenade and Allegro' for Piano and Orchestra, Programme note, Royal Philharmonic Society, May 3rd, 1869

REV. JOHN EDMUND COX

Concerning a work now quite as well known as Handel's 'Messiah', and second only perhaps in public estimation to that highly important oratorio, it is needless here to give a resumé of its various points of excellence, both as regards the consecutive nature of the circumstances connected with the prophet's life and career, or to enter at any length on the various vocal and instrumental means adopted for their descriptive elucidation. Neither would it be either useful or profitable to refer to the differences of opinion that were, and still are, expressed as to whether it is inferior or superior to the same composer's 'St. Paul'. Whilst educated musicians maintain the former opinion, public estimation will decidedly prefer the latter, chiefly because the 'book' being of more interesting construction, and of the music being almost wholly descriptive, as in many instances also exceedingly dramatic so much so, indeed, that it is said in Germany that it may some day or other be adapted to the stage—a result not at all beyond the limits of possibility, since the celebrated Bavarian Ammergau Play has served to remove many of the objections to the transfer of Scriptural subjects from the concert-room to the theatre; and assuredly the import of that play, is by many and many a degree more sacred than the history of the prophet Elijah ever can be considered. One remarkable feature of this oratorio—the holiness of its tone—seized at once upon the Birmingham audience, and has been increased on every occasion of its being repeated either in London or the provinces.

'Elijah', *Musical Recollections of the last Half-Century*, 1872

ERNEST WALKER

The main cause of the weakening of the sheer monopoly of Handelian influence was the enormous popularity of Mendelssohn. He visited this country on several occasions, and the fascination of his personal character won him hosts of friends; the first performance of 'Elijah' at Birmingham in 1845 was the crowning event of his career, and at his death a year later the English musical world talked as if the sun had fallen from the sky. For a generation more, after which a steady decline began, Mendelssohnianism remained astonishingly powerful; though it was not long before it became confined— though not to so extreme a degree as in the case of Handelianism—to a comparatively small number of works. To these two denominations all English musicians of serious aims had more or less wholeheartedly to bow the knee, so long as they did not, like Pierson, prefer a voluntary exile; even if here and there individuality declined to be crushed altogether, yet it was by the canons of Handel and Mendelssohn that the English public (even while extending a personal welcome to revolutionary foreigners like Berlioz) inevitably judged all native work, except such as frankly appealed to lower tastes, or, like that of Pearsall, presented virtually no points of contact.

A History of Music in England, 1907

ALEXANDER BRENT-SMITH

Two of the most noticeable blemishes in his music are a form of harmony which we associate with mouth-organs, and a form of accompaniment which we associate with second-rate 'morceau'-writers. For the first mentioned offence, there is no excuse or justification. . . .

How could a man who had read, learned, and edited the work of Bach, how could he perpetrate such a harmonisation of a chorale as Mendelssohn did for the second verse of 'Now thank we all our God' in the 'Hymn of Praise'? At times it would almost seem as if the man who evolved the magical harmonies for the second subject of the 'Hebrides' had learnt harmony on the vamping system. He vamps the opening of 'Be not afraid', he vamps the second subject of the Violin Concerto. Is it possible that this nauseating harmony was the counterpart of his unmanly taste for sweetmeats, especially cherry pies? . . .

His initial inspiration is rarely at fault, but the succeeding phrases, which depended upon his own arrangement and selection, frequently collapse into the insipidity of a feminine cadence, a sentimental mannerism which pleased his audiences as much as his cultivated tricks of speech coaxed his friends.

Studies and Caprices

ON CHOPIN (1810–1849)

E. PAUER

Chopin is an intrinsically subjective composer; he gives us in his music moments of his inner life which show a depth of feeling perhaps inadmissable in a classical piece of large dimensions, ... Chopin enriched the three chief elements of music—rhythm, harmony, and melody. Granting that his rhythmical expression is the result of his Polish nationality, and that particularly the Polonaise and Mazureck, those two essentially Polish dances, are the chief source of their existence, it must nevertheless be conceded that they had not hitherto been appropriated in such an effective or useful way. Respecting his harmonies, it may be observed that Chopin is fond of blending the major and minor keys ; ... His melodies are no less remarkable as evidencing his innate sense of beauty than for impressing us with the distinction and nobility of his mind. Chopin in his life never wrote a vulgar note.

Monthly Musical Record, June 1871

SIR W. H. HADOW

... Chopin can claim no place among the few greatest masters of the world. He lacks the dignity, the breadth, the high seriousness of Palestrina and Bach and Beethoven: he no more ranks beside them than Shelley beside Shakespeare, or Andrea beside Michelangelo. But to say this is not to disparage the value of the work that he has done. If he be not of the 'di majorum gentium', he is none the less of the Immortals, filled with a supreme sense of beauty, animated by an emotional impulse as keen as it was varied, and upholding an ideal of technical perfection at a time when it was in danger of being lost by the poets or degraded by the virtuosi. In certain definite directions he has enlarged the possibilities of the art, and though he has, fortunately, founded no school— for the charm of his music is wholly personal—yet in a thousand indirect ways he has influenced the work of his successors. At the same time, it is not as a pioneer that he elicits our fullest admiration. We hardly think of him as marking a stage in the general course and progress of artistic History, but, rather, as standing aside from it, unconscious of his relation to the world, preoccupied with the fairyland of his own creations. The elements of myth and legend that have already gathered round his name may almost be said to find their counterparts in his music; it is ethereal, unearthly, enchanted, an echo from the melodies of Kubla Khan. It is for this reason that he can only make his complete appeal to certain moods and certain temperaments. The strength of the hero is as little his as the vulgarity of the demagogue: he possesses an intermediate kingdom of dreams, an isle of fantasy, where the air is drowsy with perfume, and the woods are bright with butterflies, and the long gorges run down to meet the sea. If his music is sometimes visionary, at least it is all beautiful; offering, it may be, no response to the deeper questions of our life, careless if we approach it with problems which it is in no mind to resolve, but fascinating in its magic if we are content to submit our imagination to the spell. And precisely the same distinction may be made on the formal side of his work. In structure he is a child, playing with a few simple types, and almost helpless as soon as he advances beyond them; in phraseology he is a master whose felicitous perfection of style is one of the abiding treasures of the art. There have been higher ideals in Music, but not one that has been more clearly seen or more consistently followed. There have been nobler messages, but none delivered with a sweeter or more persuasive elegance.

Studies in Modern Music, 1894–5

SIR HUBERT PARRY

Chopin was born less than a month after Mendelssohn. It illustrates the branching out into many different forms and styles that men so pre-eminent in art and yet so different in musical character should have been born so near together. Chopin is one of the most conspicuous representatives of the most modern type of music, for he is thoroughly independent of the conventions of classicism in art; but he is so far from being inartistic on that account that the perfection of delicacy with which he applies all the richest resources of technique to the expression of his thoughts is almost without parallel. Moreover, though so specially notable as a master of the technique of the performance, he really has genuine musical thoughts which are worth expressing, and a genuine musical personality; and even the ornamental parts of the work—which form so important a feature in the stock-in-trade of virtuosi— in his case generally have real musical significance.

Summary of the History and Development of Mediaeval and Modern European Music, 1904

EDWARD DANNREUTHER

There is in his best work a breadth and glow as of the South wind. His fervour of spirit, the fire and force of his fancy, his pathos, and, in his lighter moods, his ease, grace, and consummate taste, are unique. Some part of his work, not a large part, appears over-refined, hectic, and morbid; a small part belongs to the Parisian salon; most is poetical work of a high order, perfect, not only in fragments and sporadically, but in entire pieces and entire groups of pieces. The music rings true. Chopin does not pose for pathos and emphasis. The sensitive delicacy of his nature kept him within the limits of courtesy and prompted him to shun the more violent accents of fashion; his canon of taste was the result of his temperament. He shrank from the robust, open-air power of Beethoven and was now and then inclined to emphasise those elements that make for sensuousness. The most artistic of romanticists, he never forgot or overstepped the limits of the art. He avoided everything that might seem pedantic, dogmatic, or theoretical. He had nothing to preach or teach, unless it be his own incommunicable gift of beauty. The fire of his genius increased in intensity as time went on. His skill 'in the use of the sieve for noble words' enriched his work and saved it from extravagance.

To a student, the perfect finish of Chopin's pieces affords evidence of the care and the labour that he expended upon them. A comparison of the rather flimsy early pieces which were published as 'oeuvres posthumes' with those that he published himself, say from Op. 9 to Op. 65, inclusive, will suffice to show that he rejected music enough to fill scores of pages. As he was fond of types such as the Mazurka, the Polonaise, the Nocturne, in which some sort of rhythmic and melodic scheme is prescribed at the outset, he virtually set himself the task of saying the same thing over and over again. Yet he appears truly inexhaustible; each Impromptu, Prelude, Étude, Nocturne, Scherzo, Ballade, Polonaise, Mazurka presents an aspect of the subject not pointed out before; each has a birthright of its own. Chopin indeed is one of the rarest inventors not only as regards the technicalities of pianoforte playing, but as regards composition. Besides being a master of his particular instrument, he is a singer in that high sense in which Keats, and Coleridge, and Tennyson are singers. He tells of new things well worth hearing, and finds new ways of saying them. He is a master of style— a master of flexible and delicate rhythm, a fascinating melodist, a subtle harmonist. The emotions that he expresses are not of the highest; his bias is always romantic and sentimental. In his earliest productions his matter and manner are alike frequently weak; in his latest now and then turgid. But in the bulk of his work, be the sentiment what it may, he makes amends for any apparent want of weight by the utmost refinement of diction. With him the manner of doing a thing is the essence of the thing done. He is ever careful to avoid melodic, rhythmic, or harmonic commonplace; and he strove so hard to attain refinement of harmony that in a few of his latest pieces, such, for instance, as the Polonaise-Fantasie, the Violoncello Sonata, and the last set of Mazurkas, he appears to have spun his progressions into useless niceties.

'The Romantic Period,' *Oxford History of Music*, Vol. VI, 1904

SAMUEL SEBASTIAN WESLEY (1810–1876)

Painful and dangerous is the position of a young musician who after acquiring great knowledge of his art in the Metropolis, joins a country Cathedral. At first he can scarcely believe that the mass of error and inferiority in which he has to participate is habitual and irremediable. He thinks he will reform matters, gently, and without giving offence; but he soon discovers that it is his approbation and not his advice that is needed. The choir is 'the best in England' (such being the belief at most Cathedrals) and if he give trouble in his attempts at improvement, he would be, by some Chapters, at once voted a person with whom they 'cannot go smoothly' and 'a bore'. . . .

The illusive and fascinating effect of musical sound in a Cathedral unfortunately serves to blunt criticism and casts a veil over defects otherwise unbearable. No coat of varnish can do for a picture what the exquisitely reverberating qualities of a Cathedral do for music. And then the organ. What multitude of sins does that cover! ...

Some would reject all music but the unisonous chants of a period of absolute barbarism—which they term 'Gregorian'. All is 'Gregorian' that is in the black, diamond note. These men would look a Michaelangelo in the face and tell him Stonehenge was the perfection of Architecture. ...

The Cathedral Organist should in every instance be a professor of the highest ability—a master in the most elevated departments of composition—and efficient in the conducting and superintendance of a choral body.

> *A Few Words on Cathedral Music and the Musical System of the Church, with a Plan of Reform*, 1849

ON SCHUMANN (1810–1856)

H. F. CHORLEY

It was said, in 1839–40, that Herr Schumann had declared his resolution of writing a work which should outdo Beethoven's Ninth Symphony. Since that time, he has produced largely; and admirers have gathered round him asserting that he has entirely fulfilled the above tolerably ambitious resolution. It appears as if the usual order of affairs has been followed in his case; as if extravagant mysticism, assumed to conceal meagreness of idea, had given way (as the composer grew older and more impatient to secure popularity) to a dullness and heaviness of commonplace, little more acceptable, not in the least more beautiful, and certainly less amusing. Opera, Cantata, Symphony, Quartet, Sonata,—all and each tell the same story, and display the same characteristics—the same skill of covering pages with thoughts little worth noting, and of hiding an intrinsic poverty of invention, by grim or monotonous eccentricity. There is a style, it is true, in Dr. Schumann's music—a certain thickness, streaked with frivolity—a mastery which produces no effect—a resolution to deceive the ear, which (as in the case of certain French composers) ends in habituating the ear to the language of dissection; and spoils the taste without substituting any new sensations of pleasure. Up to the present period Dr. Schumann's music may be said to be submitted to rather than generally accepted in Germany. A general acceptance, I must think, would imply a decadence of taste even more rapid than that which has taken place since the above sketches were made.

Modern German Music:
Recollections and Criticisms, 1862

J. W. DAVISON

The only novelty was Herr Schumann's Symphony in B flat which made a dead failure. Few of the 'Society of British Musicians' symphonies were more incoherent and thoroughly uninteresting than this. If such music is all that Germany can send us of new, we should feel grateful to Messrs. Ewer & Wessel if they would desist importing it.

Musical World, Nov. 1854

MUSICAL TIMES

The rest of the concert consisted of a Violoncello Concerto by Schumann (which, not having been put into the fire by its composer, should have been duly placed there by his admirers).

May, 1866

SIR GEORGE MACFARREN

Schumann's prominent characteristics of perspicuous design, symmetrical form, consummate mastery of

bad taste to show any hostile feeling in the immediate presence of royalty.

Musical Recollections of the Last Half-Century, 1872

MONTHLY MUSICAL RECORD

He is now generally acknowledged to stand in the first rank of the tone-poets of the present century.

Nov., 1873

JOSEPH BENNETT

More, perhaps, than the master's last symphony, this Concerto is intensely personal as regards the composer, whom it reveals in perfection, showing not only the height and depth of his genius, but his mood and fashion of thought. All the melancholy of the man, his sweetness, his poetic nature, and the sensitiveness which was, as usual, its attendant may be traced in this work. Schumann must have thrown his whole soul into the music, and now it repays him a hundredfold, for wherever the Concerto goes, there goes, also, a golden-mouthed pleader on the master's behalf.

'Piano Concerto', Programme Note,
Philharmonic Society, March 14th, 1889

SIR HUBERT PARRY

Schumann, like Beethoven, revels in a mass of sound. But his sound is far more sensuous and chromatic. He loved to use all the Pedal that was possible, and had but little objection to hearing all the notes of the scale sounding at once. He is said to have liked dreaming to himself, by rambling through all sorts of harmonies with the pedal down; and the glamour of crossing rhythms and the sounding of clashing and antagonistic notes was most thoroughly adapted to his nature. A certain confusion of many factors, a luxury of conflicting elements which somehow make a unity in the end, serves admirably to express the complicated nature of the feelings and sensibilities and thoughts of highly-organised beings in modern times. Chopin's style has coloured almost all pianoforte music since his time, in respect of the manner and treatment of the instrument; and many successful composers are content merely to reproduce his individualities in a diluted form. But Schumann has exerted more influence in respect of matter and treatment of design. With him the substance is of much greater significance, and he reaches to much greater depths of genuine feeling. There must necessarily be varieties of music to suit all sorts of different types of mind and organisation, and Chopin and Schumann are both better adapted to cultivated and poetic natures than to simple unsophisticated dispositions. That is one of the necessities of differentiation; and music which is concentrated in some especial direction can only meet with response from those who possess the sensitive chord that the music is intended to touch. There are natures copious enough to have full sympathy with the dreamers as well as the workers; but as a rule the world is divided between the two. People who love much imagery and luxury of sensation do not want to listen to Cherubini's best counterpoint, and those who only love energy and vital force do not want to listen to the love scenes in the Walkure. But as illustrating the profusion of sensations, the poetic sensibility, and even the luxury and intellectuality, the passion and the eagerness of modern life, Chopin and Schumann between them cover the ground more completely than all the rest of modern pianoforte composers put together.

The Evolution of the Art of Music, 1893

SIR W. H. HADOW

As a writer for the pianoforte he may be said to rank beside Schubert. He has less melodic gift, less sweetness, perhaps less originality, but he appreciates far more fully the capacities of the instrument and possesses more power of rich and recondite harmonisation. His polyphony was a new departure in the history of pianoforte music, based upon that of Bach, but exhibiting a distinctive colour and character of its own. The beauty of his single phrases, the vigour and variety of his 'bitter-sweet" discords, are all so many claims on immortality; hardly in the whole range of Art have we such intimate household words as 'Warum', and 'Traümerei', and 'Carnival' and 'Humoreske', 'Kreisleriana', and 'Novelletten'. His spirit, too, is essentially human. No Composer is more companionable, more ready to respond to any word and sympathise with any emotion. There are times in which we feel that Bach is too remote, Beethoven too great, Chopin too pessimistic; but we can always turn to Schumann with the certainty that somewhere in his work we shall find satisfaction.

Studies in Modern Music, 1894–5

ON LISZT (1811–1886)

QUARTERLY MUSICAL MAGAZINE

Master Liszt's extraordinary talents as piano forte player enable him to overcome with ease, difficulties that would startle most others. His lessons, therefore, require much power of hand in the performer. The variations are the least difficult parts, still, however, we must consider them the best of the two. But little distinct style is to be discovered in them, though there are to be found traces of the solidity of the German School, which shew that the composer is studying good models.

'Seven Brilliant Variations for the Piano Forte to a Theme of Rossini', Vol. VII, 1825

H   D.M.C.

FRANCIS HUEFFER

Whether Liszt's compositions possess that absolute vitality and substance which are the only guarantee of permanent life, the future must decide; that they are the immediate and spontaneous expression of a distinct individuality is not open to doubt, any more than is the fact that they have given a mighty impulse to the progress of modern music in the direction of what we may call its poetic development. Absolute mastery of technical means, large minded generosity, helpful love for the work of others, uncompromising expression of innermost feeling regardless of immediate popularity—these are the qualities which have given Liszt his place in history, and to which the musicians of this and other countries should look up to as a shining example.

Half a Century of Music in England, 1837–1887, 1889

ON WAGNER (1813–1883)

GEORGE HOGARTH

The English public had, for the first time (for we do not take into account one or two lame attempts to play one of his Overtures) a specimen of Herr Wagner's qualities as a composer. A fragment of dramatic work, transferred from the theatre to the concert room is necessarily heard to disadvantage, being deprived of the scenic spectacle and action which are requisite to display its design and produce its effect; and the more thoroughly dramatic the music is, the more it suffers from such a performance. The selection from 'Lohengrin' consisted chiefly of a nuptial celebration of the most gorgeous kind; a bridal procession with choral songs and tumultuous rejoicings, where the music is associated with all the pomp and splendour of the stage. Wagner's music, however, deprived as it was of these essential accessories had a great effect, and a most favourable reception. It was found to have much breadth and clearness, flowing and rhythmical melody, and marvellous variety and richness of instrumentation. Wagner, as it appears to us, rivals Berlioz in the power of orchestral combination, and excels him in simplicity and symmetry of form.

Daily News, 27th March, 1855

The public have been told that Wagner is a musical revolutionist whose object is the destruction of all existing greatness—who seeks to pull down from their thrones all the recognised sovereigns of the art, that he may raise himself to supremacy in their room. Such, we are informed, is the purpose of his critical writings; and, it is added, his extravagant doctrines are illustrated by equally extravagant compositions. It was with no small surprise, therefore, that the public, thus prepossessed, listened to Wagner's music on Monday evening. In place of finding it to be obscure, unintelligible, and studiedly unlike anything ever heard before, they discovered that it was clear, simple, melodious, and not at all hard either to perform or to comprehend. The audience were delighted; their prejudices were overcome by their feelings, and they applauded frankly and warmly; all but the professional 'native talent' clique, who comforted themselves by trying to convince everybody who would listen to them that the music was conventional and commonplace. Even from the slight specimen now given, it was evident that Wagner's music is dramatic in the highest degree. Such music suffers greatly by being transferred to the Concert-Room; but we felt satisfied, in listening to it, that, with the scenic action and adjuncts of the opera house, it would be as effective as the music of Meyerbeer himself.

Illustrated London News, March 31st, 1855

The overture to Wagner's much-talked-of opera 'Tannhauser' was performed under the direction of the composer, the conductor of the Philharmonic Concerts. It was most carefully executed and listened to with much curiosity and interest. Opinions were much divided with respect to its merits. Some deemed it, though wild and eccentric, a work of originality and genius, while others condemned it in toto. For ourselves, we did not, nor do we now, feel disposed to speak dogmatically. Every one acquainted with music is aware of the uncertainty of hasty opinions and their liability to be changed by better acquaintance with the subject. We found in this composition some beautiful and striking effects, mingled with (as it seemed to us) much obscurity and confusion; but how far this obscurity may be dissipated by further hearing we do not at present pretend to know.

Illustrated London News, 19th May, 1855

H. F. CHORLEY

The Opera House at Dresden, during the years preceding the Revolution of 1848, also witnessed the production of certain musical dramas, by one who has since made some noise in the world, and who is likely to make more—noise, strictly speaking,—not music. I mean Herr Wagner, whose 'Rienzi' had already been given in Dresden at the time of my second visit thither, and who was named as 'Capellmeister' by the King of Saxony under conditions of most friendly generosity. In 1840, Herr Wagner was not openly revolutionary; being in composition apparently an imitator of the least amiable peculiarities of Herr Meyerbeer, and showing, it may be apprehended, few signs of that spirit, which, in later times—those of the German riots of 1848—sent him out upon a barricade with the purpose of discrowning the very King whose bread he had been eating. 'Rienzi' was pronounced to be dull, over-charged, and very long. It was endured as a work belonging to Dresden, as other operatic pieces of dullness in other German capitals have been, but, I believe, followed the common lot of local successes, and never travelled far beyond the barriers of the Saxon capital.

It would seem as if the favour with which this 'Rienzi' was received, and the position in which its composer was placed, ripened to fever heat that desire to distinguish himself in progress by destruction which passes for a generous ambition with persons imperfectly organised or crookedly cultivated. But earlier than this, a prophet, an innovator, a celebrity, Herr Wagner had resolved to be; and—weak in musical gifts—he appears to have entered on his crest of greatness by a profound contempt of all other musical celebrities. The confessions which he has recently published, reveal an amount of arrogance and irritable disdain for all opera composers save himself, happily rare in the annals of artistic self-assertion. His point of departure was to be the union of poetry and music. Operas were to be made of an exquisite completeness in which both arts were to find the very fullest expression; and since librettists, however ingenious, are not always the best of poets, Herr Wagner (wisely enough) resolved to be his librettist.

In this capacity he has proved himself to be strong and felicitous as an inventor, though less excellent as a lyrist, than his self-commendation would have us believe. . . .

How am I to speak of the manner in which the musician has set his own drama (Tannhauser)? I shall hardly be able to represent my impressions without appearing to those, who have not suffered under this extraordinary opera in the light of one indulging in hyperbole and caricature; for, in truth, I have never been so blanked, pained, wearied, insulted even (the word is not too strong), by a work of pretension as by this same 'Tannhauser'. I could not have conceived it possible that any clever person could deliberately produce what seems to me so false, paradoxical, and at such fierce variance with true artistic feeling, a system, before I sat through the opera and read the 'Hallelujah' vented by its maker in homage to his new revelations which he has been tempted by his own vanity and by the injudicious praise of others, to put forth. . . .

But allowing this opera to be accepted as a Symphony accompanied by scenery, bearing part in a drama intoned rather than sung, I cannot find its symphonic or orchestral portion much more admirable than the wild and over-wrought recitative which it is to check, support, and alternate. 'Fidelio' may, in some respects, be called a symphonic opera also, in as much there, too, the instrumental part is more interesting than the vocal portion of the work; but who that knows 'Fidelio' does not know it by the wonderful variety and spirit of Beethoven's orchestral devices? Or, to take a newer instance, on a first hearing of Herr Meyerbeer's operas, the ear, if it can receive nothing else, is cognisant of new and peculiar sonorities. I remember, as if it were only yesterday the delicious impression first produced on me in 1836, by the scoring of the first and second acts of 'Les Huguenots'; in such scenes as the one where Raoul is among the gallants peeping through the window at Valentine or, in the interlude of the second act, precluding the grand aria of Marguerite de Valois. No such felicities did my ears derive from 'Tannhauser'. To me the instrumentation of that opera is singularly unpleasant—as too preposterous to be overlooked, too untrue to its own conditions to be accepted as a charming monster after its kind. From the pianoforte arrangement of the overture (in which, as I have said, the only two motivi deserving the name have been wrought), I had expected striking effects of crescendo, brio, and, if a noisy orchestra, a rich one also. The reverse is my impression. The sound is strident, ill-balanced, and wanting in body. An awkward treatment of what may be called the tenor part of his band, leaves Herr Wagner often with only a heavy bass to support a squeaking treble poised high aloft. He seems to be fond of dividing his violins, as Weber and Mendelssohn did before him; but neither of these masters of the orchestra considered that by such division alone richness of tone was ensured. Such a full, brilliant, well nourished sound (to adopt the French phrase), as we find in Mendelssohn's tenor orchestra, even when his theme was the wildest—as in his 'Hebridean' overture, his 'A minor Symphony', his 'Walpurgis Chorus'—is nowhere managed by Herr Wagner. There is a brilliant violin figure at the close of the 'Tannhauser' overture,—more than once used by Cherubini,—which was intended to work up the composition with amazing fire. This, however, is so stifled by the disproportioned weight of the brass instruments that deliver the Pilgrim tune in contrary tempo, as merely to produce that impression of strain which accompanies zeal without result—how different from the brilliancy which Cherubini and Weber could get in similar situations, by means of one half the difficulty, when they tried for a like effect! Throughout the opera, in short, beyond a whimsical distribution of instruments, such as a group of Flutes above the tenor voice, or some lean stringed sound to harass not support the bass,—I recollect nothing either effective or agreeable—but grim noise, or shrill noise, and abundance of what a wit with so happy a disrespect designated 'broken crockery' effects—things easy enough to be produced by those whose audacity is equal to their eccentricity.

Modern German Music:
Recollections and Criticisms, 1862

Besides appearing as conductor and critic on Monday evening, Herr Wagner also produced himself as a composer. Some fragments from his last and, we think, his best, opera were performed. . . . So far as we can recollect, these are about the only movements (belonging to 'Lohengrin', which is a long opera) in which there is even a pretext of melody—as melody was understood before it was 'emancipated' by these men of the future, and its existence asserted(?) to be independent of form, beauty, or rhythm. In No. 1 (the Prelude) the idea, if idea it be, recalls a phrase used by 'Euryanthe' and another by Halevy in his 'Guido'. This is dressed out by a division of the violins and the employment of them at the altissimo notes of the scale, so as to produce an impression of singularity rather than sublimity. Thus, also, M. Felicien David and (in his 'Attila') Signor Verdi have described dawn effects by the orchestra; thus M. Jullien has, more than once, fitted out a sunrise for one of his descriptive Quadrilles, previously to the bursting out, in all their glory, of the orb of day and of the conductor's luminous smile. Employing a like principle, it would not be difficult to paint a night picture or a descent of Proserpina into the lower regions for any maestro who had courage to use the deepest notes of united viole and violoncelli for one hundred bars; but, (as the Irish Lady asked concerning the Torso) 'where are the features?' The name of the 'Saint Grail' and the Angels nearly as good as 'the mobled queen' in 'Hamlet', and the length of such an unrelieved piece of monotony, apparently impressed a part of the audience with the idea that the Introduction was celestial and new, and they applauded it accordingly. No. 2, to our thinking, which better merited favour, pleased less. In this wedding music, a certain dignity is to be recognised; though no tone of festivity, no bridal tone. Herr Wagner has, nevertheless, tried as hard for musical climax as though he was one of the wicked effect-makers on whose destruction he is bent—and to obtain it, he has used his voices as arbitrarily as the most conventional copyist of the Rossinian crescendo. On what principle of truth are all the female singers kept still so long, when a bride is in the case, merely that they may bring up the cortege with a few bars at last—a sort of 'trot for the avenue'? And yet somehow the climax comes to nothing. The magic cauldron bubbles, but does not boil. The effect, to attain which the writer has stooped so low (trying him by his own canons) never arrives. In this music again, Herr Wagner's acute fancies of scoring give the ear more pain than pleasure.—No. 3, the entr'acte is (as we have heretofore said) the best page in the opera—but the Epithalamium, as an accomplished musician remarked to us, is as petty and pretty a tune of short phrases, as if M. Adam had flung it off for the opera-wedding of some Trianon Jocrisse with some Toinette of Marly. Dr. Liszt or Herr Wagner would be sadly puzzled to prove the propriety or truth of such a piece of common-place at nuptials so sublime, told by a poet so mystical in his meanings.—It is true that the episodical strophe sung by eight ladies, 'while the sumptuous robes of Lohengrin and Alice are taken off by their attendants,' is symphonised by certain pizzicati,—and these may possibly represent the withdrawal of diamond pins; but as a whole, the chorus is small to silliness. . . . Except, in short, for the stir which has been made in the matter, and the empiricism with which the music was recommended in the programme, these specimens of 'composition for the future' would hardly have been worth a line of analysis for any intrinsic novelty or merit they possess. . . .

Athenaeum, March 31st, 1855

Never did Germany stand more in need of a composer than at present. For Herr Wagner's operas do not please, in spite of the picturesque and sympathetic nature of their libretti—and in spite of all the machinery of wit, sarcasm, misplaced enthusiasm, and political sympathy brought to bear on recommending them. 'Tannhauser' is the most liked among them, but this principally in the holes and corners and not the high places of German opera, Dresden excepted. Curious it was, after reading the composer's letter to the Cologne manager, . . . to hear at Cologne on every side that 'Lohengrin' had proved there an entire and profitless failure. I cannot but give currency to this report, in confirmation of my idea that the new doctrine, however it may disturb young writers, blighting and burning up all their geniality by encouraging in them a humour at once blasé and arrogant—does not and cannot command a public and that, though it may represent a part of the rising generation of pseudo-artists, it has neither gone to the heart nor touched the sympathies of the great music-loving people of Germany, north and south.

Athanaeum, June 9th, 1855

EDWARD FITZGERALD

I have seen no more of Tannhauser than the Athenaeum showed me: and certainly do not want to see more. One wonders that Men of some Genius (as I suppose these are) should so disguise it in Imitation: but, if they be very young men, this is the natural course, is it not? By and by they may find their own Footing.

Letter to W. H. Thompson, Dec. 9th, 1861

HENRY SMART

There is nothing . . . against Wagner to discredit the testimony of his advocates. At least, we might safely conclude it next to impossible that one half of Germany had gone mad about nothing. The thing needed was some practical warranty for the fuss made about the greatness or smallness of the matter in dispute. To this end, the half hour's demonstration on Monday evening was worth a year of pro's and con's in the German journals. The test we have a right to suppose perfectly fair, within the prescribed limits. The composer personally directed the performance, and he would not, obviously, have selected his least-esteemed specimens wherewith to make his first impression in London. We have heard, then, what there was to hear of the 'Lohengrin' and are perfectly satisfied that, as in most such cases, there is much error on both sides of the dispute, as to this music in general. In the first place, Richard Wagner is, beyond doubt, a man of genius. He is a poet, in the broad and generic application of the term, and therefore an artist, sentiently, in everything; but it by no means follows that music has been wisely chosen for the development of his gift. To some mistake or accident of this kind only, seems attributable the extreme rarity of absolutely first-class men in any of the arts. The artist element—poetic feeling—is the same for all. Poetry, music, painting, sculpture, are but varying manifestations of the one divine spirit. Yet it is quite possible for a man, while right as to the broad purpose of his mission, to mistake the implements of its announcement. Thus Phidias might have taken to composing symphonies. . . . Wagner is, we verily believe, a chosen vessel of the sacred fire; but we can in no way satisfy ourselves that music is, in his case, its appropriate form of utterance. He is evidently full of great and profound feelings, of vast and dreamy mind-pictures struggling to acquire material vitality. Yet when he seeks to realise these in music, we feel at once that we have but a faint shadowing of his imaginings—that the tongue he has chosen is all but dumb for his purposes. We have not a word to say of his vagueness or rejection of ordinary forms; in art, all things are justified by their result. Our complaint against his music is that it does not evince the faculty of creating beauty . . . . While he keeps in cloud and mystery, those who will dream with him may recognise his power. His weakness increases with his approach to earth and reality. If he gives us a tangible phrase, it is not beautiful, if he makes trial of a familiar tune, it is common-place to the very threshold of vulgarity. If, then, as asserted for him, Richard Wagner is to take up the thread of art where Beethoven left it, it can only be by, not the expansion, but the total subversion of the world's ideas of music. The great composers have left behind them imperishable traits of melody, which will haunt men's memories to the end of time . . . . Wagner does not—cannot, we believe—produce these things; and, therefore —no matter his inward consciousness of genius—he has mistaken his mission.

(The 'Lohengrin Prelude') . . . is an instance of effect by colour alone, and without form or rhythm. It is conceived in a highly poetic spirit, and as far as such music-painting can be so, is certainly successful. But it is unfortunate for the 'music of the future' that this first specimen is by no means new. Berlioz long since commenced all this style of effect; he has repeatedly done the same kind of thing, but more perfectly. Felicien David, too, has employed nearly similar means and with quite equal results, for his description of sunrise in the 'Desert' Symphony. The 'Bridal Procession' for at least three parts of its length, fails from want of any distinct character. The chorus, which accompanies it, is sombre and without musical interest; and indeed the only redeeming feature of the piece is the crescendo with which it terminates—again solely a matter of colour—and which introduces the full force of the orchestra with powerful effect. The march-movement which prefaces the 'Epithalamium' is characteristic, but somewhat rugged and uncouth. Here, for the first time, we come across a tangible melodic point. It is a figure for the basses, afterwards reinforced by the trombones, and supported by a powerful iteration of the violins in triplets. It stands out in isolated prominence by its character of rhythmic decision yet, beyond this, is no wise remarkable for merit or originality. The 'Epithalamium' is decidedly the weakest portion of the selection, and may well be quoted as evidence of the composer's poverty in melodic idea. There was no escape in this instance from the necessity of tangible, rhythmic figure, and the only result Wagner has been able to command is a tune—if it may be so called—of the most utterly common-place description.

With a return of the March, this scene is supposed to close; so, at least, terminated this selection from the 'Lohengrin'.

We do not yet imagine ourselves to have made complete acquaintance with Richard Wagner's peculiarities; but it is, at least, fair to suppose that the selection on Monday evening was favourably made, and, if so, its result was anything but satisfactory. Any largely disputed matter of art deserves all the help that can be afforded towards a decision and on this ground the Philharmonic directors have done well and wisely. Nor should they stop the course of justice here. If Wagner has not yet shown us his best works, by all means give him opportunity to do so.... Wonders, according to the old adage, never cease; yet we think it will require more than a miraculous amount of Teutonic journalism to establish Richard Wagner as the legitimate successor of Beethoven.

Sunday Times, April 1st, 1855

We rejoice to have heard the overture to 'Tannhauser' under the composer's direction. As we presume he will not venture to call in question the quality of the orchestra, we may fairly conclude that the performance of Monday evening was a just interpretation of his work. Satisfactory as was this hearing, as a piece of musical experience, it has in no way altered—unless for the worse—our estimate of Herr Wagner's pretensions. In his musical illustration of very exciting adventure, Herr Wagner true to his principles, of course discards all the trammels of recognised form. His overture is like no other overture in shape and pattern. It is an orchestral fantasia, in which the positions and recurrences of the materials are governed solely by the order of the incidents in his story. Now, most willingly conceding that every man has a right to reject all established rules for his musical conduct the instant he can find any better, or can shew a justifying cause for his disobedience, we believe this 'Tannhauser' story to have given as good an opportunity for fantasia making, as is likely often to occur. Our complaint is, that the composer has abandoned received forms, without giving any equivalent in exchange. He has the courage to despise the ordinary shape of the overture, but not the genius to create such beauty of material as alone can render a mere fantasia endurable.

Of subject or rhythmical melody, save at one place, ... the overture to 'Tannhauser' has not a vestige. Its whole sum and substance is a mass of orchestral colour, and even in this it has the misfortune to be little else than an assemblage of palpable imitations. The opening phrases, representing the song of the pilgrims, are a mere succession of chords for clarinets, bassoons and horns, of which the whole idea is palpably taken from the 'Carnival Romain' of Hector Berlioz, except that the French composer, eccentric as he is, never blunders on to such hideous harmonic progressions as have here fallen from the pen of his imitator. The abundant melodic baldness of this theme—we must so abuse the term, for want of a better—is subsequently exhibited when it appears in the trombones fortissimo, as a species of canto fermo against the rest of the orchestra.

In the next section of the picture, the vision of Venus, the domain of Hector Berlioz has again been extensively pillaged. Let anyone call to mind the fairy scherzo in the 'Romeo and Juliet' symphony, and while hearing the vision scene of the 'Tannhauser' overture he will not fail to perceive from whence come all the effects—the continuous bustle of the violins divisi at the highest point of their scale, the capricious spurts of tone from the acute wind instruments, the occasional clash of cymbals, and the abundant jinglings of tambourines. It is all vastly effective, without doubt, as a matter of orchestral colour, but its invention is not, in the slightest degree, attributable to Herr Wagner. Furthermore, there is a grace, piquancy, and sentiment about the original, which the imitation wholly wants.

In the next point, Tannhauser's 'jubilant love song', the composer condescends to the attempt at a rhythmical melody. We have elsewhere said that whenever he does this, the result is the extreme of common-place, and the present instance makes no exception. It is the culminating point of the overture and ought to be capable of brilliant effect; but is, in reality, as lame an attempt at broad intelligible tune as often will be heard. Shortly after this, the song of the pilgrims re-commences, and proceeds to the end of the overture; but this time it is accompanied by a ceaseless stream of passages on the violins, intended we presume, to depict the 'murmuring in the air' which 'becomes more and more joyous as it gains in strength'; but which, in truth, unhappily suggests severe mental or bodily discomfort far more forcibly than the sunlight, animation, and universal happiness intended by the composer.

Sunday Times, May 20th, 1855

J. W. DAVISON

The almost impossible overture of Herr Richard Wagner introduced for the first time to an English audience and played with surprising accuracy and decision, would do very well for a pantomime or Easter piece. It is a weak parody of the worst compositions, not of M. Berlioz, but of his imitators. So much fuss about nothing, such a pompous and empty commonplace, has seldom been heard.

The Times, May 3rd, 1854

... the overture to 'Tannhauser' is a piece of vapid rhodomontade and, as Herr Wagner paints him, 'the minstrel of love' is, after all, but a clamorous and empty personage. If the general ear of 'the future' is destined to be afflicted with such music as this, it is to be hoped that charitable posterity will institute some extra hospitals for the deaf wherever Herr Wagner and his compositions are allowed to penetrate. Some of our readers may have heard the story of an unfortunate gentleman at Berlin, who, visited with a loss of hearing for which no cure could be invented, was advised by his doctor, as a last hope, to go to the opera and witness the performance of Spontini's 'Olympia'. After the grand finale to the second act the patient turned quickly round to his medical attendant and with joy in his countenance exclaimed 'Doctor, I hear!' But alas! what cured the patient killed the counsellor, who heeded not the words addressed to him. The doctor was deaf; he had taken his own medicine. We never hear the overture to 'Tannhauser' but this anecdote forcibly suggests itself as an illustration.

The Times, Dec. 11th, 1854

To wrench fragments of harmony and melody from such a work—a work written to establish the insepara- bility of the arts—was scarcely wise in the Philharmonic directors to suggest, or in Herr Wagner to permit. It was like giving you bits of egg-shell for breakfast, instead of 'the whole egg'—since, without cracking metaphor, Herr Wagner's music, to his drama, may be figured as the shell to the egg, or at least as the albumen in the music itself. This was a shell at the best—an egg-shell, without a taste of egg, and no salt to give it relish. Except a slow instrumental movement, describing the descent of the 'Holy Grail' in which the composer hovers and flits for an indefinite space round and about the key of A, like Senora Nena with the hat at the Haymarket, and which— though arranged for the orchestra with great felicity, somewhat in the manner of M. Hector Berlioz—has no definable phrase or rhythm, little else, in short, but a sort of dull continuity, there was nothing in the selection that might not have passed muster very well for music of the past or, at least, of the present. . . . Now, if there was nothing more mysterious, incoherent, abstruse, and 'tone-defying' than all this in 'Lohengrin', we should be inclined to look upon the future art-doctrine as a hoax. Happily, the scores of Herr Wagner's operas have made their way to England, and those who have perused them are well aware that the fragments which, in their wisdom, the directors of the Philharmonic Society thought expedient to place before the public as examples of their new conductor's music, constituted nearly all that it was possible to disentangle from the dreary labyrinth of accompanied recitative that make up the rest of 'Lohengrin'. As it was, the public had no opportunity of speculating on the successful revolt against keys and their relations, by which Herr Wagner has illustrated one of his most furious dogmas.

Musical World, 31st March, 1855

Such a wonderful performance, however, as that of the Philharmonic band last night would, had it been possible, have made even 'Tannhauser' acceptable; but it was not possible, and we sincerely hope that no execution, however superb, will ever make such senseless discord pass, in England, for a manifestation of art and genius.

The Times, June 12th, 1855

. . . Richard Wagner comes to London, an object of deeper curiosity, we venture to say, than was any foreign musician who ever visited us; and, having had full scope, both as composer and orchestra director, for the vindication of his pretensions, he leaves it, we also venture to say, convicted of making one of the profoundest failures on record. Of his compositions, we can only repeat what we have before said in other words, namely, that they are the clever and dashing shams of a well-read and ambitious man, who, wholly ungifted with the faculty of developing beauty—having, in plain phrase, not a particle of music in his nature—would fain persuade to mistake his idealless and amorphous ravings for the utterances of a Heaven-descended originality, and thought too profound for ordinary penetration.

Musical World, June 30th, 1855

W. H. GLOVER

In one respect Herr Wagner's music disappointed us. We expected to find it highly, if not extravagantly original, but failed to remark this quality which, in the latter, even more than the former degree, has been given it by rumour. We observed no marked individuality of style in the score, no epoch-making innovations, such as the very original literary works of the composer had taught us to look for, but instead a succession of very brilliantly-instrumented pieces, which contained nothing strikingly new either in rhythm, harmony, or orchestral arrangement. It has been said elsewhere that Herr Wagner's theories have merely been framed to suit his creative abilities; if so, the latter were certainly not by when they were measured, for a worse fit we do not remember to have seen. A great deal of this music is as excessive and needlessly luxurious in mere loudness and meretriciousness of sound, as the unhappy dancers whom he castigates so unmercifully are in show; and it assuredly contains as much that is 'unnecessary' and 'customary' as any modern production with which we are acquainted.

Herr Wagner, however, condemns his own music more than we are disposed to do; for, as we have said, it has very great merit in respect of instrumentation, and is also highly dramatic in character and expressive of the words and action it is meant to illustrate. Strikingly original, however—like, for instance, that of Berlioz—it most certainly is not.

The best part of this selection was the Introduction, the clear and beautiful scoring of which betokens an amount of strictly musical 'knowledge' and mere 'science' which we cannot but wonder the author of the 'Künstwerk der Zukunft' ever condescended to acquire. But Herr Wagner has deigned to learn even more than this, for we understand that he knows the scores of the great though erroneous masters by heart and can direct a rehearsal of their 'progressive' works perfectly well without referring to them. The selection from 'Lohengrin' was most admirably executed . . . and left the impression, at least upon us, that Herr Wagner is a very clever though not a great composer.

Morning Post, 28th March, 1855

We are perfectly willing to consider a work from any point of view which an author may require, and review it according to its pretension.

Still, there are immutable general principles and inherent rules, the violation of which can never be tolerated. Whatever be the prominent idea—whatever be the means employed in musical composition—the writer must still be subject to the laws which the art itself imposes, and without which it cannot exist. His work must be music properly so called, before it can be received as the legitimate expression of any idea; for, if not, however he may theorise or dream, the realisation of his conceptions will be simply impossible. These reflections were forced upon us by an audition of Herr Wagner's overture to his opera 'Tannhauser' last night. The discrepancy between the really poetical description of the author's purpose, and the musical illustration of it, was well calculated to make one philosophise. Picturesque ideas, charmingly expressed in words, were completely obscured by a succession of the most unhappy experiments we ever listened to. A few bars at the commencement, effectively instrumented for clarinets, bassoons and horns, may be praised; but after these we had nothing but 'confusion worse confounded'. Destitute of melody, extremely bad in harmony, utterly incoherent in form and inexpressive of any intelligible ideas whatever, we must, even whilst duly appreciating the composer's expressed intention, set down this overture as a most contemptible performance. If it be a foreshadowing of the 'music of the future' Polyhymnia is doomed to sing in purgatory of the direst kind, for none but a terribly tormented soul could send forth such shocking sounds.

Morning Post, May 15th, 1855

JOHN RUSKIN

Of all the bête, clumsy, blundering, boggling, baboon-blooded stuff I ever saw on a human stage, that thing last night beat—as far as the story and acting went: and of all the affected, sapless, soulless, beginningless, endless, top-less, bottomless, topsituriviest, tongs and boniest doggerel of sounds I ever endured the deadliness of, that eternity of nothing was the deadliest—as far as the sound went. I never was so relieved, so far as I can remember in my life, by the stopping of any sound—not excepting railway whistles—as I was by the cessation of the cobbler's bellowing; even the serenader's caricature twangle was a rest after it. As for the great Lied, I never made out where it began, or where it ended—except by the fellow's coming off the horse block.

'Die Meistersinger,' Letter to
Mrs. Burne-Jones, June 30th, 1882

SAMUEL BUTLER

Then I heard an extract from 'Parsifal' which I disliked very much. If Bach wriggles, Wagner writhes. Yet next morning in *The Times* I saw this able, heartless failure, compact of gnosis as much as any one pleases but without one spark of either true pathos or true humour, called 'the crowning achievement of dramatic music'. The writer continues: 'To the unintelligent, music of this order does not appeal'; which only means 'I am intelligent and you had better think as I tell you'. I am glad that such people should call Handel a thieving plagiarist.

Note Books

MONTHLY MUSICAL RECORD

Any music that Richard Wagner writes is sure to possess a certain amount of interest for musicians; for however much opinions may differ as to the value of his musical theories, or the rank to which he is entitled as a composer, few will deny that he is a man of real power, and an original thinker. That he is often eccentric, no one will dispute; that he is thoroughly in earnest is, we think, equally incontrovertible. The 'Kaiser Marsch', written to celebrate the recent German victories is, it is to be presumed, in the composer's latest style; and after studying the score carefully and hearing a very fine performance of the work at the Crystal Palace, we are bound to record our conviction that it is not, as a whole, successful. It is written for an enormous orchestra—the score being on twenty-six staves—and the instruments of percussion are used with such want of moderation, that in some places the noise is almost intolerable.

June, 1871

If Wagner may be taken as the representative of the Music of the Future in its dramatic phase, Brahms, Liszt, and Rubenstein may be considered as among its chief exponents in the more general domain of vocal and instrumental composition. One of the chief characteristics is their earnest striving after originality. This tendency is sometimes carried so far as to involve the sacrifice of musical beauty. Rather than not be new, their ideas will even be ugly. It is probably this constant striving after novelty which has caused Schumann to be included by many among the composers of the Future; for though in other things he differed widely from the writers of whom we are now speaking, in this respect he resembled them. Another distinctive feature of the school is the extreme, sometimes undue length of development, not to say diffusedness, which marks its compositions, especially in instrumental music. The ideas are presented in every possible form, and the episodes are frequently more important than the first subjects. Hence musical unity, as it was formerly understood, is to a considerable extent wanting; and in its place we have, as also in Wagner's operas, a series of thoughts often apparently but slightly connected, though frequently in themselves interesting and even charming.

Oct., 1871

We must, in conclusion, say a word or two about the orchestration. There is a very prevalent impression that Wagner is one of the noisiest of modern composers. Our readers will therefore probably be surprised to learn that one great feature in the score of this work is the moderation and discretion of its accompaniments. The instrumentation is always rich, often sonorous, very seldom noisy. For example, in the first hundred pages of the first act the full orchestra is only used twice—each time for a few bars; and similar reticence is the characteristic of the whole work. The ingenuity and novelty of the treatment of the wind instruments are above all praise; and the score is one of the finest studies of instrumentation to be met with in musical literature.

'Die Meistersinger', April, 1873

It was said of Mozart's operas that he had placed the pedestal on the stage and the statue in the orchestra. The same remark might with much more truth be made of Wagner's later works, for in these the instrumental part is frequently of so much more importance than the vocal, that the latter can be omitted with very little damage to the purely musical effect; though at the same time a knowledge of the words is requisite to render the music fully intelligible. Perhaps we shall more clearly express our meaning by saying that if the words were spoken instead of sung (as in a melodrama) the effect would in many cases be nearly as complete.

With regard to the form of the music, it will not be expected by those familiar with Wagner's views that there should be any detached movements in this work; and, in fact, there is scarcely one passage in the score which would bear separating from the context and using as a concert piece. But there are several themes, some of them of exquisite beauty, which recur from time to time, giving an impession of unity to the whole which could not be obtained by any other method. On the other hand, there is much in the work which on mere reading seems altogether dry and uninteresting, with respect to which we would suspend final judgement till we have the opportunity of hearing it in its proper place, and with suitable accessories.

'Das Rheingold', May, 1873

We can ... see enough to pronounce 'Die Walküre' not merely one of the finest and most original of Wagner's works, but one of the greatest dramatic compositions as yet produced.

June, 1873

The first thing that may safely be predicted of Wagner's songs, even before examining them, is that they will be totally unlike any other existing songs, and this prediction will be fully justified by the works themselves. They are in the highest degree original—too original, we fear, to attain anything like a wide popularity. Some of them are in our opinion extremely beautiful, and all are highly interesting; but the beauty and interest are for the most part such as appeal rather to the cultivated musician than to the general public.

July, 1873

Nothing like this can be found in the entire range of music. Wagner uses the orchestra with as much ease as a child plays with a little toy, and can make it do almost everything but speak. Its expression of the varying sentiments of the text is marvellous in directness and fidelity, while the constant play of colour, managed with all an artist's eye to effect, is a source of continual wonder and delight.

'Wagner Festival', June, 1877

During the life of Wagner it was difficult indeed to gauge the real value of his contributions to musical art. The worker was so identified with his work that it seemed almost necessary to combat his theories before a listener dared to admit that he became wearied of his music. True it is that few could dispute the justice of his premises, but it might be just possible to disagree with his deductions from them. . . . Wagner's operas are like a panorama, which passes rapidly before us, dazzling our senses for a minute with artistic beauty, yet leaving only the impression of a longing for the power of concentrating our enjoyment upon some definite portion of the work. It may be asserted that if the theory is true, the reduction of the theory to practice must be equally so; but theories in art should be spoken only through an artist's works, in proof of which we may say that Beethoven—who first inspired Wagner with a consciousness of the real power of music—prefaced his immortal compositions with no announcement of the true mission of the art he so ennobled.

We have no desire here to do more than direct attention

to what may be considered the vulnerable points in the teachings of a master who has drawn converts from all countries, and whose name—however we may differ in the value of his theories—will live in the annals of art, even more honoured perhaps as music grows to its true position in the world. Had he lived to multiply operas founded upon the model of 'Parsifal' we cannot now say whether he would have strengthened or weakened the cause he had at heart; but the legacy he has bequeathed to us will sufficiently attest how a great artist can work, even when he has to create, rather than to appeal to, an audience capable of rightly judging the result of his efforts.

March, 1883

SIR HUBERT PARRY

Wagner's use of the voice part illustrates musical tendencies in the same way as every other part of his work. The traditions of solo singing which still persist in some quarters imply that the human voice is to be used for effects of beauty only. The old Italian masters subordinated everything to pure vocal effect; they made the utmost of pure singing, and singing only. Occasional reactions against so limited a view, and in favour of using the human voice for human expression, came up at various points in history. Purcell is often a pure embodiment of ill-regulated instinct for expression. John Sebastian Bach's recitatives and ariosos are still stronger in that respect. The Italian reaction that followed him was all in favour of beautiful vocal sound and simple intrinsic beauty of melody; but in Schubert the claims of expression again found an extremely powerful advocate. He appealed to human creatures a good deal by means of melody, but much more by his power of general expression. He often produces much more effect by a kind of recitative than by tune. He uses tune when it is suitable, otherwise musical declamation. He appeals to intelligent human beings who want music to mean something worthy of human intelligence and Schumann does eminently the same, though he too knows full well how to express a noble sentiment in a noble melodic phrase. Wagner again takes an attitude of 'no compromise'. The voice has an infinity of functions in music. It may be necessarily reduced to the standard of mere narrative, it may have to utter dialogue which in detail is near the level of everyday talk; it must rise in drama to the higher levels of dramatic intensity, and it may rise at times to the highest pitch of human ecstasy. For each its appropriate use. The art is not limited to obvious tune on one side and chaotic recitative on the other, but is capable of endless shades of difference. Wagner makes Mime sing melody because he is a sneaking impostor who pretends to have any amount of beautiful feelings, and has none; that no doubt is a subtlety of satire; but otherwise he generally reserves vocal melody for characteristic moments of special exaltation. That is to say, the actor becomes specially prominent when the development of the drama brings his personality specially forward. The human personality is an element in the great network of circumstances and causes and consequences which make a drama interesting, and no doubt it is by far the most interesting element; but there is no need that the actor should always be insisting upon his own importance, and the importance of his ability to produce beautiful sounds. The human voice is for use, and not only for ornament. People must no doubt learn to sing in a special way in order to do justice to the beautiful old-world artistic creations; and art would be very much the poorer if the power to give them due effect was lost. But the expression of things that are worth uttering because they express something humanly interesting is much more difficult, and implies a much higher aim. Both objects require a great deal of education, but the old-fashioned singer's education was limited chiefly to the development of mechanical powers;

the singer of the genuine music of Bach, Schubert, Schumann, Brahms, and Wagner requires the old-fashioned singer's education and education of the mind as well.

The Evolution of the Art of Music, 1893

SIR W. H. HADOW

If the different Arts are to be combined into one complex result they must make certain mutual concessions. The fusion implied in Wagner's music-drama necessarily involves some sacrifice of those individual characteristics which we should expect to find in the elements taken separately. We have no right to judge the libretto of 'Tristan' by the same laws which we should apply to a poem of Goethe: to Goethe the words represent the whole medium employed; to Wagner they are only part of the medium. We have no right to judge the music of 'Parsifal' by the same laws which we should apply to a Beethoven quartett; in the quartett the music is everything, in the opera it is only a factor in the general effect. It would be almost as unreasonable to transfer the scenery of the Bayreuth theatre to a picture gallery and to estimate it by the standard of Titian or Bellini. Hence it is not fair criticism to decry Wagner's libretti after reading them in a concert room. The whole of his mature work was intended for the stage, and for the stage alone; it stands in relation to no other conditions; it can be estimated from no other standpoint. Grant that he occasionally permitted the concert-performance of excerpts from his operas: he did so under pressure of poverty, with extreme reluctance, and in the certain conviction that they would miss their aim. Again, the stage has its own laws and its own exigencies. Even such a literary dramatist as Racine loses immeasurably if we take him from the footlights; even such a supreme genius as Shakespeare has more power to impress us if we see the action and hear the eloquent cadences of the player's voice. And this is still more true of Wagner. The piecemeal analysis of the ingredients in his work is as uncritical as an inquiry into the different scraps of metal which Cellini melted down when he cast his Perseus.

It follows, therefore, that, if we hear in a concert room the 'Walkürenritt' or the 'Schmiedelied', or the death song of Isolde, we have a right to praise, but we have not a right to blame. If we can enjoy them so much the better for us, if we cannot we must reserve judgment until we hear them under their proper conditions. It is only at the theatre that we are in a position to criticize; only when we see the drama as a whole that we can judge of the effect that it was intended to produce. The principle of 'ex pede Herculem' is a very insecure basis for an adverse decision.

But the arias of Mozart and Beethoven and Weber bear transplantation to the platform. No doubt they do; Mozart may even be said sometimes to gain by the absence of a theatrical background. But this only shows that the art of these three composers is different from that of Wagner. His is a 'nuova musica', a new type which differs almost as widely from Mozart as Peri from Palestrina. In one word the creator of 'Zauberflöte' is to be judged as a musician; the creator of 'Siegfried' is to be judged not as a musician but as a dramatist.

Studies in Modern Music, 1894-5

W. J. TURNER

. . . I can confidently and in soberness declare that Wagner is a colossal fraud. And by the word 'fraud' I mean exactly what I say. To deny his immense and devastating talent would be absurd, but Wagner is the supreme example of the truth that cleverness, even cleverness raised to the nth power of genius, is not enough. All the big scenes in the 'Ring' sound to my ear so insincere, so hollow, and theatrical that I now find them hardly tolerable. Everything is planned for effect, and if it is only in 'Tannhauser' that he descends to the level of the pure back-street showman selling his sham antiques without even knowing there is such a thing as the real antique, yet in the 'Ring' he has risen only to the position of the dealer who is a master craftsman and cannot deceive the experts with his frauds.

I have given Wagner the credit for a certain genuine sensibility to nature. Even this I suspect. I think that it is too self-conscious. 'The Flying Dutchman' does not express Wagner's real impressions of the sea so much as his sense of the theatrical value of the sea. Wagner is vitiated through and through by this lack of simplicity. He cannot feel anything directly and honestly, but always it is felt with a sense of its theatrical value, of its effectiveness. If you listen with an attentive, discriminating ear, you will find that from the beginning to the end the 'Ring' is as hollow as 'Tannhauser' which is emptiness itself. I suspect even the Venusberg to be a fraud. Here is no real sensuality. Wagner was not genuine enough for that. It is an expression of excitement at the thought of sensuality. I will admit that this nervous 'frisson' is genuine, but how Wagner exploits the 'frisson' and delights in it! Take away the genuine Venusberg 'frisson' from 'Tannhauser', and what remains? The most banal, vulgar themes, the poorest of musical structure. Consider the choruses and arias in 'Tannhauser'; they are either prosy and unmusical or the clichés of those Italian operas which Wagner conducted in his early days. And what is the fundamental conception of 'Tannhauser' in the mind of its author as revealed in his work? Nothing but a blatant bid for theatrical effect.

Facing the Music, 1933

ON VERDI (1813–1901)

H. F. CHORLEY

Neither Signor Verdi's music (which is Signor Verdi's worst) nor Mdlle. Piccolomini's singing (which everyone concedes is on a very small scale) have made the fame and furore of the opera and the lady. The music of 'La Traviata' is trashy; and the young Italian lady cannot do justice to the music, such as it is. Hence it follows that the opera and the lady can only establish themselves in proportion as Londoners rejoice in a prurient story prettily acted.

Athenaeum, May, 1856

MUSICAL TIMES

Verdi's opera 'La Forza del Destino', performed for the first time in this country . . . is likely, we think, to prove attractive if not from the intrinsic merit of the music alone . . . it is useless to erect an ideal standard of art, and criticize modern operas by such a test. The public has accepted Verdi, and we, who are not of the public and have not accepted him, must be content to compare him with himself, and chronicle his successes with a mental reservation which shall exonerate our consciences from the artistic crime of having given utterance to what we do not feel. It is idle to talk of a composer being crippled from the nature of his libretto. Verdi deliberately chooses revolting subjects because it is only these that his unreal effects can be fitly wedded to; and when the intoxication of his admirers shall have passed away, the pure style which it has superseded will once more assert its sway with redoubled power from the violence of the contrast. As a spontaneous work we infinitely prefer 'La Forza del Destino' to 'Don Carlos'. The writing is less forced, the melodies, although neither very new nor very striking, seem exactly such as the situations produced without effort in the mind of the composer; and the orchestration has less of that constant straining after glaring effects so observable in most of Verdi's works. It would be impossible, and indeed we have no desire, to follow in detail the musical illustrations of a story such as we usually find in the penny 'sensation' romances which pass for literature with romantic housemaids.

July, 1867

MONTHLY MUSICAL RECORD

The announcement of two performances at high prices and on a large scale of Verdi's 'Requiem' under the immediate direction of the maestro himself, seemed a bold step on the part of Messrs. Novello, Ewer and Co.: but if we may judge from the fact that the favourable reception generally accorded to the new work led to two further repetitions of it at popular prices of admission, it appears to have been one which has been fraught with success. . . . That it has been heard in London within a year of its first performance is a piece of luck upon which Sig. Verdi may fairly congratulate himself, when we reflect that it took nigh upon a quarter of a century for 'Lohengrin' to find its way to these shores. But what is more surprising is that we should find so many speaking with enthusiasm of Verdi's 'Requiem', who in the previous week had confessed that never in their lives had they been so powerfully impressed by anything as by their first experience of a performance of 'Lohengrin'. Such a universality of taste, the possession of which might tend to make life easier and more enjoyable, is perhaps to be envied, but we confess we can lay no claim to it. With the best will in the world we have read the pianoforte score of Verdi's 'Requiem' through and through, and heard it performed, but without arriving at that satisfactory conclusion as to its merits that some have done. Some critics have already objected to the work as being of too dramatic a character for sacred music. We do not go along with them, else we should have to condemn some of the most striking choruses in Bach's 'Passion' Music, and a large portion of Beethoven's 'Mass in D', etc. But we do think that a distinction should be drawn between 'dramatic' and 'theatrical' music. . . . In his attempts at fugue writing here, as well as elsewhere, Verdi finds himself as much out of his natural element as did Rossini in his 'Mass'. Apart from these objections, it is evident that Sig. Verdi approached the task he set himself with genuine enthusiasm and deep earnestness as is made apparent by the many alterations introduced in the later editions of his work, if not also on other accounts. His orchestration which is on the most extended modern scale, is often happily conceived, but that the many experiments which he has risked in this direction are always crowned with success in their effect cannot be said. On the other hand, his skill as a perfect master of vocal art is made fully apparent by the manner in which he has laid out his vocal parts.

June, 1875

MUSICAL TIMES

If Verdi ever had a style, it is thoroughly certain that he has changed it; but it is a great question whether he did not commence and acquire his fame as a successful imitator of the styles of others. True it is that, with an innate perception of dramatic effect, he was constantly struggling to be something else than a mere slave of the popular vocalists; and when therefore he had, as much as his nature would allow it, shaken off his allegiance to the purely Italian composers, he began to found himself upon Meyerbeer, which resulted in that pretentious work 'Don Carlos'; and then upon the great prophet of the future, Wagner, which has resulted in the Egyptian opera 'Aïda', presented for the first time in this country on the 22nd ultimo. It is not likely that the inventive power shown throughout 'Il Trovatore' and 'Rigoletto'—which, as long as the destinies of Italian Opera are ruled by the vocalists, will unquestionably maintain their place—could be so trammelled by the composer's restless desire to escape from himself as not to make itself felt in the gorgeous spectacle which he undertook to 'set' for the delight of the Khedive of Egypt; but certain is it that these reminiscences are somewhat few and far between, and that although the Oriental magnificence which gladdened the hearts of a Cairo audience may have thrown dust in the eyes of Egyptian Critics, it is a fact that neither in Italy or in Paris has its production caused much excitement; nor do we believe that in England it will obtain a permanent hold of the musical public. It is a very common error to suppose that quaint streams, with certain tonal peculiarities, must represent ancient music, simply because it is not modern; and that the more ugly it is, the stronger is it characteristic of the days of barbarism; but this may be carried to an extreme; and although Signor Verdi no doubt has exclusive means of knowing the kind of music which was sung and played in the Egyptian temples in the time of the Pharaohs, we may be at least excused for saying that he has used his 'local colour' somewhat too thickly. In the impassioned scenes he is certainly successful, yet in some of his more quiet music—as for instance in the Romance for the tenor, 'Celeste Aida'—there is much to admire; and in several of the concerted pieces in which the dramatic action is carried on, occasional writing, both for voices and orchestra occurs which convinces us how legitimately he can command the resources of his art. He has certainly striven hard to give due effect to every phase of the story supplied him. We have picturesque music for the dances and processions, heart-broken phrases for the principal characters—not one of whom experiences even a brief pleasurable sensation throughout the Opera—and sacred strains for the Priestesses in the Temple; but to infer from this that 'Aïda' resembles 'Tannhauser' or 'Lohengrin' is sheer nonsense. Wagner illustrates his music by a spectacle; Verdi illustrates a spectacle by his music.

★   ★   ★

Many situations are highly dramatic; and although ... everybody is intensely miserable, the music is in several places thoroughly sympathetic with the stirring events of the plot ... the ear becomes often wearied with the weight of the score, for not only do all the principal characters sing their loudest, but the whole of the chorus as well; the brass instruments, both on and off the stage, most zealously contributing their share to the general noise.

'Aïda', July, 1876

FRANCIS TOYE

He never was lured into that over-indulgence in harmonic or orchestral ingenuity which has proved a refuge to so many second-rate composers in distress. He was forced to concentrate on the intrinsic value of the bare musical idea ungarnished by any more or less adventitious trapping. The way in which he laughed at himself and all his colleagues for overworking the chord of the diminished seventh is very revelatory in this respect. When, however, the musical ideas he had to express demanded greater harmonic freedom, he did not, like so many composers, take other people's ideas ready-made but gradually and laboriously evolved a genuine idiom of his own. His attitude to orchestration remained entirely individual, indissolubly part and parcel of what he had to say.

It was largely, then, this habit of self-reliance, and self-containedness, which enabled him to achieve the almost unique distinction ... of withstanding the potent magic of the Wizard of Bayreuth, because, with insignificant exceptions, he never borrowed anything from anybody that could not be assimilated and individualised.

*Guiseppe Verdi: His Life
and Times*, 1928–1930

ERIC BLOM

More than one earnest musician will ask whether he is worth . . . attention. Whether indeed there is anything in him to engage the critical mind outside a theatre. One can but try to convince the sceptics. Most of them will concede that inside the opera house Verdi is a satisfactory artist; but their tendency as musicians is to attribute his success to his being, as they will condescendingly allow, a magnificent dramatist, a composer endowed with unfailing stagecraft. They never seem to ask themselves whether it can be possible for an opera composer to be a magnificent dramatist without being also a magnificent musician. Is there a single instance of a theatre composer who kept his work alive for many years—to say nothing of a rebirth of his half-forgotten operas—on the strength of dramatic power alone? Indeed, what is dramatic power in opera if it is not musicianship pure and simple, properly applied to a particular purpose?

What operas of any fame are there in which dramatic interest predominates over musical? Marschner's? They are dead. Meyerbeer's? They make but ghostly appearances in the haunts of a stale repertory. Those of scores of Italians like Ponchielli, Giordano, Montemezzi, Zandonai? They are moribund. In their dead-alive company Verdi would be by this time, had he been a dramatic manipulator only, however eminent. As it is, he not only lives but flourishes more than ever to-day, and that because he was a great musician; but I hope to show that he is in the company of those absolute masters of their art whose faults one accepts willingly as part of the individual make-up of a sturdy creative personality.

With what cubbish superiority soever one may have sneered at Verdi in younger years (I plead guilty) one learns to look forward to the prospect of hearing one of his operas with a thrill. It is, one knows, going to be a meeting with genius in its apt environment, an experience such as only two other masters of music can always be counted on to offer in the theatre—Mozart and Wagner. After them, who is to be encountered there so unquestionably? Without them, is to choosing this or that man's outstanding masterpiece: Purcell's 'Dido and Aeneas', Gluck's 'Orfeo', Weber's 'Freischutz', Moussorgsky's 'Boris Godounov', Bizet's 'Carmen' or Strauss's 'Rose Cavalier', let us say. Monteverde, Handel, Cimarosa, Bellini, Rossini, Borodin, Berlioz, Smetana, Gounod, Puccini, Debussy, all give pleasure to different people in different places. Verdi, like Mozart and Wagner, is universal.

No disparagement of Wagner is implied here, even if we agree that he matured more slowly than Verdi. It must be borne in mind that the Italian settled down without protest to an accepted convention, whereas the German from the first began to grope towards a new manner. Still, the fact remains that Verdi is not only comparable to Wagner, but may be regarded from certain viewpoints as actually superior to him. It is simply a matter of creeds. The choice between the two is not determined by any radical difference of eminence, but by the question whether, as musicians, we accept the Reformation or prefer to remain Romans.

Verdi, though not a reformer, is a liberal-minded catholic. If he was not for thoroughgoing changes, he was amenable to gradual evolution along rational lines of his own. His life-work is one of steady progress. That is why, as Mr. Bonavia points out, it is wrong in his case, if indeed it can be right in anybody's to speak of three styles.

As for the current theory that Verdi was indebted to Wagner in his later years, it is not worth refuting nowadays. Verdi is the opposite pole to Wagner. Much of the disparagement to which serious musicians have disparaged him is due to their failure to recognise this fact. They dislike him because he is not like Wagner instead of admiring his independence, and where that can no longer withold admiration, they must needs seek an approach to Wagner in his work.

Their great objection to Verdi is that he is theatrical— a terrible indictment indeed to level at a man who writes for the theatre! If they intend the term to designate quite literally something for the stage, they may well use it, so long as they agree to imply that it is suitably written; but if they are thinking of something aesthetically inferior to music of absolute worth, then the answer is emphatically that they are arguing on a false postulate.

Well, the word theatrical does convey some sort of obloquy and this will not do for Verdi. Let us say, then, that his operas are not theatrical but dramatic. So is the Requiem in a smaller and from a composer's own point of view, quite permissable degree. It is worth observing here that a purely superficial stage device which occurs regularly in the operas is entirely absent from the Requiem. This is the long protraction of closing chords in rhythmically broken patterns at the end of a scene or act, which is simply the dramatist's 'curtain' converted into music. Verdi knows this to be a necessary evil and never makes the mistake of the inferior musician, who will use a convention without knowing what it stands for.

'Verdi as Musician,' *Music and Letters*, Oct. 1931

ON STERNDALE BENNETT (1816–1875)

SIR R. P. STEWART

Before I proceed to address you upon the subject chosen for the present lecture, namely 'Stringed Key

Instruments of Music', I would wish to pay my tribute of respect to the memory of one whose loss we have recently mourned, a most talented composer for and performer upon keyed instruments—Sir William Sterndale Bennett, or, to give him that more familiar title, by which we first knew and loved him, Sterndale Bennett. That the late Cambridge Professor was a man estimable in all relations of life, an honour to our art, a cultivated gentleman, and a pride of the ancient university in which he filled the chair of music, will be admitted by all; my own pupils and friends at least know how I have long admired him; and how, in as far as my own influence extended, I have never ceased to recommend his beautiful pianoforte music to all with whom I come into contact. It is only of late that it has fallen to my lot to have the command of an instrument at all adequate to the execution of his truly admirable orchestral works. Such a genuine masterpiece as his overture 'The Wood Nymphs', which I intend to have performed at the next Philharmonic Concert—alas, that it should be in memory of him from whose pen we can look for no more!—such a work, I repeat, could only have emanated from a true musical genius. But, of late, Sir Sterndale Bennett pursued too quiet, too unobtrusive a life, and devoted himself almost entirely to teaching—a state of things surely to be deplored, for giving lessons, although perhaps a necessary evil, is at best but mechanical employment—an employment which might well be entrusted to those who are incapable of creating music. The time of Sterndale Bennett belonged of right to his country, and was far too precious to be wasted in lesson-giving. For a man thus gifted to continue teaching, as he did, for from six to ten hours per diem, instead of rather producing such noble overtures as 'Parisina' or the 'Wood Nymphs' or such works as the fine Concerto in F minor for Piano and Orchestra—this cannot but be deemed a talent misapplied. Amid all the extravagant expenditure of our nobility, could nothing be spared from yachts and race horses for the advancement of the noblest music in England? Was there no Maecenas, no English Esterhazy to emulate the magnificent Duke of Chandos who, more than a century ago, to his immortal honour, maintained an orchestra, a chorus and a composer, and will never be forgotten, no, never while Handel's name survives? It appears not: although many of the English nobles seem absolutely not to know what to do with their money, not one of them ever dreamed of laying it out thus.

And yet what incalculable benefits has not the world derived from Chandos, Esterhazy, and the Arch-Duke Rudolph, the respective patrons of Handel, Haydn, and Beethoven? It is quite evident that but for two of these truly 'noble lords', we should never have had the twelve Chandos Anthems of Handel, or the more than one hundred Symphonies and eighty quartets of Haydn. As for the Arch-Duke Rudolph, and the amiability of that Austrian Prince who humoured Beethoven, and loving the man for his art's sake, bore with the oddities of that deaf and somewhat crusty old bachelor—all this is matter of history.

However, Sterndale Bennett is now far above all human patronage; let us, then, not altogether sorrow over his tomb, since, knowing the character of our dear departed friend, we may the more happily conclude this brief tribute of our love and respect. So, giving expression to our sure and certain hope, let us borrow the words inscribed upon the tomb of Henry Purcell (near whom he now reposes in Westminster Abbey), and say that Sterndale Bennett is 'gone to that blessed place where only his harmony can be exceeded'.

At Trinity College, Dublin,
Monthly Musical Record, April, 1875

W. GARDINER (—?—)

It is certainly unwise to neglect the productions of genius, to whatever period they belong. Yet, as music, like every other branch of art, and knowledge, is progressive, it cannot surely be expedient constantly to refer to the works of our forefathers, as the only models of excellence.

The Philharmonic Society is established exclusively for the study of MODERN instrumental music, and whoever has had an opportunity of listening to its orchestra, composed of the first masters in the country, can hardly fail to recognise the superiority of later times in this department.

To do perfect justice to the works of the great modern composers, it is requisite that they should be executed by men, similar in musical taste, and genius, to themselves. So different do they appear in the hands of this distinguished society, from the style in which they are usually exhibited, that the effect resembles the pure effulgence produced in the recent experiments of Sir Humphry Davy, when compared with the 'dusky beams' of ordinary brightness.

Note in a *Life of Haydn*, 1817

ON GOUNOD (1818–1893)

MUSICAL TIMES

The second part consisted of the work which was presumed to be the real attraction of the evening—'Tobias' —a sacred drama. To this we have two objections to make—first, that it is not sacred, and secondly that it is not a drama. The music might be written for the most conventional libretto of an Opera ever placed in the hands of a composer. . . .

There is . . . some exceedingly clever instrumentation

scattered throughout; but the somewhat lugubrious orchestral movement descriptive of young Tobias performing the miracle had a somnolent effect upon the audience in our immediate neighbourhood which all the joy of old Tobias, at his sudden restoration to sight, could not afterwards completely shake off. The last chorus is effective; but hardly of sufficient musical importance for the conclusion of a sacred work. So weak a composition by a weak composer could have little claim upon our attention; but from a man who has shown us that he can do better things, it possesses an historical interest which fully justifies his admirers in producing it.

March, 1866

Gounod's new opera 'Romeo and Juliet' produced for the first time in this country on the 11th ult considering the deserved popularity of its composer was certainly one of the most interesting events of the season. A great deal is always said about the temerity of a composer who selects a subject already immortalised by a great poet; and we think it would be well if those who have already obtained a certain reputation were to weigh this matter well before they committed themselves for trial under such disadvantageous circumstances. That composers have succeeded in many of the settings of previously well-known poems and plays is no proof that they have been wise in attempting the task. . . .

. . . in spite of the . . . unquestionable merit of much of the music, we do not predict for it a lasting popularity with the English public.

Aug., 1867

MONTHLY MUSICAL RECORD

M. Gounod's sacred music may be described as a mixture of the old ecclesiastical style with that of his 'Faust'.

June, 1870

I 2

D.M.C.

REV. JOHN EDMUND COX

To this hour I maintain the opinion that from beginning to end the 'Faust' is nothing else than a delightful piece of musical mosaic, dovetailed together from the compositions of every class of musical composer, right and left, but with so much ingenuity that it presents, especially in the 'garden' scene, a perfect picture, brimful of beauty, although somewhat overloaded with a profusion of melody that is at times all but cloying to the senses. It would be impossible to say how many times I have heard the 'Faust' since its first production at Her Majesty's Theatre, but rarely have I been disappointed with it, although I have never failed to detect fresh plagiarisms which, although distinct enough, may be forgiven on account of the admirable manner in which they have been utilised.

Musical Recollections of the last
Half-Century, 1872

MUSICAL OPINION

... perhaps the most disappointing work of modern times, and which it may be at once said is a stagy imitation of Bach's sublime 'Passions Musik' from a Roman Catholic point of view. ...

Gounod's attempts at choral writing are of the most humble description, resembling brief 'part-songs', and without the slightest address in the march of the inner parts. ...

The impression after listening to Gounod's 'ouvrage de ma vie' must be faithfully chronicled—it is one of dull monotony.

'Redemption', June, 1883

W. S. ROCKSTRO

... there is one great French composer, upon many of whose compositions the world has already had ample time to pass judgement, and actually has passed judgement, with no uncertain voice, a composer to whose genius the French School is mainly indebted for the high position it has maintained since the death of those who had long been looked upon as its most efficient supporters, and whose earnestness of intention has been the means of infusing into it a reality which is likely to be soon forgotten. For it may be safely said, that, from his 'Messe Sollenelle', first publicly performed under the direction of Dr. Hullah in 1851, to the 'Mors et Vita' written for and first sung at the Birmingham Festival of 1885, M. Charles François Gounod has never given to the world one single Composition, great or small, which does not bear witness to the earnestness of his desire to do honour to the Art he loves: and in the presence of power like his, earnestness means a great deal, and he has effected a great deal.

History of Music, 1886

JOHN RUSKIN (1819–1900)

In music especially you will soon find what personal benefit there is in being serviceable: it is probable that, however limited your powers, you have voice and ear enough to sustain a note of moderate compass in a concerted piece—that, then, is the first thing to make sure you can do. Get your voice disciplined and clear, and think only of accuracy; never of effect or expression: if you have any soul worth expressing, it will show itself in your singing; but most likely there are very few feelings in you, at present, needing any particular expression; and the one thing you have to do is to make a clear-voiced little instrument of yourself, which other people can entirely depend upon for the note wanted.

'Music for Girls, What they are to aim at', Sesame and Lilies, Preface, para. 9

Then, in art, keep the finest models before her, and let

her practice in all accomplishments be accurate and thorough, so as to enable her to understand more than she accomplishes. I say the finest models—that is to say, the truest, simplest, usefullest. Note these epithets: they will range through all the arts. Try them in music, where you might think them the least applicable. I say the truest, that in which the notes most closely and faithfully express their meaning of the words, or the character of intended emotion; again, the simplest, that in. which the meaning and melody are attained with the fewest and most significant notes possible; and, finally, the usefullest, that music which makes the best words most beautiful, which enchants them in our memories each with its own glory of sound, and which applies them closest to the heart at the moment we need them.

On 'Music, What Kind the Best is', *Sesame and Lilies*, Lecture II, 'Lilies, Of Queen's Gardens', para 79

... true music is the natural expression of a lofty passion for a right cause; that in proportion to the kingliness and force of any personality, the expression whether of its joy or suffering becomes measured, chastened, calm, and capable of interpretation only by the majesty of ordered, beautiful, and worded sound. Exactly in proportion to the degree in which we become narrow in the cause and conception of our passions, incontinent in the utterance of of them, feeble of perseverance in them, sullied or shameful in the indulgence of them, their expression by musical sound becomes broken, mean, fatuitous, and at last impossible; the measured waves of the air of heaven will not lend themselves to expression of ultimate vice, it must be for ever sunk into discordance or silence. And since, as before stated, every work of right art has a tendency to reproduce the ethical state which first developed it, this, which of all the arts is most directly ethical in origin, is also the most direct in power of discipline; the first, the simplest, the most effective of all instruments of moral instruction; while in the failure and betrayal of its functions, it becomes the subtlest aid of moral degradation. Music is thus, in her health, the teacher of perfect order, and is the voice of the obedience of angels, and companion of the course of the spheres of heaven; and in her depravity she is also the teacher of perfect disorder and disobedience, and the Gloria in Excelsis becomes the Marseillaise. . . . among the many misbegotten fantasies which are the spawn of modern licence, perhaps the most impishly opposite to the truth is the conception of music which has rendered possible the writing, by educated persons, and, more strangely yet, the tolerant criticism, of such words as these: 'This so persuasive art is the only one that has no didactic efficacy, that engenders no emotions save such as are without issue on the side of moral truth, that expresses nothing of God, nothing of reason, nothing of human liberty.'

'Definition of Music', *The Queen of the Air*,
Athena Chalinitis, para. 42

For although purity of purpose and fineness of execution by no means go together, degree to degree (since fine, and indeed all but the finest work is often spent in the most wanton purpose—as in all our modern opera—and the rudest execution is again often joined with purest purpose, as in a mother's song to her child), still the entire accomplishment of music is only in that union of both.

'Perfect Music, unites fine execution with purer purpose', *The Queen of the Air*, Athena Ergana, para. 141

. . . music was, among the Greeks, quite the first means of education; and that it was so connected with their system of ethics and of intellectual training, that the God of Music is with them also the God of Righteousness;

the God who purges and avenges iniquity and contends with their Satan as represented under the form of Python, 'the corrupter'. And the Greeks were incontrovertibly right in this. Music is the nearest at hand, the most orderly, the most delicate, and the most perfect, of all bodily pleasures; it is also the only one which is equally helpful to all the ages of man—helpful from the nurse's song to her infant, to the music, unheard of others, which so often haunts the deathbed of pure and innocent spirits. And the action of the deceiving or devilish power is in nothing shown quite so distinctly among us at this day—not ever in our commercial dishonesties nor in our social cruelties —as in its having been able to take away music, as an instrument of education, altogether; and to enlist it almost wholly in the service of superstition on the one hand, and sensuality on the other.

'Music in Greek Education',
Time and Tide, Letter, para. 61

The continual advertisement of new music (as if novelty were its virtue) signifies, in the inner fact of it, that no one now cares for music.

Cestus of Aglaia, VIII, O. R. I, §§ 388, 389

The law of nobleness in music and poetry is essentially one. Both are the necessary and natural expression of pure and virtuous human joy, or sorrow, by the lips and fingers of persons trained in right schools, to manage their bodies and souls. Every child should be taught from its youth, to govern its voice discreetly and dexterously, as it does its hands; and not to be able to sing should be more disgraceful than not being able to read or write. For it is quite possible to lead a virtuous and happy life without books, or ink; but not without wishing to sing, when we are happy; nor without meeting with continual occasions when our song, if right, would be a kind service to others.

Rock Honeycomb, Preface

QUARTERLY MUSICAL MAGAZINE

It is indeed refreshing in these days to meet with an original composition, and that, too, in *score*. We repeat, that it is refreshing for 'weary wretches', like ourselves, to fall on such a work in times when we hardly hope to hear of any thing but Variations, adaptations, and hashing up of every description, which are poured out upon us, in all the fertility of mechanical dulness, till even the task of looking at title pages becomes laborious and distressing. When is such a state of things to come to an end? When will our countrymen learn, that there are some among them who should disdain always to write for the shops? And when will they be brought to depend on the resources of their own minds, and feel themselves above the pitiful necessity of constantly borrowing from the genius and invention of their predecessors?

If we have hitherto refrained from visiting this practice with all the reprobation, it is first—to that large portion of the milk of human kindness which we are well known to possess—and secondly from the hope most people are given to entertain, that 'times may mend'.

Vol. IV, 1822

ON BRAHMS (1833–1897)

MUSICAL WORLD

... 'Schumann's Folly' ... has composed and published a good deal more.

May, 1864

MONTHLY MUSICAL RECORD

... the first thing that strikes us ... is that Herr Brahms is a very unequal writer. By far the best of the compositions before us is the sextett for stringed instruments. The ideas are original throughout, and often very striking, and the work is to a great extent free from that over-elaboration and diffuseness which seem to be Brahms' great fault. The opening movement is charming, from beginning to end . . . . He is evidently a man who thinks for himself, his subjects are always unborrowed, but there is a want of clearness of form, and a tendency to over-development which seems more or less to character-ise all the modern German school of composition, and which greatly impairs the effect of the whole. We do not forget that the same criticisms were made with reference to Beethoven's music at the time of its appearance; and it is possible that the time may come when Brahms' works may be accepted as a model; but until thought and idea comes to occupy only a secondary position, and elabora-tion is considered the one thing needful, we do not see how this can take place. Melody in all these works except the sextett is subordinate to harmony; and the vagueness of the thematic treatment causes them to resemble a series of fantasias for three or four instruments rather than classical compositions such as we are accustomed to meet with. There is much in all of them that will be interesting to musicians; but we doubt if they, or any similar works, are destined to effect the revolution in the art which Schumann predicted.

April, 1871

. . . an examination of some of the instrumental works . . . had led us to form an opinion of his abilities that was not altogether in his favour. We are bound, therefore, in justice to say that, after a careful and somewhat minute examination of the present work, we consider it definitely superior to anything of its author's that had previously come under our notice. . . . The 'Deutches Requiem' has undoubtedly two great merits—it is original from the first bar to the last, and the music is admirably suited to the words. . . . We may as well say at once that the one great fault we find with it is its diffuseness. It is a somewhat remarkable thing that the same failing seems characteristic of nearly all the modern German school, of which Brahms is one of the most illustrious writers. In many cases it is, we fear, that an attempt is made to conceal the want of ideas by over-elaboration. Such is not the case with the present work, in which ideas are abundant; but some of the movements would, we think, have certainly gained in effect by judicious curtailment.

May, 1871

MUSICAL TIMES

Brahms' Serenade in D is a work so unequal in merit as to make us doubt the permanent position of the music of 'Young Germany', even where such undoubted marks of genius are shown, unless the representatives of the school can be prevailed upon to believe that the worth of a piece is not to be estimated by its length. A Serenade in eight movements is too much for an English audience, however it may be endured in Germany, and in spite, therefore, of the undoubted merits of many of the movements—especially the Minuetto and Scherzo—the last note of the work was unanimously hailed as a relief.

August, 1872

MONTHLY MUSICAL RECORD

Among the composers of the recent German school we are inclined to award the first place to Johannes Brahms. Though in some points all that we have seen of his music fails to satisfy us fully, he must yet be credited with great originality and inventive power, often with considerable poetic beauty of idea, and invariably with a thorough mastery of the technicalities of composition. If he can be said to be a follower of any of the great masters, we should consider him under the influence of Schubert and Schumann than of any one else. By a certain dreamy romanticism, perhaps we should rather say 'Mysticism', he reminds us (in the spirit more than in the letter) of the latter composer, while he resembles Schubert in the extreme, often undue, development of his movements. Indeed, his great fault which, to our mind, at least mars the effect of nearly all his instrumental music, is diffuseness. . . . his Serenade in D, Op. 11 for full orchestra—a work full of the most delightful thoughts, but of which every movement is spun out till it becomes absolutely tedious. We can recall no modern German music more beautiful in its themes than the slow movement of this Serenade; yet, for want of condensation, the effect in performance is tiresome in the extreme. Had Brahms but the faculty of self-criticism and the power of knowing when he had said enough, his compositions would possess a much higher artistic value than is actually the case. We have before had occasion to remark upon this tendency to extreme development as one of the characteristics of most modern German musicians. We cannot at present see that it portends an enlarging of the limits of the art—'Beginning', as it has been said, 'where Beethoven left off'; our impression rather is that it is too often a sign of weakness and an attempt to hide the poverty of invention. We are not, however, impervious to conviction.

Feb., 1872

It is a composition of such novelty, both of form and treatment, as to render it somewhat difficult to speak of it decidedly after a single hearing. The impression produced on ourselves was that it is a work in places diffuse and laboured, yet on the whole of great power and originality. The first movement struck us as the least successful; both the Adagio and Rondo are charming.

'Piano Concerto in D minor', April, 1872

SIR GEORGE MACFARREN

It is impossible in the space of these comments even to hint at all the extraordinary merit, technical and aesthetical, of the composition under our notice; let, at least, the admiration, the reverence, they aim to express indicate to the reader that the work abounds in matter for high esteem, and invite him to do himself the justice of leaving his attention open to the perception of its beauties . . . . When the German Requiem becomes known, the lovers of music in England will feel, indeed, that their art has a living representative, that the greatest masters have a successor, and that the line of Purcell, Handel, Bach, Haydn, Mozart, and Beethoven, and those great men who have yet shone since and through the blazing of his transcendent light, is not extinct.

'Requiem,' Programme Note, Royal
Philharmonic Society, April, 1873

MUSICAL TIMES

Brahms' 'Requiem' and Mendelssohn's 'Walpurgis Night' were the principal attractions. Were we inclined to hazard an opinion upon the 'Requiem' from a single hearing, we certainly should not do so when performed as a concert-piece, surrounded by compositions in such violent contrast; and we must content ourselves with saying that the unemotional character of the subjects, notwithstanding the brilliancy of the instrumentation, produced a feeling of weariness in the audience, which although we cannot accept as tacit criticism of the work, sufficiently evinced that the Philharmonic concert-room is not the place for a funeral service.

May, 1873

MONTHLY MUSICAL RECORD

. . . as an artistic production for this particular combination of instruments, in the judgement of musicians, it is certainly in advance of the earlier work (Sextett in B flat, Op. 18) and at the same time has equal attractions for the general listener. Indeed, it is one of Brahms' main characteristics that he has always something to say, and generally says it pleasantly, and in a manner which both interests musicians and at the same time appeals to the least initiated. On these accounts it is satisfactory to feel that this clever composer's works are surely, though slowly, making their way in England.

'Sextett in G, Op. 36', Jan., 1873

Of all the living and producing musicians of Germany who, regarding the past as the beacon of the future—as Mr. Macfarren tersely expresses it—adhere to traditional forms, Johannes Brahms, born at Hamburg in 1833, has of late been frequently spoken of as one of the most worthy of consideration. . . . One cannot but remark, especially in the first movement of this concerto, the influence of Bach and Beethoven, which is apparent from its breadth and grandeur of form, coupled with a severity almost amounting to grimness. There is real beauty about the slow movement and the Finale is animated and taking. One misses, however, much of the charm of subsequent works by the same composer.

'Violin Concerto', August, 1873

The introduction here of a work by a living German composer which was heard for the first time in Vienna so recently as November last, certainly points to the fact that we are less behindhand in musical matters than not long ago was the case with us. . . . To a composer so thoroughly versed in counterpoint, harmony, orchestration, and all other secrets of his art, so ingenious, and at the same time so largely endowed by nature with strong musical feeling, the themes selected for treatment would be inconsequential. In the present instance Brahms may fairly be said to have proved the fallacy of the proverb that 'it is impossible to make a silk purse out of a sow's ear'. This, be it said, with all respect for Haydn. For once let a 'Sow's ear' be accepted merely as a symbol of simplicity. These variations, nine in number, are as interesting on account of the cleverness and ingenuity of their construction as for the originality and effectiveness of their instrumentation, and have the additional merit of being very pleasing to listen to.

'St. Anthony Variations', April, 1874

Being less diffuse in form and more original in character than the same composer's Serenade in D, Op. 11 for full orchestra, of the two it is certainly to be preferred.

'Serenade in A', Op. 16, August, 1874

MUSICAL TIMES

This fine work was heard for the first time in England at Cambridge on March 8th, 1877 . . . whether as a whole it will ever be 'popular', in the sense in which that term is applied to the Symphonies of Mozart and Beethoven, may be doubted; Brahms' style is too reflective, at times too abstruse, to meet with universal appreciation. But the real traces of genius which abound in this symphony, and which become more apparent on each repeated hearing, are such as to secure for this great work a place in the esteem of musicians second to that held by the symphonies of Schumann, with whom Brahms has much in common.

'Symphony in C minor', April, 1877

Next came a novelty of the highest interest—a Rhapsodie (Op. 53) for alto solo and chorus of male voices by Herr Brahms, performed on this occasion for the first time in England. . . .

There is no need to assert Brahms' mastery over the orchestra; but it must be said that in this wild and gloomy music we have his genius as a tone-painter fully declared.

Not a ray of light illumines the dark prospect, and before the end arrives the hearer longs, even amid his interest in the musical technique, for change and relief. How happily the change comes, and what a relief it brings with it, when the poet makes his passionate appeal to the Divine mercy . . . .

Enough that Brahms so uses the language of human emotion that emotion responds to it, and whenever music has this effect its great end is attained.

June, 1877

MONTHLY MUSICAL RECORD

The greatest admirers of the composer can, we think, scarcely deny that there are very many passages in this 'Requiem' which are laboured and diffuse; but these are more than compensated for by whole movements the pathos of which seems to come from the whole heart. It may be conceded that the almost uniform sombreness of the text renders the subject almost impossible to be successfully grasped save by the highest order of genius; but an artist can be judged by results, and the true position of Brahms' 'Requiem', therefore, will depend not upon the rash and enthusiastic judgement of the present, but by the calm and silent verdict of the future.

Oct., 1877

The work is the work of Brahms, and with all respect to the German critics who declared, upon the first hearing, that they could trace a resemblance to Mozart, especially in the finale, we submit that this statement is founded in error. It is as clear and as definite in construction as a work of Mozart, but contains nothing more in point of similarity. To those who look for the impetuosity and formlessness of the modern erratics, the new symphony may appear to be mild and lacking in grip, but the workmanship is everywhere clever, and if the material fails to satisfy, will stand as a proof of the master's increased ability.

'Symphony in D', Nov., 1878

As far as the great work of the day, the new Concerto for Violin by Brahms, can be judged of at a single hearing, there is every reason to believe that musical literature will be the richer by a new and important contribution. It is original in treatment, full of rich fancies and masterly scoring, and the opportunity it affords for the exhibition of virtuosity on the part of the soloist . . . is such as will make it a favourite with all those players who possess sufficient technical skill to master its difficulties.

March, 1879

It has much that is worthy and fresh in the character of the scoring and so forth, but all its worth is apparent on the surface, for the second hearing does not create any very high or augmented impression as to its permanent worth.

'Violin Concerto', April, 1879

MUSICAL TIMES

With the solitary exception of opera there is no branch of composition in which Brahms' genius failed to find vent. To say in which he excelled most is no easy task, but perhaps there is a wider consensus of opinion as to the supreme merit of his concerted chamber music as to anything else he wrote. Here even the most unsympathetic and antagonistic critics have been constrained to express their reluctant appreciation of such pieces as the sextetts and the great Clarinet Quintette.

His extensive contributions to the literature of the pianoforte illustrate the uncompromising aspect of his genius more markedly than any of his compositions.

May, 1897

SIR HUBERT PARRY

An overwhelming loss seems to make a void in the musical world which we cannot hope to see filled in our time. The great heroes of the world are so rare that it is fortunately but seldom in the brief spell of our lives that we have to try and realise what parting with them means. When the career of a great hero ends we stand amazed, and wonder how the immense powers it represented can have really ceased.

When we think of the vital force which the work of a man like Johannes Brahms represents, we can scarcely bring ourselves to face the fact that there will be no more symphonies, quartets, 'Schichsalslied', requiems, songs, sonatas, part-songs, nor any other treasures of art marked by the strong and noble individuality of that particularly heroic tone-poet. Not heaven itself, nor all the combined ingenuity of all the cleverest scientists and artists in the world can ever produce one single work which would represent truly and adequately the noble type of thought and the essentially characteristic qualities in the now familiar works of that single-hearted man.

The life-work is ended and nothing of quite the same order can again be done in the world. The mortal part of him lies fitly in close proximity to the resting-places of Beethoven and Schubert in the cemetery at Vienna. And what comfort have we? Truly, the comfort of heroic work heroically done—a noble life lived out in untainted devotion to generous ideals. The knowledge that here was a man who formed the most exalted ideals of art, and carried them out unflinchingly; who never coquetted with the mob or the 'gallery'; who accepted the exalted responsibilities of knowing what was first-rate, and never belied himself by putting trumpery catch-phrases into his work to tickle the ears of the groundlings and gain a little cheap popularity. And it is something to comfort ourselves with that, notwithstanding the wrath of the

Philistines and the ribaldry of the frivolous and the vain, there is still enough wholesome energy left in humanity to give the highest place in honour and loving reverence to the work of the last of the great German heroes of musical art.

The man Johannes Brahms has gone from us, but his work and his example are our possession still, and will be, not for us only, but for the generations that come after us. The example enforces the pre-eminence of the individual element in art. For, even as it is said that faith without works is dead, so art, without the stamp of a strong personal character, is stillborn. The grandest distinction of specially notable men is that this particular work can be done by no other man whatsoever in the world. A man may utter artistic things with the technique of a superman conjuror, and if he have not temperament and character of his own he is become but a spinner of super-fluities and a tinkling cackler.

And it is worth remembering that it is in that respect that the English race is so peculiarly deficient. In the intensity and fervour which gives the full nature without stint to the expression of artistic ideals, foreign natures have much better aptitudes. We are too cautious and reticent to abandon ourselves to the full absorption in a musical thought or expression. We have too much respect for grand and wide principles of organisation to give our individuality full scope.

But here, too, the example of Johannes Brahms is full of encouragement for us. His was no nature always laid open to receive any chance external impression. He was no expansive, neurotic, ecstatic, hysterico-sensitive bundle of sensibilities, but even as full of dignified artistic reserve and deliberate artistic judgement as the most serious of our own people. But he joined with it the great nature, the cultivated, comprehensive taste, the imagination fostered and fed by dwelling on noble subjects and keeping far from triviality and conventions. To all, it is open to follow the example—in small things as well as great. You know how one of the profoundest of men said;

> 'To thine own self be true . . .
> Thou canst not then be false to any man.'

But it is not only by being true to yourselves that you will be true to one another; it is, in art, a higher truth that it is only by following the highest native qualities and being true to them that you can ever arrive at a genuine niche of your own in your art. As far as true happiness is concerned, it will not matter much whether the niche is high or low, so long as it is your own. Every man has some personal characteristics which mark him from his fellows and some lines of endeavour into which they are impelled. And it is by following out these lines and developing these characteristics that a man is happiest and most likely to be of service to his fellow-men. It is when convention and indolence stifle them that men become torpid, bored, useless, insufferable. You must try to see things with your own eyes, not to take even what wise men tell you as so many formulas you have to learn by rote, but try to see through what look like formulas at first into the principles and truths that they really express. Then you may rise above the mere knowledge of details into the genuine appreciation of great artistic ideas, and be worthy of belonging to the brotherhood of artists of which Brahms was the greatest and most noble member in our time, and feel without false presumption the honourable exaltation of belonging to the same calling as he did.

College Addresses, May, 1897

J. S. SHEDLOCK

There was, however, a higher step to take, and that was to write a symphony. Mozart, Schubert, and Mendelssohn, while yet boys, rapidly wrote off symphony after symphony, but when they grew up to manhood they took longer over such work, and were far less prolific. Beethoven was more than thirty years of age when he published his first symphony in C, and before the C minor of Brahms appeared the latter had passed his mature age of forty. He, in fact, approached that most difficult of tasks after writing music of similar structure, yet, by reason of the smaller numbers of instruments employed, and the proportionally fewer contrasts of colour, less complex. Great is the pathos and power of the C minor, great the charm and nobility of the D major. The music, constructed with care and skill, is at times bold, yet free from all eccentricity; while attentive listeners, who have grasped even only the outlines of form, can follow it without serious trouble. These two works, as Dr. Deiters justly remarks, have won for Brahms 'his place in Beethoven's domain of art'. In the third and fourth symphonies there are many points of interest—for whether inspiration be strong or weak, Brahms, by his solid, masterly workmanship always commands attention. I feel, however, strongly inclined to think that while popular interest in the first two will increase, in the last two it will decrease.

Monthly Musical Record, May, 1897

J. A. FULLER-MAITLAND

Never, since music was a conscious art, have the ideals of its structure been so continually fulfilled as they were by Brahms. His power of handling his materials so as to bring out every beautiful aspect of every theme, is surpassed by none of the older masters, not even by Beethoven. That power is none the less conspicuous because, for the most part, the usual types of musical form, those which are called classical, have been employed, Brahms, being in no straits for new ideas, had not the need which Liszt and other 'advanced' composers had, of altering the classical forms or experimenting in new ones, for as long as he lived the old forms, so far from hampering his genius or confining his inspiration, seemed to suggest fresh outlets for development, and while there is no slavish adherence to the moulds in which Haydn and Mozart cast their thoughts, there is no opposition to the classic model. Any alteration is in the direction of amplification, the groundwork of the structure being virtually in conformity with the rules laid down long before. This is especially true of the 'first-movement' form, which, in all the many examples in the work of Brahms, is identical with that used by the classical masters, though in many instances some increased interest is imparted to the regular design by the presence of a motto-theme (neither first nor second subject, but dominating both) or by incorporating part of the development with the recapitulation. A third point of great importance with Brahms is the coda, and no more striking instance of his most successful innovation in form can be pointed out than the third symphony, where the motto pervades the whole work, and the coda of the last movement introduces new matter, fusing it with the old in a manner it is impossible to forget....

... the more deeply it is studied, the more enthusiasm will be called forth by his skill in the development of his themes, sometimes from quite unpromising germs, but more often from some melodic strain already so beautiful in itself that we might expect it to be spoilt by any process of alteration. In this special art of development we may perhaps see the highest achievement of human intellect in music. It requires not merely a complete mastery of every harmonic and contrapuntal resource, and the insight to detect in the poetic invention to control the different phases of the theme, and to present them in such a succession as will enhance their beauty or eloquence.... Nothing is more remarkable throughout the work of Brahms than this splendid art, ...

Brahms, 1911

H. V. JERVIS-READ

I like to place on record my own feeling that Brahms by nature was a lyrical writer for the piano, and that his work is the direct opposite of Beethoven's epic sonatas and symphonies, and that, like Chopin and Debussy, he composed at the piano. I feel that when Brahms was not writing for the piano and at the piano, he was colourless, obvious in sentiment, and often insufferably dull (no 'profound psychological import' about Brahms!). In this respect that is to say as an orchestral writer, he seems to me to be of a different quality and of less calibre than pretty nearly any composer who has written, or who writes at the present time, for the orchestra at all. Brahms lacks the quality that I admire most: emotional candour. (Elgar has it and markedly; it is a part of the hall-mark common to both creative and interpreting artists.) As a piano writer, and from every point of view as a piano writer, Brahms is superb.

The Arrant Artist, 1939

ON BIZET (1838–1875)

MUSICAL TIMES

... the composition is never dull, never at a loss in describing strong emotion and never commonplace. In some of the numbers are to be found distinct resemblance to the style and manner and even the phrases of Gounod and Meyerbeer, especially the former: but this is not so very material when such good, sound, musician-like work as Bizet's is forthcoming. He was clearly never at a loss for ideas and had a facility for expressing them far beyond the average of his contemporaries. His scoring is sound, scholarly and elegant; and about his music from the first to the last page of this opera, there is a healthy, honest vigour that contrasts very favourably with much we have heard of late years. The music of 'Carmen', despite of the traces of Gounod has a freshness, a dramatic applicability to the situation, and a true ring of inspiration, with undoubted cleverness of construction, that should do everything for Bizet's permanent fame. It carries the listener onwards with undiminished pleasure to the very end of the opera, although it has, almost as a matter of course, its comparatively weak places, as, for instance, the finale of the second act. Without being a work of over-powering genius, 'Carmen' is an opera that may be heard with pleasure and profit, and this is more than can be asserted of many productions of the modern school which have been accorded the honour of representation abroad and in London. There are absolutely no barren places in the four acts. The opera is, as we have said, deeply interesting throughout, and the proof of the composer's talent was found in the enthusiastic reception given to his work. The public is seldom wrong in its unanimously favourable estimate, and that the opera has made its mark in the first representation does not admit of a doubt.

July, 1898

ON TCHAIKOWSKY (1840–1893)

MONTHLY MUSICAL RECORD

In every respect this Concerto of Tchaikowsky's is a very remarkable work, and one, which, when it has become familiarised, will, we think, be warmly appreciated. . . . As regards the general texture of M. Tchaikowsky's subject-matter, which bears the unmistakable impress of a Slavonic temperament acted upon by the extremes of heated passion and depression, it may be characterised as tunefully melodious and as grandly harmonious as a constant change of key will allow.

'Piano Concerto in B flat minor', April, 1879

MUSICAL TIMES

The overture to 'Romeo and Juliet' by the Russian composer, Peter Tchaikowsky, which concluded the concert, is a most elaborate composition, which requires repeated hearing and careful study to be appreciated. It is full of beauties, but at the same time contains much that is hard to be understood.

Dec., 1876

MONTHLY MUSICAL RECORD

There is general agreement as to the great merits of Tchaikowsky's compositions—taking melodies, striking rhythms, skilful harmonies, and in works written for orchestra, picturesque scoring. And to all this the Slavonic element, now of excitement, now of depression, adds a certain charm, for in the works with which we are acquainted it is never introduced to excess. A certain tendency to diffuseness seems to be his chief weakness, and it, perhaps, is somewhat characteristic of modern Russian composers generally. But whatever his merits or demerits, Tchaikowsky deserves the high esteem in which he is held, both in his own country and abroad.

Nov., 1892

MUSICAL TIMES

. . . fiery exaltation alternating with languid melody, a fondness for huge outlines and barbaric gorgeousness of colour.

Dec., 1893

GERALD ABRAHAM

What was Tchaikowsky's conception of music, then? First and last, the spontaneous, lyrical idea whether embodied in a short theme or, as was more often the case with his own compositions, in a fairly long-breathed melody. The art of composition was to him the craft of dressing up and fitting together such ideas in the most effective way. He disliked music that lacked this inward lyrical feeling or in which it was, in his view, smothered by elaborate technical treatment. He disliked genuine programme-music that is to say, music with a literary or pictorial as distinguished from a merely emotional programme—probably because the impulse to it came from outside, as it were.

. . . wonderful as his flow of melodic inspiration was, Tchaikowsky over-tapped it by his habit of 'working like a cobbler, day in, day out, and often to order', as he put it. Every period of his career is marked by a quantity of work inferior in inspiration though seldom perfunctory in craftsmanship. And towards the end of his life he began to subject his melodic inspiration to yet another strain: that of more definite emotional expressiveness, the almost extra-musical expressiveness—struggling for the precision of words. . . .

The skill with which Tchaikowsky dressed up his melodic ideas is as striking as his failure to build them into large-scale instrumental forms. Except when he writes for the piano, his 'facture' is usually irreproachable. Of the easy assurance of his part writing I have already spoken; of his mastery of orchestration, garish though it is at times, there is no need to speak. But something must be said of his harmony, which was often commonplace, sometimes spicy, as in 'Francesca', and not without individual traits. He himself told Mme. von Meck that 'every melodic idea brings its own inevitable harmony', and it is quite true that with him melody and harmony play into each other's hands more frequently than with most Russian composers. (With the 'Mighty Handful' harmony seems always inessential to the original idea, a mere support or decoration.) The pull of appoggiaturas and suspensions, for instance, is frequently felt in Tchaikowsky's melody. But his harmonic thinking is curiously limited. He feels the great tidal pulls of the tonal system as little as the members of the 'handful'. He is conscious only of the more limited forces of gravitation within the key. Typical Tchaikowsky harmony more often than not consists of a comparatively short progression of apparently complicated chords gravitating towards tonic or dominant, more often the latter . . . . A favourite harmonic device of his was the simple alternation of two chords. The ninth variation in the trio is almost entirely based on two chords—everyone will remember the poetic effects Tchaikowsky produces in this way in 'Romeo and Juliet' and the first movement of the B flat minor Concerto; and it is hardly an exaggeration to say that the harmonic germ of the whole of the first movement of the fifth Symphony consists of the alternation of the minor tonic chord with the sub-dominant. This last, a peculiarly 'weary' effect, frequently occurs in Tchaikowsky, the subdominant chord being sometimes the simple triad or inversion, . . .

'Tchaikowsky: Some Centennial Reflections',
Music and Letters, April, 1940

CONSTANT LAMBERT

In my opinion Tchaikowsky had a gift for thinking naturally in musical terms which has been granted to few composers in the course of history. His melodic faculty was as spontaneous and as rich as that of Mozart and Schubert, composers with whom he has more in common than is generally supposed.

This gift is seen at its best in his ballet music, notably 'The Sleeping Princess', in which he creates a world of timeless beauty which can without any disrespect be compared to the world created by Mozart in such an opera as 'The Magic Flute'. But Tchaikowsky was a man at war with himself in more senses than one. The need to express his own tortured personality struggled

K

D.M.C.

with the purely lyrical side of his music. Moreover his emotional capacity was greater than his romantic capacity. When it came to romantic self-expression he was unable to forge a form of his own like Liszt or (to a minor degree) Berlioz, with the result that his symphonies for all their fire and inspiration are incomplete artistic utterances. Half the time he is trying to tell a story about himself, half the time he is trying to remember what various professors had told him to do. This is particularly noticeable in his first movements which hover uneasily and (from the technical point of view) a little timidly, between personal romanticism and scholastic formality. Not until his last symphony, the Pathetic, did he begin the experiments he should have started years before. He is far happier in his slow movements and scherzos where his lyrical talent is less hampered by technical considerations. Yet for all their faults, his symphonies still maintain their hold over the public and one must certainly admit that the public is right, just as it is right in the case of Puccini. The capacity to hit people below the belt is one that the most intellectual musician must envy and in each of these cases the capacity is due to a vitality of musical imagination which counterbalances a number of intellectual short-comings.

The Listener, May 2nd, 1940

ON DVORAK (1841–1904)

MONTHLY MUSICAL RECORD

... only one novelty was introduced, namely, some Slavonian dance music by a composer new to an English audience ... who is called Dvorak. There is a considerable amount of fascination in the melancholy tone of the melodies of these Slavonian dances, and the constant change of rhythm and the alteration of slow and rapid movements has an effect not at all unpleasing. There is no great pretension in the work as a musical composition other than that which aims at the representation of a national peculiarity, and the reproduction, in a quasi-classical form, of things that are in their origin popular.

'Slavonic Dances', March, 1879

Firstly, it is to be noted that the composer has returned to the style of the 'Stabat Mater'—that is, in the individuality of the working out of slight thematic material; and, secondly, the conception and treatment are throughout of the most solemn, and even ecclesiastical character. Abounding in beauties, these are all touched with the gloom which pervades the whole. . . . Hearing it, I was reminded of the old musician who, finding fault with the sweetness of the 'Benedictus' in Mozart's 'Requiem', said 'If I had to write a Requiem, do you think I would make it sweet? No, sir, I should see the corpse in front of me'.

'Requiem', Nov., 1891

SIR W. H. HADOW

His treatment of the classical forms is much influenced for good by his long and patient study of Beethoven. In the more highly-organised types he certainly falls short of his great master: he lacks the perfect balance that marks the first movement of the Appassionata or the A major Symphony; as we should naturally expect, he tends rather to restlessness of tonality and to a page over-crowded with accessory keys. But, in spite of this, his instinct for structure is real and genuine; it ranks higher than that of Chopin—far higher than that of Lizst or Berlioz; and his outline, though not always in complete symmetry, is firmly drawn and filled with interesting detail. . . .

This feeling for colour and movement, which appears partly in his rhythms, partly in the use of the scale, partly in his preference for lyric and elegiac forms, may also account in some measure for his unquestioned and supreme mastery of orchestration. Here at least there is no counterchange of victory and defeat, no loss in one direction to balance gain in another; here at least every achievement is a triumph and every work a masterpiece. Nor has he alone the lesser gift of writing brilliant dialogue for his instrument, of making each stand out salient and expressive against a background of lower tone; he is even more successful in those combinations of 'timbre' which harmonise the separate voices and give to the full chord its peculiar richness and euphony. When we think of his scoring, it is not to recall a horn passage in one work or a flute solo in another—plenty of these could be found, and in a master of less capacity they would be well worth recording—but it is rather the marvellous interplay and texture of the whole that remains in our memory and compels our admiration.

Studies in Modern Music, 1894–5

ON SULLIVAN (1842–1900)

MUSICAL TIMES

Mr. Sullivan has a talent which should not be trifled with. He has thoughts which so dazzle him by their brilliancy that he is a little too prone to reflect whither they lead him. His instrumentation—never weak or conventional and often remarkable for novel and effective combinations—enables him to dress up those thoughts so attractively that he can calculate with certainty upon their effect. . . . To us it appears that Mr. Sullivan, relying upon his natural qualifications, writes seldom and quickly; and that he rarely subjects his works to that rigid self-examination which alone can enable him to do full justice to his powers.

Dec., 1866

... this firmly cemented union between author and composer is detrimental to the art-progress of either; ...

... Sullivan has in him the true elements of an artist which would be successfully developed were a carefully framed libretto presented to him for composition.

June, 1878

MUSICAL OPINION

Sir Arthur Sullivan's music which, though here and there too classically good for a popular entertainment, always relents with following numbers by melting in exquisite melodies.

'Princess Ida', Feb., 1884

MONTHLY MUSICAL RECORD

The title of the new opera by Gilbert and Sullivan was withheld from the public until three days before the representation .... When it was announced, everyone was astonished. Many were disgusted. 'Ruddy-Gore' or 'The Witch's Curse' does not look elegant in the bills of a Transpontine melodrama of the old but now defunct type. ...

At the first performance there were many of the best known people in art, literature, and music; but they did not laugh much. The gallery hissed, and at the conclusion uttered wolfish yells, indicative of dissatisfaction. ...

The music should draw all who love melody. Beautifully harmonised and richly and dramatically scored, it is among the best things that Sullivan has as yet accomplished, and it proves conclusively that if his COLLABORATEUR's powers are showing signs of 'paying out', his own are gaining in freshness and originality with each successive effort.

Feb., 1887

DAME CLARA BUTT

'Oh, the "Light of the World"! It is so grand and so touching; people in the audience generally weep. Even I myself after singing one or two of the solos feel rather choked.'

'Which is your favourite of the grand operas?'

Unhesitatingly came the answer,

'Verdi's "Othello", and among the oratorios, the "Light of the World". There is a grand part for me in it, and the audience always appreciate the music.'

In an interview, South Wales Daily News,
Sept. 19th, 1895

MUSICAL TIMES

It may be asserted without fear of contradiction that Sullivan was a most successful composer. One of the chief secrets of his success was his great and natural gift of melody. . . .

Form and symmetry he seems to possess by instinct; rhythm and melody clothe everything he touches; the music shows not only sympathetic genius, but sense, judgement, proportion, and a complete absence of pedantry and pretension; while the orchestration is distinguished by a happy and original beauty hardly surpassed by the greatest masters.

Dec., 1900

MUSICAL OPINION

Never in the history of the art has a position such as his been held by a composer; and it was earned simply and solely by his own achievement, unaided by interest or side influences of any kind. For all the English speaking races —with the exception of a very small and possibly unimportant class—Sullivan's name stood as a synonym for music in England. . . .

No one who had any ear for music at all could fail to appreciate the grace and fancy which always marked Sir Arthur Sullivan's work. Trained musicians delighted in the marvellous cleverness and resource of the orchestration; the critic and student found new beauties at every fresh hearing; What captivated the majority, and set Sullivan in popular esteem far above all the other English composers of his day, was the tunefulness of his music; that quality in it by which, without ever descending to mere trickery of commonplace 'catchiness', it found its way to the ear at once, and was immediately recognised as a joyous contribution to the gaiety of life. . . .

Many who are able to appreciate classical music regret that Sir Arthur Sullivan did not aim consistently at higher things, that he set himself to rival Offenbach and Lecocq instead of competing on a level of high seriousness with such musicians as Sir Hubert Parry and Professor Stanford. If he had followed this path, he might have enrolled his name among the great composers of all time.

Jan., 1901

ON GRIEG (1843–1907)

MONTHLY MUSICAL RECORD

Recalling the favourable impression it then made, and the opinion very generally expressed at the time that no more original or more effective work of the kind had appeared since Schumann's Concerto in the same key, one cannot but feel surprised that it should not have been heard again. We happen to know, however, that many of our resident pianists, taking example from Mr. Dannreuther, have set to work to study it. That it will eventually take its place as a stock piece among the best pianoforte concertos there can be little doubt.

'Piano Concerto', May, 1875

The principal attraction at the first concert, on the 22nd ult, was Grieg's Pianoforte Concerto, which was played by Mr. Dannreuther with an earnestness and artistic finish which indicated that he estimated the work at a higher value than did the majority of his auditors. We cannot certainly say that definite themes are wanting in the Concerto, but many of them are uncouth—the first, especially, with the ascent of two augmented fourths in consecutive bars—and they appear thrown together as if the composer had resolved to use up all the melodies he had jotted down at various times in his sketch-book. Occasionally we have some excellent writing, and the orchestration is exceedingly effective in many parts; but the composition left a sense of weariness upon the audience which somewhat checked the well-merited applause which the executant received at the conclusion of his difficult task.

March, 1877

MUSICAL TIMES

We could readily forgive the Philharmonic Society for ignoring the claims of our native composers, if strenuous efforts had been made, as in the older times, for procuring the highest-class works of foreigners; but when we find that the season has been chiefly occupied in reproducing compositions which are already known, or in presenting such an elaborate and pretentious work as the 'Dramatic Symphony' of Rubinstein, we cannot but believe that the Society has abandoned its true mission and entered the lists as a mere concert-giving Association without any definite notion save the idea of making the performance pay.

'On Philharmonic Society Policy', Aug., 1876

The Nineteenth and Twentieth Centuries

War is having the customary depressing effect on musical events.

Monthly Musical Record, Jan., 1900

ON MACKENZIE (1847–1935)

The 'Rose of Sharon' is an epoch-making work; the composer has reflected the traditions of the past, and at the same time he has remembered the spirit of his age, and so has produced not a mere mixture but a true compound, a work that will endure, and that may, and probably will, point the way to yet higher achievements.

Nov., 1884

FRANCIS HUEFFER

Mr. Mackenzie's maiden effort in opera, 'Colomba', showed dramatic qualities of a very high order indeed, as did also the first and fourth acts of 'The Troubador', and the so-called Dream Scene of the oratorio 'Rose of Sharon'. If the promise here held out has not been altogether fulfilled in other works by Mr. Mackenzie, the fault lies perhaps less with the composer than with the circumstances in which London musicians are compelled to work surrounded as they are by the turmoil of the largest city in the world, and impelled by competition to produce against time and in excess of the degree of spontaneous inspiration allotted to man.

... it must be hoped that Mr. A. C. Mackenzie, the new principal (of the Royal Academy of Music) will differ from his predecessor, Sir George Macfarren, by conducting the institution more in accordance with the spirit of the age.

Half a Century of Music in
England 1837–1887, 1889

On Thursday April 17th 'Colomba' was given, and the composer came expressly from the Continent to conduct it. In noticing this opera when produced last season, Mr.

F. Niecks said, 'It will live, and be the more appreciated the better it is known.' Well, the judgment he formed was a correct one; the receptions given both to the work and the composer this season show that 'Colomba' has life in it, and that it will probably hold a high place in English musical art. We do not say the highest, because Mr. Mackenzie is at work on a second opera, and it is only natural to suppose that he may surpass his first attempt.

May, 1889

ON PARRY (1848–1918)

THOMAS F. DUNHILL

Parry's consummate mastery in part-writing and his power of controlling massive choral forces led some of his admirers to speak of him as 'the English Bach'. The compliment was doubtless appreciated. It is probable, however, that it gave him more pleasure when his old pupil Vaughan Williams (then studying at the Royal College) declared, in making a presentation from the students on the occasion of his receiving the honour of knighthood, that those who loved his music best preferred to think of him as 'the English Parry'.

The truth is that Parry's music was, almost from the beginning, an intensely personal expression. That is, perhaps, why those who knew him personally were almost invariably the most ardent admirers of his art. To others it seemed on a lofty plane of isolation which was remote from the world. They understood him when he gave play to exuberance and that bluff geniality which was the most openly apparent quality of his personality. To his highest flights they were somewhat coldly responsive, recognising the nobility of manner rather than the deep conviction which lay behind it. Parry's attitude as an artist was uncompromising and not of the kind that quickly wins popular acceptance. He did not write to please, but to express. He was, I think, devoid of any kind of vanity. He would not have been human had he not appreciated the good opinion of the discerning and of those who consistently admired his work, but for any other kind of applause he seemed to care nothing. . . .

Profound alike as scholar and musical historian, hotly impulsive and vigorous in his music, and inspiring in his influence upon all who were in any way associated with him, Sir Hubert Parry's example still lives and shines amongst us—'a presence which is not to be put by'.

Monthly Musical Record, Nov., 1918

MUSICAL OPINION

Of the technical mastery, and the ease with which he managed large effects, it is superfluous to speak. He wrote with exceeding quickness, but no one was more careful to revise what he had written. Just accentuation was with him a fine art, and the carrying out of large and elevated ideas almost an obsession, none the less so because it was unaffected and not a deliberate aim. With Parry effect for the mere sake of effect was a thing to be despised, a principle as sound in music as it is in architecture; but possibly he carried it to a length which militated against the immediate popularity of many of his works. He was so intent upon the expression of his idea that sometimes he left his audience behind him, creating the impression that he was talking or writing above their heads. That in itself is no reproach—the same thing has been said of other composers, Beethoven among them— and it is true that 'easy come and easy go' is as valid an apophthegm with regard to music as to money. Music that has enduring qualities repays study.

The question is, has Parry's music that quality which will win for it appreciation in the long run? To dogmatise would be futile; it is only possible to state one's personal belief and to express sympathy with that writer who said

he believed that there was 'a future for Parry's music'. . . .
One may agree that had he consented to attach a little
more importance to the manner in which his ideas should
be presented, his music would have stood to gain in
every way, but it is hardly possible that works of such
lofty conception should not eventually wax in public
estimation as they become better known.

Nov., 1918

SIR W. H. HADOW

Every great artist, painter, poet or musician is to some
extent the child of his time and his country, and the
genuineness which marks his originality will itself be
influenced by his inheritance and by his surroundings.
He will use the style and idiom which come most naturally
to his hand: he will express through them thoughts and
feelings which he shares, though more fully and deeply,
with the rest of his countrymen. And this is exactly what
Parry has done. He represents in music the essential
sanity of the English genius: its mixture of strength and
tenderness, its breadth, its humour, its entire freedom
from vanity and affectation. It is idle to compare his
gifts with those of the great Continental composers,
'great in their way, not ours nor meant for ours': one
might as well compare the serenity of an English landscape with the glow of sunset on the Apennines or the
Aegean.

Paper read to the Royal Musical
Association, June 17th, 1919

H. V. JERVIS-READ

In the history of English music Parry's name stands
out. He served music well, and as a historic figure, if for
no other reason, he deserves to be remembered.

Parry, aided by Stanford, started the emancipation of
English music, and with them began its movement away

from Handelian and Mendelssohnian influences, and, as earlier, a recognised and recognisable school of English composition arose. These two men were the first to write notable, as opposed to derivative, secular music since Purcell. True, there is Sterndale Bennett: an honoured name. Sterndale Bennett though did not possess Parry's sturdy disposition, nor Parry's independence of mind and outlook.

If one speaks of Parry as the liberator, one must think of Handel as the enslaver; and if one thinks of Parry as establishing one epoch, one must think of Purcell as the highest conception: the apotheosis of another. And between Purcell's period and Parry's epoch is Handel.

The Arrant Artist, 1939

ON STANFORD (1852–1924)

MONTHLY MUSICAL RECORD

... Mr. Stanford's music failed to arouse the enthusiasm of the audience. As in the 'Canterbury Pilgrims', so here, he adopts the Wagner system of leit-motiv. The danger of trying to imitate the German master is obvious: Mr. Stanford has effective themes ... but before the close of the Opera one feels that they are pressed into service; they do not grow in interest, as in Wagner, by means of constant modification and surprising combinations. ... in spite of many interesting passages, he fails to sustain the interest of the listener. We attribute this partly to a lack of individuality in the music, and partly to a certain labour and heaviness in his accompaniments. We have nothing to say against the orchestration, which is throughout skilful and often very effective.

'Savonarola', Aug., 1884

Mr. Stanford has boldly adopted the general style and mannerisms of Wagner. He makes abundant use of the leit-motiv and in each act there are no breaks in the music. It would be mere affectation on the part of composers to ignore Wagner's art theories, and on the other hand it would be risky for them to follow the German reformer in his determination to avoid concerted music as much as possible.

'The Canterbury Pilgrims', June, 1884

SAMUEL BUTLER

... next to him was Villiers Stanford, whom I disliked.
'A Johnian at Trinity', *Note Books*

MUSICAL OPINION

Stanford's music might or might not appeal to everybody—that was a personal matter—but there was no gainsaying the fact that here was a master of his craft, one who knew what he wanted to say and knew how to say it: a combination which is not so common at any time that we can afford to underrate it. It might be that he was not always inspired: what composer is? But he was ever the accomplished musician. It might be that sometimes he appealed more to the intellect than to the emotions, but he could never be ignored. In judging an artist we must be guided by his best work and not by that which may fall below it in merit: and at his best Stanford was a composer who surely came very near to genius, if indeed he may not be considered to have possessed it.

May, 1924

ON ELGAR (1857–1934)

ERNEST WALKER

We cannot help noticing here and there a lack of sustained thematic inventiveness, a deficiency in the power of broadly organic construction, even when, in a way, quite original, the material sometimes consists of scraps of music, neither individually nor collectively of any particular interest beyond mere colour, joined together by methods not altogether convincing. Occasionally also there seems an undue reliance on a rather hot-house type of emotionalism, that every now and then comes near degenerating into a somewhat forced pseudo-impressiveness; the melodramatic bars that depict the suicide of Judas in 'The Apostles' set on edge the teeth of listeners who have felt to the full the dramatic power of the pages that precede them, and there are parts of Gerontius' confession of faith that, although sincere, nevertheless suggest an atmosphere of artificial flowers. Sometimes the splendour of the frame tends to hide the picture; and in the picture itself, when we do see it, the gorgeous colour tends to hide in the drawing. His most inspired excepted, it is not altogether paradoxical to say that even the late Elgar is a light composer compared with the classics; the relatively sensuous elements seem often to be the main consideration and it is very rarely that he shows anything of the bracing sternness that lies at the root of the supreme music of the world. The path of picturesque emotionalism is beset with snares, and Elgar has not escaped them every one; but, when all is said, an unmistakably new and living voice of high genius is something for which we must needs be lastingly grateful, and—remembering his astounding progress in the last ten years—we cannot but believe that there is still a further future before this youngest of our leaders.

A History of Music in England, 1907

ERIC BLOM

With all that is traditional and even reminiscent in Elgar there is no other composer's dominating influence to be found in him. Eclectic as his music is, we can never lay a finger on any passage and say positively; this comes from such and such a master. His melody is sometimes redolent of Tschaikowsky, his spirituality of Franck; he has the grandeur of Beethoven and the aloofness of Brahms; his use of the 'leit-motiv' comes from Wagner; his mastery of orchestration reminds us of Berlioz; yet there is no actual likeness, not even a profound sympathy with any of these composers to be found in his work, which has always that peculiar, indefinite and yet palpable Elgar quality, a thing so characteristic that even its mannerisms have a curious attraction. The artifice of the sequence, for instance, which merely annoys us in no less accomplished but far less individual composers like Saint-Saens or Glazounov, loses its artificiality at the hands of Elgar and grows into a typical personal feature. The 'leit-motiv', too, is in his blood and so natural to him that he instinctively associates definite musical themes with people of his acquaintance.

To describe Elgar, who all his life had mercifully escaped systematic teaching, and whose very visit to Leipzig was but a holiday, is not only absurd but, in spite of his addiction to form, absolutely unjust. His method is certainly meticulously correct, but he obeys no rule other than his own, according to which nothing is forbidden that sounds right and conveys the artist's meaning. He goes to the point directly and will transgress freely against any scholastic regulation, if by breaking it he finds a short cut to his goal. He will not write consecutive fifths merely to vex the professors, but if by doing so he gains just the effect he needs, he will be as reckless about it as an author who prefers a well-spaced split infinitive to a clumsy avoidance of it.

There is not a more suspicious figure in art than the man surrounded by admirers who find, or pretend to find, no blemish in his work. Elgar is not one of these. He certainly is dull on occasions; but so is Bach. He is grandiloquent at times; so are Beethoven and Wagner. He has, in fact, plenty of defects; but so had all the great masters, whose faults as well as their qualities have gone to the making of their definite personalities. It will have to be recognised sooner or later that Elgar is one of them.

Chesterian, June, 1922

J. H. ELLIOT

It is generally admitted that the obvious influences which have been concerned in Elgar's development are foreign ones—principally Brahms and Franck. It is, however, the Elgarian qualities in which they are absorbed that must chiefly concern us. What, then, are they? Elgar is, of course, emotional—'Too emotional', Professor Dent has told us, 'for English ears.' Certainly he is, I think, too emotional to act as spokesman for the English people as a whole. The ordinary Englishman might possibly allow himself the luxury of expressing inward joy in Elgarian tunes such as those in the finale of the second symphony; but he would never dilate them with such zestful rhetoric: he would retire at once shame-facedly into his shell. Indeed, neither the classical forms nor variations upon them square with English sentiment, in that they imply either expansiveness of expression or academic patience, or both. Nor is the blend of the two within our policy of compromise. We are not actually unemotional, nor are we afraid always to express emotion. But it must be done with dispatch; we do not care to dwell upon it, with or without a temper of intellectual restraint. We need a Sibelius to voice our feelings without making eloquent commentaries upon them, and to pass on to the next matter without fuss, relying upon the logic of musical thought rather than upon derivations from a form evolved in Central Europe during the seventeenth and eighteenth centuries.

Professor Dent has complained of Elgar's pomposity. One need not utter protest on musical grounds; the composer's 'nobilmentes' and 'grandiosos' are almost invariably rich and satisfying. But they are not English. We are not so demonstrative a race. The formalities of our patriotism, for instance, are conducted with inward discomfort and external sheepishness. We shuffle awkwardly to our feet when the National Anthem is played, and cheer only under the conviction that we are making asses of ourselves. Our patriotism consists of a sublime unawareness of any conceivable challenge to what we fondly imagine to be our superiority; all foreigners are people at whom half-bricks may be heaved— or, better still, who may be contemptuously left alone. We do not insist upon this supposed priority: we just believe in it and assume that the rest of the world believes in it likewise. We English, collectively and individually, have too much humour, or too much conceit, to employ the grand gesture, however intensely we may admire it in Continental architecture or in Elgar's music.

Elgar is essentially un-English in the magnificence of his rhetoric; and the concentrated speech of his later works—the 'cello concerto is a notable instance—is due more to a hardly-won technical economy of style than to a restraint rising from inward impulse. I would even go further, and contend that Elgar not only speaks, but thinks differently from the average Englishman. That is, his initial ideas are not characteristic of his race. There is an ornateness in his melody, a ripeness in his harmony, that do not accord with British sentiment generally. Look at the typical Elgarian phrase, how it dips and rises in voluptuous curves, or languishes with sinuous grace, quasi-Oriental in general contour! Even his heartiest rhythms, therefore, are apt to blaze into the florid rather than the robust; they have not, for instance, the honest bucolic roll that Holst sometimes contrives. Not that we are a rusticated nation, but we are too far west to utter anything that savours of the ecstatic.

I venture to submit, therefore, that while Elgar is indubitably the greatest English composer, and as indubitably among the giants of all countries, he is in no sense a nationalist; and that the music-loving English accept him simply and solely on the strength of his genius as a creative musician.

'Elgar and England', *Sackbut*, Oct., 1931

REV. BASIL MAINE

In many ways the cases of Sibelius and Elgar are parallel. Elgar, too, expresses national identity without resorting to folk-song for material. Even in the works which are deliberately patriotic in motive, he avoids the error of relying upon tunes that once were folk-music but are no longer, and instead writes tunes of his own, one of which has already become a representative folk-tune. Because he has done this, he is upbraided for being a purveyor of merely popular folk-song enthusiasts. If the term 'folk music' conveys anything, it is that once upon a time this was popular music. But if a composer of our own time writes a tune that is popular without being ephemeral, he is accused of playing down to the public. 'Land of Hope and Glory' and the big tune in 'Finlandia' are looked upon as crimes which the composers must expiate. So completely inverted are our standards!

It is easy enough to bring a charge of Jingoism against Elgar in connection with the 'Imperial March', 'The Banner of St. George', 'The Crown of India', and 'Land of Hope and Glory' (although, incidentally, the accusation is never brought against Purcell for writing 'Fairest Isle'), but it is another matter to prove such a charge against the symphonic works. There are those, howbeit, who talk of the symphonies and concertos as if the content of each work had been mysteriously communicated to them in terms of a definite programme. Having received this ghostly communication, they naturally turn to it to support their own argument, since those who oppose the argument have no way of disproving the communication and perhaps lack the audacity to forward a ghostly communication of their own. Without a moment's misgiving, then, these diviners of the unknown give out that beyond the shadow of a doubt, the content of the symphonic works is also jingoistic. If it is tactfully suggested that quite possibly they have been guilty of reading the meaning of the avowedly patriotic works— those with a text to provide the clue—into the symphonic works, they answer by reminding us that to them, and not to us, has been vouchsafed the literal meaning of those works. We have no alternative, but to express surprise and doubt, and at the risk of appearing irreverent we claim the right to state our own case.

To refer to Elgar's symphonic works as being the expression of Jingoism is to under-rate the function of symphonic style in a composer's development. The fact that it frequently represents a late stage in that development indicates not only that symphonic form calls for an exceptional mastery of technique but also that it is a medium especially suited to the expression of matured experience. . . . In spite of occasional outbursts of impatience at the stupidity of the British public, for many years Elgar was its obedient servant. He did not betray the trust which had been implicitly placed in him by common consent. As faithfully as any Poet Laureate he sang and celebrated and mourned with the people of his land. He did so consistently through years that saw constant change in social, political and international ideals. . . . The Violin Concerto, the Second Symphony, 'Falstaff', and the Violoncello Concerto are none the less individual as achievements because they belong to a period which also produced 'The Coronation March', 'The Crown of India', Polonia', and 'Carillon'. Nor do they appear any the less great if they are regarded as works of purely musical content and design. Criticism which attempts to bring about a depreciation in the value of the most important of Elgar's instrumental works, adopts one of two methods: either it takes the attitude of denouncing the use of the holy vessel called Symphony for the purpose of unconsecrated Romanticism, . . . or it examines these works in the context of the other less important works, (less important, that is, as expressions of the composer's individuality) and, following the line of least resistance, reads into the great works the distasteful ideas which can so easily be pilloried in the others. The second method is open to anyone who can wield a journalistic pen. Musical judgement is not a requisite, since the distasteful ideas can be readily discovered in the titles or texts of the one group of works and fancifully applied to the other group. By this method of juxtaposition Beethoven's Seventh Symphony can be criticised in terms of 'The Battle of Vittoria', and Wagner's 'Siegfried' in terms of 'The Kaisermarsch'. When, therefore, the charge of Jingoism or of aggressive nationalism is brought against the symphonic works of Elgar, the accuser must be prepared to support his case with definite evidence. It is not enough to state baldly that this or that theme or episode suggests (to the accuser) this or that distasteful idea. It is possible, by such a method, to explain any piece of music in terms of any preconceived idea. Obviously the method is too easy and arbitrary to be of any value to serious criticism.

'Elgar and the Edwardian Age,' from
Elgar: His Life and Works, 1933

CONSTANT LAMBERT

In Elgar, the first figure of importance since Boyce, we get an example of a composer, in touch both with his audience and his period, expressing himself nationally in an international language. It is more than probable that, but for the social and spiritual changes brought about by the war, Elgar would have been a more potent influence on English music than Vaughan Williams; but the aggressive Edwardian prosperity that lends so comfortable a background to Elgar's finales is now as strange to us as the England that produced 'Greensleeves' and 'The Woodes so Wilde'. Stranger, in fact, and less sympathetic. In consequence much of Elgar's music, through no fault of its own, has for the present generation an almost intolerable air of smugness, self-assurance and autocratic benevolence.

Music Ho! 1934

ON PUCCINI (1858–1924)

CECIL GRAY

In many essential respects Puccini's artistic development recalls that of Verdi. For although, unlike his great predecessor, his works from 'Manon Lescaut' onwards reveal a continually growing pre-occupation with theatrical effect and a correspondingly marked decline in musicianship generally—a progression which 'La Fanciulla del West' (surely one of those works which one could safely assert without fear of contradiction to be one perpetual and unrelieved nausea from start to finish, from its sticky beginning to its sloppy end) represents the culminating point or rather the nadir—his recent recovery in the so-called 'Trittico' is all the more welcome because it was so wholly unexpected.

It is not only in his belated development that Puccini suggests a parallel with Verdi, but also in the spirit in which these works are written. He seems to have set himself, probably quite consciously and deliberately, to Italicise modern impressionist composers in the same way that Verdi Italicised Wagner. But while in the latter's case the attempt to prolong the existence of the old Italian tradition, then lying gasping and emaciated upon its death-bed, by means of a kind of artificial rejuvenation or transfusion of blood from a younger and more vital organism, resulted in the production of two supreme masterpieces—surely sufficient in themselves to justify the somewhat dangerous and unnatural experiment—the operation in Puccini's case, performed by a less skilful and steady hand, has hardly turned out so successfully. At best the success has only been partial, though sufficient to prove an abiding possibility. . . .

In Puccini's later works the two elements, native and foreign, seem to exist side by side without coalescing, as with Verdi, into a homogeneous and wholly personal style; like oil and water they refuse to blend, but exist together on a basis of mutual toleration and tacit understanding. The one does not intrude upon the other's domain. When Puccini is in his lyric vein he writes wholeheartedly in the old 'cantilena' style; when it is necessary to be dramatic he writes in the 'modern' style. This duality is highly characteristic of modern Italy, of the antagonism between Past and Future—to the discomfort of the immediate Present—which is exemplified in every walk of life, whether political, social, or intellectual. Every Italian seems to reproduce in microcosm this constant struggle for supremacy between two hostile and irreconcilable forces; every Italian carries within himself a Vatican and Quirinal. Futurism and passéism are both expressions of this dualism, are even fundamentally the same thing. They are both of them based upon the disheartening certainty of their inability to escape from the past—the one accepts it, the other tries to revolt against it. Puccini and Malipiero, D'Annunzio and Marinetti may seem to the superficial eye very different, but essentially they are the same.

Puccini gives the impression of continually trying to escape from the past to which he naturally belongs, and with which he is in secret sympathy. The 'modernities' with which he besprinkled his pages so lavishly seem to have been conceived and carried out in a spirit of disagreeable necessity. One is certain that he dislikes having to do it, but feels that it is incumbent upon him to keep up to date and move with the times. We almost see him setting his teeth as he writes them.

'Three Modern Italian Composers',
Sackbut, Oct., 1920

A. WALTER KRAMER

It has been their fashion to speak of him contemptuously. He has been accused of every manner of thing of which successful men—whether in the arts or in other fields—are open to being charged with. In his case, his musicianship has been questioned, his mastery denied, etc, etc. All bootless charges. Puccini sinned in these things at times as all humans sin, but his greatest sin was that of lack of taste at times where the possession of it would have won the day for him. The great and the small in opera-composers stand or fall in the final analysis not because of the approval given their work during their lifetime by a group of what for a better word we would call 'highbrows', but because of their ability in coming years to interest succeeding generations of opera-lovers. . . . Harmonically he began rather falteringly, but before he had reached fifty he developed a keen harmonic sense as 'Madame Butterfly' and 'La Fanciulla del West' prove and later the three one-act operas comprising the 'trittico'. But above this harmonic development, which he seems never quite to have mastered, his broad flow of melody, frequently unrefined and banal, emphasised by the mannerism of scoring so much in unison with the whole string body of the orchestra playing along with the singing voice, stood out for the masses, touched their hearts, won their favour, in short, made him 'their Puccini'.

. . . Puccini's influence has been felt in more than a single composer's music, not only in his own country but also in other lands. Erich Korngold in Austria revealed it and Franz Schreker too; and other men whose names are perhaps less widely known. A deep influence he could not exert, for it was not his kind of opera that others strove to compose; the influence was rather a type of melody that crept into their output unconsciously as the result of their having familiarised themselves with his music.

He stands to-day where a composer equally admired in his time stood when he left his work behind to preserve his name for a later day. That composer was Giacomo Meyerbeer. Praised in his day, performed as frequently as Puccini in our time, the first Giacomo has paled into boring fustian, his endless operas of dull theatrical music, bombastic and unreal, have dwindled into nothingness. I would call Puccini 'the other Giacomo', for his contribution to operatic literature is not unlike that of Meyerbeer. Both Giacomos were men of the theatre and that alone. Their operas brought no message, new and vital, they explored no untrodden ways, they blazed no new paths. Both of them were successful in a special field in which they laboured untiringly, and both had fame and fortune during their lifetime. . . .

A figure in present-day operatic music striking and sincere was Giacomo Puccini. Even when he first used the vocabulary of modern French harmonic development, he used it 'fortissimo' in his own lusty way, and did not pose as an impressionist, knowing doubtless how ridiculous a figure he would cut were he to try it. But no matter. I will not praise him because he has given so much pleasure of a certain kind to so many millions of people throughout the world. But I am in deep admiration of his honesty of purpose, his sincerity as regards his place in the world of music of his day, and his always appropriate music to a given scene. There are not many composers who can boast of that, I dare say.

'The Other Giacomo', *Chesterian*, Jan.–Feb., 1925

F. STEPHEN CLARK

Puccini's great success may be attributed largely to a blending of Italian and German styles in music. The Italian style of Opera is, as everyone knows, melodious, but somewhat lacking in depth. The German, on the other hand, is masterly in construction, but often somewhat lacking in melody. Puccini achieved an almost perfect blend of these two styles, and, furthermore, gave full significance to the orchestra without neglecting the singers.

Compared with the work of other composers, Puccini's output is not great, but this is accounted for by the great pains he has taken to make his works perfect in every detail. Although his works were few, he made over a million pounds out of them. . . .

It is not exaggerating to say that Puccini was the greatest of Italian composers since Verdi. He was a great artist, and his music lives as everlasting evidence that he fully deserved the title that was his—'Il Maestro'.

Monthly Musical Record, Jan., 1925

ON MAHLER (1860–1911)

HENRY BOYS

Gustav Mahler is a key-figure for the understanding of one of the great crises in musical history. He was the last of the great German line to express himself in the old idiom, but he also found forms which pointed a way towards the transformation of this seemingly exhausted idiom into a new one of great potentiality. Thus there is much music being written to-day which depends on some knowledge of Mahler for its full comprehension.

The music of no other composer of the late 19th century, not even Busoni's, reflects all the problems of technique and aesthetic of this most complex and problematical period more completely than Mahler's; and not even in the case of Berlioz is opinion more sharply divided between those who worship at the shrine on the one hand, and the unsympathetic who can see only the defects of his virtues on the other, than it was over Mahler the man and still is in the case of his music. When he was director of the Vienna Opera, this was due to his fanatical and uncompromising zeal for the perfect realisation of his ideals. His commanding personality left few people who came into contact with it neither hot nor cold, and it is only to be expected that the music of such a personality will affect people similarly. For there can be no doubt that Mahler's music often gives the impression that he is compelling the listener to feel things to the same intense degree as Mahler felt them himself. Those who understand and sympathise with it get from it an inspiration as great as from any other music. Those who do not feel in the same way, or who do not want the revelation Mahler seeks to give, will feel that they are being bullied, or will be embarrassed by what they take to be mere 'rhetoric' and sentimentality. . . .

Mahler's work, . . . , is very precariously poised, and more vulnerable than most to unsympathetic treatment. When such ideals are so highly pitched as Mahler's, their complete realisation is undoubtedly a triumph, but the least fall becomes disproportionately great. His rhetoric, when used properly, is magnificently convincing; its sincerity is never in doubt; but rhetoric easily falls into a flamboyant grandiosity. If in the means, in the choice of material or in the technique, there is anything in the smallest degree lacking, 'extase' appears as little more than exaggerated attitudinising. And such inner conflicts as beset Mahler can become too much even for his prodigious musical gifts to organise, yet in his best work the drama is superb. The Ninth Symphony, like 'Das Lied von der Erde', is free from these defects of Mahler's virtues. Apart from his many perfect songs, they are his most perfectly realised and intimately personal works.

Mahler and his Ninth Symphony, 1938

HERBERT ANTCLIFFE

Sentimentality, morbidness! What has art to do with these? A sentiment that is not healthy is as much out of place in a work of art as is an unhealthy organ in the human body. A morbid expression is merely a sign of an inward morbid character and immediately condemns the work in which it appears. And of all modern works which have achieved any serious popularity those of Mahler suffer the most in this respect.

The popularity of Gustav Mahler's music among certain classes of people in Austria and Holland is easy to understand, if one knows these people. Except for a number of Semitic characteristics, which, as they are much purer than one usually finds in the work of the average Jew, must derive from a very remote ancestral train, the music of Mahler is essentially Teutonic with all the sentimentality which we find in a greater or less degree in every branch of the old Teutonic family. This, apart from the ubiquitous and urgent propaganda of the friends and disciples of the composer, has aroused unbounded admiration especially among the weaker types of music-lover. At its best it is a healthy expression of thoughts and feelings which the normal person has or ought to have, with a strong tendency to the sombre side of life. At its worst it never falls below a certain standard of technical mastery which implies a power of making mere repetition effective—a power of which the supreme examples are to be found in the works of two other essentially German, or Teutonic writers, Schubert and Beethoven. This is one of the few good qualities which remain in Mahler's worst compositions, and in this category is one of the biggest and one of the most popular.

'Das Lied von der Erde' is the work of an old man, of a man worn out before the normal time; and it has all the worst qualities of premature senility. . . .

. . . Out of the six numbers two, the third and fourth, have some character which approaches healthy beauty, these two being the least original of all. For the rest the expression of the sentiment is strained, and, apart from the question of the balance, or the lack of balance, between voice and orchestra (it has been said that Mahler, in view of the music he has written, should have altered the close of 'Der Trunkene in Frühling' into 'Lasst mich'—that is, the singer or his voice—'ertrunken sein'), much of the vocal part, even with the most accomplished Wagnerian singers is impossible to sing—it can only be screamed. . . .

A still surer sign of the artistic senility is in the weakness of the themes and the lack of character of his melodies. Some of them are meaningless and apparently aimless sounds which, were they less sordid and less pathetic in their lack of inward significance, would be comic. Most of them, however, do not call for such a description but are merely banal. Had they been written by an English or American commercial ballad writer to feeble love poems, they would have achieved a success that would have made a fortune for both the composer and his publisher.

Dominant, March–April, 1939

ON DEBUSSY (1862–1918)

MRS. FRANZ LIEBICH

Realising as he does the unlimited power of suggestion, possessed by the art of music and understanding in a very subtle degree its capability of giving a fleeting existence to immaterial, abstract ideas he has invariably chosen delicate, intangible subjects and flights of fancy which gain pre-eminently an added and prolonged eloquence in music. To those who would attempt to define the unknowable, and who would limit the arts to precise expression or imitation of what they call realities, Debussy's choice of poets, his association of ideas in music, even his Nature studies and impressions, must seem antagonistic and incomprehensible. He is averse to binding music down to the exact reproduction of set programmes, but has rather chosen to amplify and expand evanescent, shadowy thoughts—to distil their essence and then capture and protract it in sound. . . .

'L'Après-Midi d'un Faune' is an encomium in verse of the imperishable dominion of fancy and dream and of the artist's power to evolve a world of his own from his artistic creations. These subjective thoughts are given an archaic setting and are made objective in the illusions of a mythological faun. A cursory glance at this extremely difficult symbolic poem, the conventional association of ideas connecting a faun with antics, Debussy's unusual harmonies and progressions, and prejudiced criticisms consigning music and poem to the void and the inane were, of necessity, in the natural order of events. . . .

A veil of palpitating heat seems to be suffused over the composition, and corresponds to the glow of Eastern sunlight in the poem, and also to the remote, visionary nature of the poet's imagery and fancies. The tone poem also recalls the golden noon of an idyll of Theocritus. All through the piece the composer preserves this feeling of elusiveness, of mirage: he attains it by the use of delicate unusual harmonies and by the silvery, web-like tracery of the phrases. The frequent use of the scale of whole tones and the unresolved dissonances produce a distinct charm of their own. The chords are of exceeding richness and present a depth of glowing colour. The interspersed solos for violin, oboe, clarinet, cor anglais, resemble dainty broidery, and portray intimately the ramifications of doubt and longing in the faun's mind, which he likens to a multitude of branches with slender pointed sprays and sprigs.

Claude Achille Debussy, 1908

No composer of eminence, with the possible exception of Berlioz, has ever possessed so little true harmonic sense as Debussy. This may seem to some a mere paradox, but a moment's reflection will show that it is an actual truth. Few indeed among modern composers have actually progressed further than the earliest tentative experiments of medieval musicians; the principle on which their harmonic writing is based is, almost without exception, nothing but that of organum and its offspring 'Faux bourdon'—for it obviously makes little difference if seconds, sevenths, and ninths are thrown in with, or instead of, mere thirds and sixths. Debussy often uses harmony as Bach used instrumental colour in his writing for orchestra; whole passages and sometimes even whole pieces such as the 'Voiles' from the first book of Preludes are harmonised almost throughout on one single chord, and 'Pelleas' has with justice been called 'the land of ninths'. Indeed, in his harmony, Debussy is as curiously limited, monotonous, and restricted as in his melody.

His rhythms too are singularly lifeless and torpid as a general rule, and this fault is generally admitted by his greatest admirers; such exceptions as there are in his work, like 'Fêtes' and the finale of 'Iberia', strike one as being either not altogether successful or not particularly characteristic of the composer. Debussy lacks entirely the leaping pulse and vitality which constitute Strauss' greatest asset, and even the factitious vitality and machine-like energy of Stravinsky.

In short, it cannot be too emphatically insisted upon that the objectively musical interest of Debussy's music is almost as slender and tenuous as Hans Andersen's 'Emperor's Clothes'. He consistently sacrificed every constituent element of musical language to the expression of a particularly restricted order of sensations and emotions. He achieved his purpose by means of a narrowing and not a broadening of artistic scope. The fact remains, however, that he did in many works achieve it, and ultimately nothing else matters very much, provided always that what he has to say was worth saying. And on the whole one can safely say that it was; the world would be the poorer without such works as the 'Nocturnes', 'L'Après-Midi', the string quartet, 'La Mer', and a small handful of songs and piano pieces.

A Survey of Contemporary Music, 1924

ON DELIUS (1862–1934)

PHILIP HESELTINE

Anyone who has ever heard a work of Delius will know that his chief power lies in his extraordinary harmonic resources. One might almost say that the CHORD is to him what the NOTE was to the polyphonic composers, and that the melodic LINE is always seen in a higher dimensional aspect, so to speak, of changing chords. Yet Delius has no harmonic system which can be defined and analysed as readily as those of Debussy or Scriabin. His range of expression is infinitely wider than theirs and his limitations far less apparent. Harmony with Delius has always been more of an instinct than an accomplishment and, although his chromaticism is not radically of a different order from that of Wagner and Chopin, it would not be altogether true or just to say that it was derived and developed from the study of these two masters. Delius' harmony lies just within the boundaries of tonality; but it never crosses them—in the sense in which we regard the later works of Schonberg as lying definitely beyond them. The principle of modulation, though not discarded, is pushed to the farthest extremity of chromatic licence, and it is the continual shifting of the tonal centres that gives his music its elusiveness and that peculiar quality of reticence which imparts to every phrase a suggestiveness and a hidden meaning that is never actually uttered. Polyphony with Delius is not the CAUSE of the harmony as it is in true contrapuntal writing, but its apparent effect. Harmonic variation takes the place of what one may call the usual linear thematic development, counterpoints appear as decorative comments upon, rather than as integral factors of, the harmonic structure—and the very melody of a passage is often obviously dependent upon and conditioned by its harmonic background. . . .

As Beethoven is the morning and Wagner the high noon, so Delius is the sunset of that great period of music which is called Romantic. And there is a spiritual image in this historical superscription. The art of Delius belongs to the evening of a great period. It has its roots upon the descending arc of life; it is cadent but not decadent. Its image is rather to be seen in the rich colours of the sunset fires than in the cool dim greys of twilight from which all fire and brightness has faded away. But it is neighbour to night: it looks before and after, seeing the day that is past mirrored upon the darkness that is approaching.

Frederick Delius, 1923

SIR GEORGE DYSON

It is said that we are too stupid or too inept to understand Delius; that he is better appreciated abroad. This may be so, though if the number of performances of his works given on the continent be divided by the number of orchestras and choruses available, not to mention the number of opera houses, England may not emerge from the comparison so incorrigible a sinner as might at first sight appear. We are certainly no worse than Paris, to say the least. No, the present reputation of Delius is a phenomenon not of our locality but of our time. How far has he himself contributed to it? He is not aggressively an innovator, yet he distinctly belongs to the modern school.

He seems indeed to represent, among the many crudities and exuberances of experiment, that ideal mean which should appeal to a similar level of public appreciation. Where lies the fault?

In the first place, Delius has written little or nothing for the piano, or for those small combinations of instruments which are a very potent factor in the contemporary dissemination of music. There are admirable piano arrangements of most of his works, but they have to be read or played with imagination. His peculiar values, his essentially orchestral economy, suffer greatly when divorced from their proper medium. He also makes formidable demands on the technique of performance, on the understanding and on the aesthetic sensibility of listener and performer alike. If one is not alert enough to listen, Delius will not periodically surprise one into wakefulness. He has no facile tricks, no seductive emotionalism, no nervous intoxication to offer. Neither is he telling a raw tale, nor cracking jokes. He is not overcome with a sense of his own technical capacity. All is not grist to his mill. There are many things now fashionable which he does not, nor will not say. Complaint is sometimes made that there is so little one can carry away, so to speak, from Delius. But how much can one carry away, in this sense, from an unfamiliar work by Bach? Delius has a melodic gift, but it is usually rhapsodic. He has an amazing harmonic instinct, but it is diffused. He does not distil his thought into a single line, nor into a striking passage. Delius is concerned primarily with texture, just as Bach was. It is a sustained atmosphere that he seeks, and texture is his approach to it. His method is harmonic; Bach's was contrapuntal. But however fundamental this divergence may be technically, and however much one may doubt whether, so long as we think and play our parts horizontally, the more disparate impressions of harmony can hope to rival the sustained perfection of melodic counterpoint, this does not alter the fact that texture as such has aesthetic values of its own which may be derived neither from those of the single line nor yet from the reflected light of powerful harmonic themes. We do not demand from Bach the values either of Mozart or of Wagner. Delius learnt his art away from the schools, away from the fashions of his day. His diction has in it a tinge of aloofness, even of vagueness, which to some temperaments is a real difficulty. But he has at least one quality which is perhaps above all others scarce in our time; he has a deep, a quiet, and an intrinsic sense of beauty. Is it this that our generation has lost or is losing? His idylls 'On hearing the first cuckoo in Spring' and 'Summer night on the river', and a dozen other movements of tranquil yet enchanted fantasy, were not born of the tumult of to-day. Like the idyll of Siegfried, they must be tasted without passion, without impatience. Delius is not of the market-place. So homogeneous is he that it is sometimes hard to tell where folk-song ends and Delius begins. It is hard to tell where is melody and where harmony. His is often a rhapsodic art, but still more is it at times an art of pure contemplation. And an art of pure contemplation is not easy to practise in this twentieth century of ours. *The New Music,* 1924

EDWIN EVANS

Delius' music needs for its true appreciation a greater degree of passive acceptance than that of any other great composer. The analytical faculty must be given a holiday, or it will become entangled in labyrinthine processes which will dull the emotional and sensuous receptivity. There is only one way to enjoy Delius' music, and that is to let it float past you as a dream-vision of ineffable beauty, the source of which lies in some indefinable region beyond the world of logic and reason; the moment you bring reason to bear upon it the vision begins to fade. . . .

In what, then, does this beauty exist? The technical equipment by which it is accomplished consists of an extraordinary intuitional command of harmonic colouring which, without method, achieves a thousand and one shades which method could not have achieved; a natural aptitude for what might be called plastic variations, that is to say, variation which derives not so much from melodic or harmonic modifications as from a kind of re-shaping of the sonorous mass; and a ready invention of arabesque. Delius was not a great melodist, nor yet a musical architect—two of the attributes with which other composers have attained to greatness. He developed in himself something that was neither one nor the other, but of which he made an expressive medium capable of the most subtle shades of emotional meaning. It is this that makes him, of all composers, modern or historical, the most difficult to describe in language. One cannot explain such subtlety in words. One can only say 'Go and hear it', and if the person to whom you offer that advice does not hear what you have heard, you have no remedy.

Chesterian, Sept.–Oct., 1934

BERNARD VAN DIEREN

The most curious point . . . is that, however much he tried to escape from England and English influences, the one being insular and the other stifling, he could not hide the essential Englishness of his being. Whether he knew it, or whether he wished it, is of little importance. What matters is that with every succeeding work he became more characteristically English. All the talented composers in England during the last few centuries had been trying to be very German or very Italian, or very international. Most of them had succeeded in being merely epigonic, sycophantic, and insignificant. The greatest talents among Englishmen of Delius' generation represented two classes. Some of them were, according to the old traditions, very Irish, or very Welsh, or very Scotch; others were more cosmopolitan than anyone had ever been before. Delius, who had no direct interest in either school, and who gave German and French and Scandinavian titles to his works, became by the virtue of his peculiar genius the most representatively English of them all. He might sing the praises of red wine, of yellow vermouth, of green absinthe: every English ear would at once recognise the colours of the ox's blood, the cowslip, and the clover, and the praise of 'good ale and old'. He might dress his fairies in Nordic garb; one knew at once that they belonged to the glades of Windsor. And wherever, by outlandish titles and texts, by hints and asseverations, he asks us to follow him, we find ourselves back with him in the lanes and the fields of England. Shelley, Wordsworth, and Keats could not call forth the magic of the English landscape and the fullness of English life with greater certitude than Delius' music does.

He did not put folksong embroideries over his musical texture. No heigho's and bosun's mate business. He let no pudding get cold in Ludlow, and he did not kneel with Salvationists in London slums. But, although his 'Summer Night' may have been experienced on a Norwegian river, the authentic atmosphere of English waters enfolds it. His 'Sea Drift' may have been inspired by the transatlantic scene, but every English heart will recognize the waves that beat against the rocks of the Western coasts. His 'Summer Garden' may have been conceived in the Ile de France; only an English garden could have the shimmering loveliness we recapture there. And no 'First Cuckoo' ever called in a more purely English spring than the one Delius heard. Since the golden period of English music there has never been a composer who was so completely, and in the best and truest sense, national.

Monthly Musical Record, July–August, 1934

ON SIBELIUS (1865–)

J. H. ELLIOT

The moods of the music are not painted by arbitrary means or expressed in classified symbols: they are implicit in the substance, the very conception, of the music's aesthetic. The despair and desolation of the wonderful fourth Symphony hang in the air like tangible things: they do not agitate the personal feelings after the manner of Tschaikowsky's 'Pathetic', with its comparatively crude (albeit sincere and forceful) expression of individual sorrow and hopelessness. Sibelius attains to a level of emotional implication more profound, more nearly objective. His music, moreover, lives on one plane, and retains a unity of expression despite its multifarious changes of spirit. Like Wagner, who imposed a distinctive atmosphere upon each successive work without departing from his own intensely personal mode of speech, Sibelius gives each Symphony an individual character while sustaining the whole compass of his art upon a level that is remote, noble, and aloof.

It is in the matter of formal procedure that Sibelius most obviously departs from precedent. Where other aspects of his music are concerned, we know, without precisely recognising its nature, that a deep originality lies at the root. Even his scoring, which is supremely effective, is unique in character and at one with the austerity of his whole artistic outlook. Where form is concerned, however, one may immediately discern the radical nature of the rift. Sibelius is totally unconcerned with anything cut-and-dried in the way of formal progress. If an exposition is made, the matter has been dealt with; why should one develop, elaborating a speech already uttered, still less recapitulate? This seems to be his attitude to conventional symphonic form. His own symphonies are extraordinarily concentrated; the traditional machinery—which, needless to say, has been justified only by the vitality with which genius has endowed it—is useless for his own peculiar purpose. Nor can its absence be counted against him for unrighteousness. The lack of formal thematic development never results in a weakness of texture, as it so often does in such cases as Meyerbeer and Berlioz; the abandonment of the principles of sonata-form, where Sibelius is concerned, does not mean that the music straggles and sprawls, spreading itself indefinitely in all directions. He has destroyed, but only to re-erect.

As I conceive it, there is a positive formal principle in all the symphonic music of Sibelius, none the less potent because it is removed from conventional terms—and, indeed, changeable in its conditions. The form of a Sibelius symphony cannot be forecast. It is useless to stand by with labels marked 'first subject', 'second subject', and so forth, with a few blanks for subsidiary matter. The official marker is given small excuse for dipping his brush into the paste. The form arises from the content in a different way from that of works cast in the classical mould or palpable derivations from it.

'Jean Sibelius: A Modern Enigma',
Chesterian, Jan.–Feb., 1931

CONSTANT LAMBERT

In Sibelius . . . we have the first great composer since Beethoven whose mind thinks naturally in terms of symphonic form. Coming at the end of the romantic movement, he is as far removed from the apex of the romantic past as Beethoven was from its future. His symphonies, then, though subjective in mood, are free from the tautological emotional repetitions of romantic music cast in the classic mould. Though their grim colouring clearly owes much to the composer's nationality and surroundings there is nothing in them that can be considered a folk song. Therefore, without being eclectic they address an international audience and are free from the conflict between local colour and construction which is to be observed in the Russian school. Finally, Sibelius is the one important figure of our times who has not been influenced by the Impressionist revolution—even 'The Oceanides', though pointillist in orchestration and superficially Impressionist in form reveals on close analysis a construction as firmly knit as any of the symphonies. He has concentrated on the integration of form and has not wasted his energies on the disintegration of colour.

This formal strength explains why, unlike all other composers, who belong equally to the pre-war and post-war periods of modern music, Sibelius' work does not split itself into two periods, and shows no sign of the definite reaction that we associate with the last ten years. One soon reaches the end to the possible dissection of technique and elaboration of vocabulary. This end was reached for all practical purposes in 1913, and since then the revolutionary composers having pulled the clock to pieces and being mentally incapable of putting it together again have taken to arranging the wheels and levers in neat little patterns.

Formalism is only the complementary reaction to formlessness, and montage follows naturally enough on disruption. But a sense of musical form, the power not only to arrange sounds tastefully but to think in them vitally, is a living and generative force which reaches no such dead end, and Sibelius' symphonies in consequence show a steady and logical process both formally and emotionally. The Olympian calm of No. 7 may seem in contrast to the bitter and tragic quality of No. 4 but technically speaking it is the logical result of the process of concentration and integration that is to be observed from the second symphony onwards.

Music Ho! 1934

ON ROUSSEL (1869–1937)

EDMUND RUBBRA

There seems to be in most countries a blind spot in musical appreciation which leads to an inability to recognize certain significant figures of other nationalities, although recognition is granted to others whose claim may be far less. Thus one may search Parisian concert programmes in vain for the appearance of Delius' name, in spite of the fact that this composer long ago adopted France as his home. Similarly, Roussel's works seldom figure in English programmes. This neglect is curious, because Roussel, who in many ways departs from traditional French thought, has a pronounced liking for the English language; he has often chosen English words for his songs, and for his setting of Psalm 80 he deliberately used the English Biblical version.

Certain it is that Albert Roussel is one of the strongest of the French composers writing to-day. Each new work of his shows a fresh exploration: not, however, as in the case of Stravinsky, an exploration of other and older styles, alien in spirit to his real musical nature, but an exploration into further and finer fields along paths already indicated in his earlier works. In other words, his music shows a consistent evolution, and however far removed in spirit his later compositions may be from the earlier, yet one can always see the same mind at work, a mind that has steadily enlarged its scope of expression.

This evolution has taken the form of a gradual dispensing with external nature as the starting-point of inspiration. French composers seem particularly sensitive to the influences of environment, and have thereby obtained some of their richest inspirations (Couperin and Debussy are two whose names come to mind), but Albert Roussel, although he too started from this more objective side of his art, has, in his later music, sought his inspiration more and more in his own being. His later works, although they have lost the pictorial element so skilfully and beautifully used in his First Symphony ('Le poème de la forêt,' 1904–1906) have become far deeper in musical expression, and are to be judged as abstract shape and sound, with only a musical-emotional significance. Roussel himself has said 'What I would wish to realize is a music completely satisfying in itself, divorced from all picturesque and descriptive elements, and far from any localization in space.' And again, 'Art should change like the seasons of Nature, and be ever renewed.'

His music is deeply thoughtful. He refrains from any display of that superficial brilliance into which a great command of technique has tempted many a musician. Every element that is not necessary to a vivid presentation of an idea is eliminated, and this gives to his music a starkness not readily associated with French music. Even Ravel's pungencies have their mitigations, but the cacophony of Roussel's music remains unrelieved by any softening overtones. This almost continual cacophony, however, is no obstacle to one's enjoyment of the music, because of the tremendous, almost primitive, rhythmic drive behind the sound. One can accept almost anything in the way of sound-combinations if the rhythm is vital. (Is the lack of this what ails the Schonberg school?) Moreover, Roussel's harmonies are logical constructions from that corner stone of all Western music, the triad. Strange shapes the chords may sometimes assume, but their parentage is never doubtful.

Monthly Musical Record, Dec., 1932

W. H. MELLERS

The key to the technique of Roussel's late work is by way of what M. Hoérée calls its 'polymodality'. Most types of defective scales are to be found in hindoo music, the most modally fecund, and the scales of hindoo music are almost all exploited in 'Padmavati'. Greek modes are used in 'La Naissance de la Lyre', the pentatonic scales of Chinese music in 'A un jeune gentilhomme' and *passim*. But to catalogue the various modes employed by Roussel is futile, and, moreover, impossible, since like Fauré, Roussel evolved his idiom quite spontaneously and it is not true to say that modalism influenced the shape of his melodies but rather that the shape of his melodies—and behind that the mould of his sensibility—precisely determined their modality. He seldom writes melodies on one specific mode, but his melodic thinking tends towards modality in the way in which his tunes oscillate round a fixed point, generating other related figurations (the basses of 'Padmavati' by this process vitalize the whole score despite their apparent immobility; and *cf.*, the 'Danse des Nymphes' from 'La Naissance' and the 'Sarabande' from the Suite in F); in the undulating contour of the melodies, their abrupt leaps particularly of sixths and sevenths), their irregular accentuation, their sinewy chromaticism, and above all in their perpetual modulations and tonal instability.

Roussel's conception of his art is essentially melodic, rather than thematic. He works on a principle of melodic evolution by modal alteration, independent of the customary procedures of repetition, transcription, and development. This trick of incessant transition from one mode to another by means of 'modes altérés' is a distinctive feature of his principle of modulation and hence of his harmony.

(The major scale with the flattened sixth is used in, for instance, the second Violin Sonata, and the minor scale with the augmented fourth *passim*, that is, the tritone, in the later work, has become as much a melodic as a harmonic idiosyncrasy). All this means of course, that Roussel's phrases tend to be of exceptional length and sustained power. In this respect his technique resembles Fauré's in a more 'advanced' form. Though his melodies are tonally much freer than Fauré's they too are never

Atonal since even his most complex departures from diatonicism can be referred back to some scale system or chordal structure. . . .

I think it is significant that though his language was universally recognized as an accomplishment utterly dependent of and comparable in importance with, the various revolutions of the most influential of modern composers—Stravinsky, Schönberg, and Hindemith—this language has had absolutely no influence on practising musicians—and this despite the fact that young composers looked to him, as a commanding personality, for guidance. (Satie took a course of strict counterpoint under Roussel but if there is any question of influence involved here it is . . . the pupil who influenced the master. And it is not as surprising as it superficially appears that the Parisian-American, completely anti-traditional revolutionary Edgar Varese, should have been among Roussel's pupils). In his way, Roussel was as lonely a figure in his generation as Sibelius.

'The Composer and Civilization',
Scrutiny, Sept., 1938

ON VAUGHAN WILLIAMS (1872–   )

EDWIN EVANS

As a craftsman he is intensely practical, sometimes hampered by a lack of dexterity, but not in the least disposed to turn to theory for assistance. In that, his compositions are an accurate reflection of himself, as they are in many other traits which are easily recognised by those who have the privilege of his acquaintance. Among them is economy of speech. He expresses himself without circumlocution, and seldom speaks unless he has something definite to say. This does not restrict him to brevity in form, as on a great subject there is always much to be said. But he dispenses willingly with what may be called the argumentative resources of music, and rarely troubles to expend much labour upon establishing the connection between successive ideas whose relation to each other is, in his mind, sufficiently clear. This results sometimes in a seeming disjointedness analogous to conversation between friends who understand each other too well to be needlessly explicit. The same applies to a certain ungainliness which sometimes affects his musical speech. It is the exact opposite of the carelessness of style which in some composers results from volubility, and it corresponds to the speech of one whose power of thought is not matched by his power of words. Another writer has aptly described his music as 'sane in conception, weighty in utterance, and blunt in expression'. That again proves its intimate relation to his personality, for his outlook upon life is eminently sane and free from cant: the things that interest him are those things which are most worthy of interest and what he has to say about them is generally blunt and to the point. If the measure of all music is its expressive power, then the music of Vaughan Williams must be accounted great, for it is a perfect expression of the man even in its occasional failure to find polished expression for what is in his mind—which by no means results in failure to make himself understood. He would wear the honour with an ill grace.

Musical Times, April, 1920

H. C. COLLES

I first came across Vaughan Williams as a student of the Royal College of Music in the 'nineties, and I seem to remember that no one expected wonderful things from him. His music made no impression comparable to that of Coleridge-Taylor or W. Y. Hurlstone, who belonged more or less to his generation.

Chesterian, Feb., 1922

E. C. ROSE

Vaughan Williams has every reason to be the happiest of modern composers. His music, original and novel as it is, bears in itself such an appeal to all classes of his countrymen as has not been made since the days of Byrd and Gibbons; an appeal not based on the ground of contemporary music (though couched often enough in modern terms), but reaching back to a broader social basis, an older and commoner idiom, a speech at once simpler and more subtle. The 'Dream of Gerontius' and the 'Enigma Variations' are the work of a great genius, not necessarily of an Englishman; but the 'Pastoral' and the 'London' Symphonies are English in the sense that 'Tess' and the 'Return of the Native' are English: they have Hardy's grand simplicity of line, and that intense humanity which is so much the more universal because it is so completely local. Modern music and modern art are full of people marching out of dolls' houses into a great doll's world; these two English stay-at-homes have been farthest and seen most. Had Hardy abandoned 'Tess' and started talking about the Rustic Problem, he would have ceased to be universal, he would have become provincial. Because Vaughan Williams has neglected the idioms of Stravinsky and Ravel for an ancient and commoner speech, he has achieved, after due effort, a method of expression as English as the Great Bible. What is perhaps more important, he has shown that it is possible for a man to speak naturally, and even trivially, in a world perpetually at an artificial strain; where science confronts expressionist art, Capital confronts Labour, and everyone seems suffering from some cosmic dichotomy as rigid as the division of their hours in work and play. There is the art-song and the folk-song artist and audience, and a host of artificial distinctions, amongst which (as Mr. Gill pointed out in his recent illuminating essay 'The Church and Art') one of the most pernicious is the conception of

Art produced by a special kind of superior person. Vaughan Williams cuts across all this: his art-songs are folk-songs, and I have never met an artist who was a more persevering audience, or who more consistently refuses to be edged on to the Superior Person's pedestal for his own and everybody else's convenience. He has burrowed under the ant hill of our perplexities and come up farther on; and if the field he has tunnelled to is considerably like a very much older field, perhaps it is because Merry England is wider than we had imagined.

Sackbut, July, 1926

A. E. F. DICKINSON

First, he is one of the most downright composers that ever lived. At every stage of his work he has shown his determination to speak plainly, in both senses of the word, and to speak about something fundamental. He chose London and the country, or Walt Whitman and the Bible, as his 'subjects', because he felt he could sincerely concentrate upon them all the vital experience at his command. His continual revision of past work is the sign, not of a low standard of past achievement, but of an increasing determination to know himself—which, after all, is the chief business of living. He has thus, in general, not only meant what he said, but also said what he meant. The absence in his music of every form of rhetorical address, of all those 'effects' which are really so monotonously ineffective, is the expression not of incompetence but of the belief that every individual conception must have its own unique presentation. He has his mannerisms, but they never distract the listener from the essence of what he has to say.

Secondly, he speaks (whether he likes it or not) to the twentieth century. Purposive address is an essential quality of art. It is an address to an ideal audience, not to any actual audience, nor, again, to the class of audience which an outworn and out-of-date phrase stigmatizes as 'the gallery'. But if it is true, as a thoughtful writer has maintained, that 'the passion of the artist is dimmed by the leagues and the years', then it is for the ideal audience of the present that Vaughan Williams's music is most clearly meant. The present age, rudely shaken out of its complacent self by the War, and by all the hidden forces let loose by the War and now at large, is an age of fierce and purposeless sensationalism, but also of fierce and purposive idealism. And I feel, though I cannot prove, that Vaughan Williams's music is likely to make a special appeal to the men and women of fierce ideals, to the explorers, to the people whose experience in the last ten or twelve years has taught them the grave danger of playing for safety, whether in art or in the ordinary walks of life. Moreover, for those who, reacting from the crude sensationalism of the day, are trying to refit their minds for the more permanent ecstasies of the emotions felt, or at any rate crystallized, in tranquillity—for those Vaughan Williams can present, with the freshness of a vital experience, the eternal beauty of nature, ('The Pastoral Symphony' and 'The Lark Ascending'), or the eternal romance of spiritual adventure ('Toward the Unknown Region', 'A Sea Symphony', 'The Shepherds of the Delectable Mountains', 'Sancta Civitas'), or the outlook which will give new life to common things ('On Wenlock Edge', 'Hugh the Drover', and, technically, the Mass in G minor). No doubt, some people will prefer Elgar or Holst for spiritual adventure, Delius or Bax for quiet beauty, Ireland for homely strains. Of all living composers, however, Vaughan Williams appears to me to provide the most consistently what is solid and refreshing.

An Introduction to the Music of Vaughan Williams, 1928

REV. BASIL MAINE

Disciple. I cannot think that my difficulty in approaching the music of Sibelius is altogether due to the fact that he is a foreign composer, for, truth to tell, I sometimes have that same difficulty in appreciating Vaughan Williams.

Epictetus. Ah! That is a mind which has never been easy to know.

D. His 'Pastoral Symphony' and 'Tallis Fantasia' are comparatively simple matters, and I love both works. But when it comes to such works as the 'Concerto Accademico', the 'Benedicite', and the 'Three Choral Hymns' I find the music forbidding. As for the Pianoforte Concerto and the Fourth Symphony, never in my life shall I learn to love either of these works.

E. I should say that in the slow movement of the 'Concerto Accademico' the essence of the man's mind is to be perceived, its sensitiveness, depth, ruggedness, above all, unworldliness. In the 'Benedicite' and the 'Choral Hymns' it is more starkly revealed. I can understand that you find these forbidding. The adorning details of the 'Benedicite' do not soften but emphasize the straight, strong lines which run through the texture. But I cannot agree that the 'Choral Hymns' are forbidding, unless you are going to rule out from music everything of an austere nature. Stern, yet resourceful, these praising hymns are, as is so much of Vaughan Williams' sacred music.

D. My objection is not that these works are austere, but that they are puzzling.

E. Puzzling? That is a description I should have reserved for the Pianoforte Concerto and the Fourth Symphony. To a certain extent I share your perplexity there. Certainly the Concerto is like no other written for the keyboard. In the sense that in these two works Vaughan Williams has moved so far as to be temporarily out of his followers' sight, they may be taken as representative of a phase comparable with what is conveniently called Beethoven's 'third period'. But we have yet to learn whether it is a directly forward move or not. My own suspicion is that the spiritual stress of present-day life has driven this always sensitive composer down a side-track.

D. You do not see my problem, then, in coming to grips with a work like the Fourth Symphony?

E. I see it, yes; for my own first impression of the music was that it was so pungent in its statements, so spare in its development of these, that it apparently lacked important parts of speech. In brief, the logic was too closely set forth to be immediately comprehensible.

D. Sibelius' trouble again.

E. There is a certain similarity between the method of Vaughan Williams's Fourth Symphony and Sibelius' Fourth. Only you are wrong to speak of Sibelius' trouble. It is for the listener to trouble himself if he wishes to follow the close logic of Sibelius. This applies equally to Vaughan Williams.

D. You said just now that Vaughan Williams's mind has never been easy to know. Perhaps I didn't gather all that you meant by that.

E. I mean that many of his works require us to look past mannerisms and an occasional roughness of his technique, in order to appraise their peculiar imaginative quality. Even in the case of the Fourth Symphony I find that hearing it later, I was appreciably nearer to an understanding; and I was helped, I confess, by an appreciation written by an American critic.

D. That critic, probably, was afforded a direct approach to the work by the fact that he was unaffected by the environment of English music.

E. Granted.

D. But what did you subsequently perceive in this Symphony, which I find so unlovable?

E. I perceived a spirit grappling with an essentially

personal problem. I also perceived the working of a most original and forceful mind.   *New Paths in Music*, 1940

ON HOLST (1874–1934)

EDWIN EVANS

To me he appears more of an idealist without ideals —far too practical to encumber his philosophy with imagined ideals, but at the same time so keyed as to be an idealist without them, serving a high purpose but always less conscious of its height than of the demands of its service. I find it difficult to imagine him carried away by any elation other than that of the artist content with his work. And here begins an apparent paradox, for, just as vagueness and diffidence are often associated with a morbid degree of self-criticism, one might imagine this calm self-possession to reflect a lack of it. But precisely because Holst knows his purpose so well he is a severe judge of the degree in which he has achieved it. Concerning a recent work, of which little has been heard, he confessed to me that he had been in some doubt whether it was music or not, and was gradually inclining to the latter view. But I have preserved a card which came with a newly printed score, 'Hope you will like it, I'm afraid I do'. There speaks, not the man who is sometimes querulously dissatisfied with his work because it does not fulfil an aspiration which is probably nebulous to himself, but the man who knows his task, is the best judge whether he has performed it well or ill, and at the same time sufficiently objective to be able to deliver either verdict without any disturbance of equilibrium. That this calm sense of values should be associated with an outward manner suggesting diffidence to the point of timidity is only the obverse aspect of the same apparent paradox and equally explicable.

The Dominant, April, 1928

BERNARD VAN DIEREN

One thing which seems astonishing is that Holst, with his practical experience of the orchestra, and living in full activity during the period when, all over Europe, composers' dearest ambition was to write instrumentally characteristic 'symphonic poems', has in spite of his craving for local colour—exotic and otherwise—never produced anything startling or even at all brilliant in orchestral writing. The explanation would seem to be that his mental processes are apt to seek well-worn grooves; the idea which at its inception possessed originality is during the subsequent phases forced into some standard shape. This inevitably results when the conventionalizing prejudices of timid and conforming mind are not neutralized by the ruthless ardour of creative urge. Where the balance might be uncertain, any threatening spiritual rebellion is crushed by the obsessing fear of offending the ant-heap traditions of the herd. Docility is rewarded with benevolence. It may mean professional ostracism, and perdition to the chances of otherwise negotiable music, if a writer with an acknowledged training places the flutes an octave below the horns. Should the occasion present itself, a discreet composer would think so many times before committing a similar outrage against instrumental morals that he would never reach the conclusion that the risk might be justifiable. But this is the state of mind that creates needles' eyes all around for a man who, even if he does not happen to be a full-sized camel, cannot successfully persuade himself that it would be better to be one than to seem to be one.

The Dominant, Dec., 1928

RICHARD CAPELL

I have heard it said that Holst's music 'lacks mystery', what was meant being that there is nothing cryptic about it. For it remains, in spite of the aestheticians, a mystery why a concatenation of notes should repeatedly charm, exhilarate, or move the mind, which is what many of Holst's works do not fail to do in a good number of us. It is true that there is nothing or little hidden in this music. There are no twilight scenes in which more and more is revealed as the eye accustoms itself. This music either imposes itself or does not; it does not grow on one. But then surely there are cities one likes at once and never tires of; persons one falls in love with at first sight; and great music in the same case as Holst's. If music can so win a listener as—to take the smallest example—Holst's 'Four Medieval Songs' did at Miss Henschel's first performance (in that Byzantine crypt somewhere behind Westminster Abbey), surely nothing more need be asked of it.

Can a thorough-going admirer put down briefly the reasons of his faith? Well, there is the splendid technical confidence of the man who uses the many instruments of his craft so often audaciously but, as the upshot always proves, knowledgeably and justly. And—since there is really no separating the technics and the spirit of a work of art—at the same time his spiritual confidence. This music can stride. It is not hedged round with doubts It tells, often, in its great dancing movements, of the pride and pleasure of sheer living—that very proper pleasure and pride which we all know it to be perverse to deny.

While inclined to fight shy of the sentimental chord (as who should say that it has been struck too often and too long), so brave and little self-conscious is it that it never thinks of hesitating to sing a song in public. This music is so well-bred as to be always natural. It can pray simply and naturally. That must be an enviable gift.

In a distracted age it manages to be an optimistic music. Perhaps a pessimistic artist is a contradiction of terms. How should a creator not believe in life? 'Everything has been said—it only remains to refine on the manner.' This, or words to that effect, was said to me not long after the war by two composers, both young and clever as possible. Holst cannot be thought of as passing any such remark. The creator knows that nothing, so far as he is concerned and is a creator, has been said before, since what is to be said can only be himself. It happens that cleverness is very prevalent, much more so than creativeness.

Holst has made this very clear in his music of the last twenty-one years. He is your friend or not, according to your taste. Perhaps your friend must be a more subtle or a more sensuous mind. But that the Holstian self of this great mass of work is a musician and a man is plainly impossible to deny.

The language of his art, his idiom, has sharp references to the music of the past and sharp divergencies from it. Such references are the means of the new artist's communicating with his audience, and they also give the measure of the divergencies. The degree of the sharpness of the references indicates the intended breadth of the artist's appeal—whether it is to a knowing few or generally to his fellow-men. Holst feels nothing of the typical modern artist's aversion from fellow-men in any numbers; but he might possibly be intimidated in a smart studio. The aesthetes are left cold by his music, so it is said. Diaghileff has never asked him for a ballet.

The Dominant, Dec., 1928

ON SCHÖNBERG (1874–   )

ROLLO H. MYERS

The baffling element in his music is not so much the harmonic audacities in the parts as the apparent incoherence of the whole.

Not only is his language strange; we are at a loss to understand what feelings move him to employ it, and what kind of effect he hopes to produce upon our minds. In other words, his aesthetic ideal is obscure. He is clearly not aiming at sensuous beauty, at 'sound for sound's sake'. Not a single Schönbergian discord appears to have been chosen for the sake of its sonority. . . .

. . . the general aims of the composer appear to be less obscure than some of his technical processes. A piece of music finishes where it might equally well have begun; one dissonance succeeds another apparently for no particular reason; the 'mood' even of this music is frequently elusive and baffles definition. Add to these features a disconcerting lack of rhythmical interest, and all that can be said on the negative side has now been said.

But if this were all, no musician need bother his head about Schönberg any more than he bothers about the latest popular composer of musical comedies or about the constitution of the board of examiners for the degree of Mus. Doc. in the University of X. Every serious musician however, knows that this is not all, and that Arnold Schönberg cannot be dismissed in a few words either as a nonentity or as a crazy eccentric. There is something in his music which commands attention. It is so obviously serious, so carefully contrived, so technically accomplished, that one instinctively feels that if only one had the key to the composer's intentions it would all become as clear as day and that, moreover, one's curiosity would be richly rewarded.

In the case of 'Pierrot Lunaire' one is conscious that the work contains at least the elements of greatness; its effects are so sure and so convincing; the texture is so closely knit and of so level a quality, and the music so pregnant and concise that the listener is left with the feeling that he is in the presence of a real work of art, the author of which, though speaking in an unfamiliar idiom, yet has assuredly succeeded in achieving what he set out to do.

There is nothing tentative or uncertain about this

music. It goes straight to the point without any beating about the bush. Each number is as full of matter as an egg.

'Pierrot Lunaire,' *Chesterian*, April, 1922

CONSTANT LAMBERT

There is a strong flavour of the Black Mass about Schönberg. He has the complete lack of humour of the diabolist, while a glance at his earlier works indicates how devout a believer he once was. His later eccentricities are in direct ratio to his early conventionalities, just as the excesses of a revolution are in direct ratio to the previous oppression.

There is no composer whose early works, superficially examined, display so great a contrast to his later development. Debussy's early piano pieces and Bartok's early orchestral suites may seem conventional enough when compared to their more mature work, but they contain the seeds of their later efflorescence. But in Schönberg's early works such individuality as he had was completely stifled by the overbearing influence of German romanticism. There is always a temptation to be wise after the event and to detect in some innocent early work the flavour of a later masterpiece, but in Schönberg's case the smell that detaches itself from his early 'Lieder' is the familiar Teutonic aroma of stale pot-pourri prevented from leaving the room by the heavy curtains and double windows. These songs belong essentially to the nineties and in that, rather in any intrinsic merit, lies their interest for the student of Schönberg. The fin-de-siècle quality of these works is a constant factor in all Schönberg's music—at least up to the war—and the more advanced and revolutionary his methods become, the greater is our sense of the spiritual conflict between his subjective and sentimental vision and his objective and mathematical technique.

If, while admitting the superficial contrast between

Schönberg's earlier and later works, we examine their technique in more detail, we find that Schönberg, although sabotaging the conventional tonal sense of German romanticism, has in many ways retained its general texture and rhythm. Although it may seem a far cry from Schumann's 'Frauenliebe und Leben' to Schönberg's nightmare 'Herzgewachse', there is no denying a certain resemblance in shape between Schönberg's melodies and those of the romanticists. The rhythm is the same and the placing of the wider intervals is the same. A typical Schönberg phrase bears far more resemblance to the preludes to the first act of 'Tristan' or the third act of 'Parsifal' than it does to the work of any more recent composer. It is this that makes so much of his music disturbing to listen to, and gives it a curious flavour of morbidity that reaches its climax in the operas.

Music does not strike us as abnormal unless at the same time it recalls the normal—as in Strauss' 'Salome' and 'Elektra'. We can listen to Bartok's 'Amazing Mandarin' without a qualm, for we accept the composer's statements directly without referring them back to conventional experience. We do not feel that we are listening to Liszt or Dvorak 'gone wrong'. But in many of Schönberg's transitional works we do emphatically feel that we are listening to Schumann and Wagner 'gone wrong'. To hear a performance of the 'Kammer Symphonie', for example, is as disquieting an experience as meeting a respected family friend in a state of half-maudlin, half-truculent intoxication. Even in 'Pierrot Lunaire', one of the masterpieces of our time, there is a slight touch of a 'Lieder' recital that has taken the wrong turning. Yet 'Pierrot Lunaire' undoubtedly owes its force to the curious conflict of outlook and method. It is like an explosive formed out of two elements that in themselves are anodyne, and only develop their disruptive power when mixed in precisely the right proportions. In many of the earlier works the emotional force has not received the definition given by the technique, while in too many of the later works the technique is unleavened by any emotional force.

Music Ho! 1934

ON RAVEL (1875–1937)

NORMAN DEMUTH

Ravel has always been considered a small master and this, with a certain amount of disparagement. Certainly, if we regard a 'Master' in the light of vast frescoes and symphonies, we cannot estimate him as in any way comparable with Beethoven, Berlioz, Brahms, Wagner, Elgar, or Sibelius. In his own country he could not be considered in the same category as d'Indy, Saint-Saens, Roussel, or Dukas—and for the same reason Debussy must also be excluded from the list of those who can be called 'great'. However, it may be argued that the French 'goût' does not run along these lines and that if a composer reflects the characteristics and temper of his own country in a faithful manner, then the substance of his music, provided that its quality is of an adequate sufficiency, may credit him with a kind of national greatness.

It has been said that pioneers very often miss greatness because they are unable to crystallize their ideas and bring them to a complete state of fruition. The ability to say something new which is worth saying at all is, surely, a proof of greatness—if, indeed, this search for the quality is worth while. It must be remembered that Ravel's most loved works were all written before 1918. 'Jeux d'eau' was composed in 1901, the Harp Septet in 1906, 'Gaspard de la Nuit' in 1908, 'Daphnis et Chloe' in 1909–1912. What other French music appeared round about that time? Was not Ravel as much ahead of his day as it is possible to imagine? These works are by now established. They said something new, and they still retain their freshness.

By reason of his early works and the influence they brought to bear on the general outlook of French composers of their immediate following, and the stamp imprinted on French music by them, Ravel may truly be said to be a candidate for greatness. The substance of them is rich. Let us admit that his orchestration is mostly effect and glitter; no one had thought of the particular effect and glitter before him. The harp glissandos, the adroit touches on the glockenspiel, the imposing sweeps of violin arpeggii, all these are Ravel himself. They are his hall-mark, his signature, and to decry them must be to decry Ravel himself.

On the piano he brought a romantic imagination to bear as fertile as that of Schumann, and while we may tire of the 'Sonatina' because every budding pianist has it thrust before him or her, we can never tire of the sombreness of 'Gaspard de la Nuit'—the eerie 'Le Gibet', the dazzling 'Scarbo'. It may be that the substance of 'Miroirs' is not profound, but there is a place in music for exquisite taste and judgment, for the picturesque, for romanticism separated from introspection. Why cannot it be acknowledged that Ravel had greatness in the very slenderness of his textures?

He has suffered at the hands of pianists who see in everything something that is not there. Ravel himself demanded a perfectly cool and even performance of the 'Pavane' and the 'Sonatina'; he was driven to fury when he heard pianists romanticising and sentimentalising them beyond recognition.

Everything he did, he did well. It is all so well organised, so completely 'apt'. The taste is as near perfection as can ever be attained. There are no loose ends or jagged corners. Polish and still more polish. If this element of polish and refinement is the characteristic of the French style and manner, then Ravel is the most consummate artist in music that France has ever produced.

'Daphnis et Chloe' is a work apart. Ravel himself thought of it as a fresco, a symphony. That it was composed for the theatre makes no difference except that probably he had the vision in front of him of a spectacle which one day would be actuality. If he were incapable of imagining an extended music, of producing thematic breadth, and mixing in a sense of colour, no amount of ambitious feelings could have brought this work and all it contains to completion, in the style we have it.

It is no use placing him against such figures as Tchaikovsky and Brahms, Saint-Saens or d'Indy, and measuring his stature against them. The first two viewed music from an angle of introspection, the second from one of academicism. Only one French composer has succeeded in combining tradition with his own national spirit and has formulated a style of his own and of no one else, and that was Albert Roussel. Ravel was not by nature 'symphonic', but that he could write symphonically when necessary he showed in 'Daphnis et Chloe': Later on he had an outburst of the grand manner—the principal subject of the Piano Concerto for the Left Hand, but this was a flash from which he recoiled.

There is a tendency to concentrate on the 'délicieux' aspect of his music. True, the Septet, the Quartet, the Sonatina, and to a very small extent, 'Tzigane' have this element to a marked degree; 'La Valse' is decried for its glitter and brilliance—but was it not designed for choreographic purposes? This justifies it from all viewpoints. Yet he showed considerable strength in 'Le Tombeau de Couperin' and vigour in the 'Chansons madecasses', to say nothing of the exquisite diatonic beauty of the slow movement in the Piano Concerto (for both hands). This slow movement is unique in music. It is far too simple to take its place in a Concerto, *per se*, yet completely in keeping with the spirit of the work as a whole. Nothing could be more simple, and nothing more typically FRENCH.

He suffers, still, from being coupled with Debussy, with whose music he had nothing in common. Debussy waited until the end of his career before he turned to abstract ('cold') music. Ravel produced it at several points in his life, culminating in the two Concertos. These Concertos have weaknesses as well as good points. It is easy to observe the frivolity and superficiality of the first and last movements of the two-handed Piano Concerto (although he wrote thus advisedly) and overlook the tenderness of the slow movement. It is equally easy to remark the commonplace jazz effects of the Left Hand Concerto, and pass by the dignity, opulence, breadth, and nobility of the principal subject. Ravel more than any composer offers loopholes, but his vulnerability is resilient. Every hole can be justified. Each one is Ravel himself, a genius, an artist of the first water, a mind refined and polished to its highest degree.

The music illustrates the man. Surrounded by 'knick-knacks', both genuine and spurious, dressed faultlessly, brisk and energetic, Ravel LIVED; he did not exist. The world was there for his enjoyment and in return he gave it his genius. He was generous, light-hearted and gregarious where his intimate friends were concerned—and no one ever caught him composing!

Some say that he could never have felt anything deeply because his music and his outward attitude to life were apparent to all comers. He was not one of those to put his heart on his sleeve, and he did not consider his innermost feelings of any interest to anyone except himself. To his friends he was just 'Ravel', and his music has a humanity about it with which no basically elusive and aloof composer could ever have endowed it.

Many of those who admire his music may not consider him a great composer; but he was a great French composer —this is undeniable.

Ravel, (in the Press)

ON BELA BARTOK (1881–1945)

CECIL GRAY

The pre-eminently arresting quality which the examination of Bartok's works instantly reveals, and one which distinguishes him sharply from his contemporaries is that he has no set and invariable method of procedure, no fixed and determinate style. He employs no outworn 'clichés', whether of the academies or of the modern Franco-Russian academy, neither is he, as Arnold Schönberg occasionally is, a slave to his own individual mannerisms or idiosyncrasies. It would be more accurate to say that when he does make use of them they cease to be 'clichés'. He possesses that rare quality of mind which illuminates everything he touches, transforming it into something rich and strange. At one point he is writing a melody which no more tolerates harmonic support than a 'pur sang' folk song or plain-chant; at another constructing a harmonic tissue of great subtlety and complexity. He is a master in the art of weaving rich and dazzling sonorities into an elaborate yet closely knit orchestral web of dazzling brilliance and grace; yet when the occasion demands he is equally capable of the most exquisitely wrought polyphonic texture revealing an austerity and restraint as impressive as they are rare. In short he is a master of all modes of expression, yet he has made each of them entirely his own. All this catholicity of style results in a quite unusually individual utterance, because it is at the service of a rich and masterful personality. His originality is the outcome of inclusiveness, not of exclusiveness; it is not one of these delicate hot-house plants, consciously cultivated and jealously sheltered lest the slightest breath of wind from the outside world should wither its precious and anaemic blossoms. Bartok is a great stylist precisely because he has no style. His utterance is moulded by the particular conception which he desires to realise. He seeks only the exact registration of his thought, nothing more or less. He is, in fact, the musical exponent of the 'mot juste'—the doctrine taught and practised in literature by Gustave Flaubert, prince of stylists (and, incidentally, of Stylites) half a century ago. 'Le style est qu'une manière de penser; plus une idée est belle, plus la phrase est sonore. La précision de la pensée fait celle du mot ... Si vous saviez précisément ce que vous voulez dire, vous le diriez bien.' And if we examine or analyse any work of Bartok we shall find that its elusive yet wholly characteristic charm resides in its expressive purpose, in an indefinable quality of thought behind the notes as it were. Never before has there been a clearer or a more convincing demonstration of the truth that in music as in any other art, beauty is only relative, depending upon and resulting from the relativity of the symbol to the expressive purpose. ...

On a first acquaintance, accustomed as we all are to the flatulent and plethoric redundance of most modern music, Bartok's art may perhaps appear unconscionably bare and crabbed to some, even to the verge of childishness. It is only after a time that we begin to recognise and appreciate the amazing subtlety and unobtrusive artistry which inform it. There are, indeed, few parallels in music, of any period, to this affecting simplicity and directness, frequently more incomprehensible than the most superficially complex musical structure to the average musician who has been so long in the habit of accepting the symbol for the reality and the image for the god that he is baffled and disconcerted by this deliberate rejection of everything that he had hitherto deemed essential. Bartok is an iconoclast, in the true sense of the word—a breaker of images. He has freed music from the tyrannic conventions of musicianship which are in reality its negation—all these superfluous counterpoints, meaningless figurations and all the other familiar forms of 'remplissage' which have so long inhibited all native freedom of expression,

M

like a kind of elephantiasis. He has had the courage to throw off all the vast hampering accretions of musical conventions, the parasitic accumulation of centuries—the musician's fatal legacy from the past—and has discovered a fresh enchantment in that ultimate sincerity which is forever done with eloquence and rhetoric.

Bartok is not afraid to appear crude or uncouth because he knows well enough the value of what he says. It is only the composer who distrusts himself and doubts the intrinsic worth of his ideas, who overlays his work with superfluous and irrelevant accessories in the vain attempt to conceal its hollow emptiness. As a generalisation one may confidently assert that the better a composer knows what he wants, the simpler his style will be, and vice versa.

Bartok is self-evidently an incorrigible Romantic, though many of the more superficial aspects of Romanticism are not to be found in him. His Romanticism is purged of the besetting sins of over-emphasis and exaggeration. Expressing it figuratively one could say that although his music comes from the heart, he does not carry that estimable organ on his sleeve, in his boots, or in his mouth. He bears much the same relation to the Romantic school that post-impressionists bear to Manet, Pissarro, and Monet. In fact, one might define him as a post-Expressionist. He has none of the nostalgic yearning and 'Weltschmerz' which is perhaps the most characteristic element common to the best art of the past generation, and which has attained such perfect expression in the work of Delius, Verlaine, Yeats, and others too numerous to mention. On the contrary, Bartok possesses at times an heroic strength and virility which had almost lapsed from music altogether of recent years. He is sensitive without being neurasthenic; his strength never degenerates into vulgarity; his passion is without sensuality or sentimentalism; his whimsical humour never runs riot into irreverent buffoonery. Above all, he is never sensational. In short, his art has none of the qualities which make for

immediate popularity, though it requires no other
passport than sympathy and a mind disengaged from
prejudices, whether ancient or modern.

There are many great artists, differing from each other
widely in other ways, who are alike in this, that by virtue
of the very unsurpassable perfection of their achievements
they are apt to engender in their successors a feeling of
profound discouragement and finality. One feels that
they have exhausted all the possibilities they had opened
up and that there is nothing left for those who come after.
Such are Bach, Mozart, Wagner, Chopin, Delius. Others,
among whom are Beethoven, Berlioz, Liszt, Moussorgsky,
give us hope and renewed vigour; their actual achievement, great or small, is less than what they suggest and
inspire. And Bartok is of this number. For a few of us at
any rate he reveals new possibilities. He has cut a path
through the 'selva oscura' wherein so many modern
composers have gone so hopelessly astray. Over and
and above his actual tangible donation, he gives us a sense
of liberation, fresh hopes, and new energies with which to
realise them.

Sackbut, Nov., 1920

ON STRAVINSKY (1882–   )

HENRY BOYS

Stravinsky never had a grudge against emotion as such.
But he very strongly protested against the working-up of
emotion as an essential principle and as an end in itself.
He knew that emotion is a result of art and helps to form
the material of art, but that the deliberate pursuit of that
result and the too great reliance upon emotion as a
constituent tended to take the mind off the object and
thus lessen the intensity of the whole.

His supposed indifference to material is again only an
indifference to material regarded as an end instead of as

a means. The work makes the material, and not the material the work. 'Indifference to material' used by the note-spinners as a slogan means that the material makes the work, not the work the material, for the reason that for them the work is material in itself. Stravinsky never allows his matter to direct or modify the form in his mind, but sets out to relate the matter in such a way as to show forth the most clearly that form. The clarity of the form we see on the paper is the best indication of the authenticity of the conception. For, as Blake says, 'the more distinct, sharp, and wiry the bounding line, the more perfect the work of art, and the less keen and sharp, the greater is the evidence of weak imitation, plagiarism, and bungling.' So far from there being a hiatus between spontaneity and artifice in his latest work, the nature of his artifice makes an artistic problem strong enough to intensify his creative vigour.

If the above indications are true, then Stravinsky's idea of the way to make music comes near to being a mystical attitude, which is indeed the most probable explanation of his exactitude, of his indifference to human emotion, of his limited appeal, of his intensity, of his asceticism, of his austerity. His latest works follow a sequence. They are a series of proportioned wholes, whose subject-matter is a great variety of different experience, always regarded from the same very specialised angle by a very mature intelligence with immense technical power using extremely sure, perhaps even limiting, methods. Hence, both the disconcerting separateness and the stylistic sameness of each work in the series. Stravinsky has said of this period: 'There is nothing to discuss, nor to criticize; one does not criticize anybody or anything that is functioning. A nose is not manufactured; a nose just *is*. Thus, too, my art.'

To analyse the being of each work would be to judge the value of the rather remote subject-matter, profounder in some works than in others, but only to be intuitively apprehended, a purely individual matter. For his remark quoted above means that in his opinion the works satisfactorily show forth what they were intended to show forth, in other words that they are infallible.

Monthly Musical Record, Jan., 1934

CECIL GRAY

A strong initial attraction ... is succeeded only too often by a subsequent aversion, and it is certainly a fact that those artists who most powerfully attract the public by means of their highly personal style at first, generally suffer ignominious eclipse once their work has been familiar for any length of time, and give place to new idols who, in their turn, give way to others, and so on. Observing this, M. Jean Cocteau in his 'Coq et Harlequin' put forward the following ingenious method of circumventing it: 'Je propose l'absence d'un style. Avoir du style au lieu d'avoir un style. C'est ce qui permet de tourner le dos à l'œuvre précédente, et de courir à chaque nouvelle œuvre les chances d'un début.' By changing thus his style every few years and becoming a blushing débutant with each successive work, the artist escapes the melancholy fate of those who have a recognisable style in everything they do, attracting at first and subsequently wearying the fashionable audience which to-day makes and unmakes artistic reputations overnight, like the 'tricoteuses' who sat at the foot of the guillotine in the days of the French Revolution.

It is by means of the adoption of this technique that Stravinsky has succeeded in holding the attention of the arbiters of musical fashion for such a long time. They are kept in a state of continual expectation, excitement, and suspense. What is he going to do next? that is the question. What it actually is matters little so long as he keeps them guessing, so long as it is always something different, something new—above all something unex-

pected. With each successive work he thus remains 'the
latest thing' and never becomes a back-number.

'Individualism', *Predicaments*, 1936

ON BAX (1883–   )

ERIC BLOM

It is . . . surprising to find, on closer acquaintance, that
all the composer's different modes of expression are
compelled to submit to his individuality, and that everything that passes through his hands is transmuted into his
own characteristic idiom. Arnold Bax stands quite alone;
whether he writes Celtic music, or Russian music, or
harmonises old French Folk-Songs, he always remains
essentially himself. He has passed unscathed through the
most complete academic training and, on the other hand,
he was left entirely unscathed by any outside tendencies,
all of which he was led by his insatiable curiosity to study.
If his means are modern, they are so simply because
modern technique suits him for what he has to say, and
not because he feels that he ought to be up-to-date. He
can afford to scorn all striving after originality, because he
is original by quite simply and sincerely setting down
what he feels. He is the disciple of no man and the leader
of no school, for he is strong enough to stand by himself.

One of the most engaging features of Arnold Bax's art
is the complete absence of that hothouse atmosphere from
which so much music suffers. It is true that some delicious
plants have grown in the conservatory (I am merely
retaining the metaphor and not referring to the musical
conservatory, to which I am afraid my remark hardly
applies), plants which, although they cannot endure the
open air and have not the strength to blossom perennially,
are yet worth having while they last and bear in them the
seed of new beautiful flowers. But it is refreshing to go
back to nature itself now and again, and we certainly find

nature and the love of it in Arnold Bax. Not that in the work of a composer of these isles we must expect perpetual sunshine. But there is nothing so wearisome as an everlastingly blue sky, and the fair weather is, after all, only one of the many manifestations of the beauty of the earth. Arnold Bax has understood this, and he is indeed particularly fond of indefinite, misty landscapes with subdued colours and half-lights. This delicately vapoury atmosphere, though it has been mistaken by some critics for vagueness or even obscurity, cannot but reveal itself to the careful observer as the intentional expression of certain aspects of nature which are things of beauty precisely because of their indefiniteness. Let us by all means condemn lack of clarity that has its root in incompetence, but indecisive outlines, where they are applied with judgment, must be reckoned with as artistic assets of a peculiarly beautiful and subtle quality. If we go to the Hebrides, we do not expect to see the burning skies and glowing colours of Italy, but to be thrilled by the grey and misty loveliness of the North.

Chesterian, Feb., 1920

L. HENDERSON-WILLIAMS

Just why Bax's music yields as well as its admittedly musical value a mental exaltation, or stimulation, common in the experience of all thinkers may, perhaps, be made clearer by an endeavour to point out the differing psychical states produced by listening to the music of Holst or Vaughan Williams.

I do not think any contemporary composer shows an output in which periods and individual works differ so extraordinarily and are even so much at variance with one another in conception, and in the audience to which, consciously or unconsciously, they are addressed, as Holst. Taking only the more recent output, we find works written from two standpoints, both predominantly intellectual. Sensuous beauty has apparently little value for Holst; spiritual beauty he conveys, but always with a certain remoteness. To illustrate with an opposite: where love is the very life-thread of Delius' music it is absent in either aspect of Holst's, except when he is in league with a poet. He reflects Humbert Wolfe but does not reinforce him, except in such songs as 'Journey's End', or in 'Betelgeuse', where he outdistanced him, being on his own peculiar mental ground. The Fugal Concerto (Wind) and the Double Concerto for Two Violins may be taken as illustrative of one standpoint which limits itself to manipulation of form and ingenuity of technical construction. The other, as in 'Egdon Heath' expresses by means of music the spiritual aspect of Nature without seeking to explain it. Both aspects of thought are devoid of the warm humanity of Bax's. Holst stands curiously aloof from his work. His is the cosmic point of view. He is, in a manner, beyond seeking; swallowed up in a tremendous acceptance. He gives us truth that we receive with sincere appreciation of its quality; but it remains at a distance; we do not take it away with us. Bax is not remote, not of a starry indifference; we experience his thought within ourselves as the sympathy of an intimate friend.

Vaughan Williams's concern with folk-tune has deepened to an obsession. On its stream he had drifted into a backwater of life. But while he was writing out of his own experience he, on the one hand, re-created the spiritual environment of a Bunyan, on the other, magnificently reinforced the more passionate exaltation of a Whitman (Sea Symphony). He is on the opposite side of Bax from Holst, heart and soul everywhere taking the lead of head. A devotional predisposition removes from him that urge to seek and probe that is ever tormenting Bax. He hopes more than he fears, and with all his mysticism he is more easily comprehended. He is larger, but not deeper, hearted. He takes you with him to the borderland of mortality or on the illimitable seas 'further, further out' and then, as on a Mount of Transfiguration, you feel for a moment 'It is good for us to be here'. But it is a white glow, a special moment and attitude in life. Bax is the common life of all, shot through with something splendid, something that is the very essence of humanity at its highest, but is capable of descending with it to its despair. Bax's music speaks for the inarticulate: it asks more explicitly than the tormented soldiers in 'The Silver Tassie': 'Why are we here?' Vaughan Williams accepts mysticism as an escape from the responsibility of thought. Bax does not. He must escape also; for the pressure of thought is more than mortal can endure for long. But he escapes by gates of sensuous beauty, as a student lifts his head to a window, refreshing himself with the serenity of sun on sward. Again and again in his music we meet this sudden turning away from tragedy, this lift from un-remitting discord to major harmonies of extraordinary sweetness and simplicity. But we know it for an escape, not a resolution; and in that, again it is stuff of our common experience. . . .

Extraneous thought could not, of course, be simul-taneously present in a mind creatively engaged, and it is not for a moment implied that a conscious philosophy informs Bax's music. It is the essence of past thought that, having become one with the nature, emerges fused with purely musical expression. This is not the same thing as inspiration. 'Inspiration' is the creator being used by a creativity greater than his own. One does not explain it. It is one of those facts of experience known to all actually creative minds; a knowledge as completely denied to the most sincere, most accomplished craftsmen. The active state of preparedness in which artists await this 'coming of the Holy Ghost' is frequently recognisable in their work, and it is in work of this stage that a man's characteristics are most clearly seen. All his acquired enrichment of nature expresses itself along with the habitual tendency of his mind. By far the greater quality of an artist's work

D.M.C.

belongs to this stage, and is accomplished in this practically 'normal' state. So, inferentially, is the greater part of Bax's, in which we, with him, wait for the withheld light. This aspect of his art is not less profoundly interesting; it is so passionately human. The travail of spirit is communicated and becomes fused with our problems. We also are submerged in that darkness of bass harmony; we also escape by diatonic stairways to the sunlit upper air.

One instance in which conscious labour became suddenly lifted occurs, I think, in the unaccompanied motet, 'This Worlde's Joie'. Up to 'All go'th but Godes will' at the close of the second verse, it moves on a broad and even road of no arresting quality. Suddenly, with the bass enunciation of this line, we are aware that something new has entered the music, at first seemingly out of character. But it becomes of increasing significance; it dominates. An elemental weight of evil, more mighty than any skill of craftsmanship could devise, issues from the music and beats almost unbearably upon our hearts, inescapable as death itself. Slowly the tide recedes . . . the creative fire dies down, and the prayer for salvation comes in weakly. The spirit that sometimes possesses Bax, breaching his human boundaries and speaking through him some illimitable, universal thing, has just carried us, too, beyond our little, predetermined limitations. But it has passed on and the world closes in. We see again a man, graving with man's tools his small designs . . . alone.

'Bax, the Philosopher's Musician',
Sackbut, March, 1931

ON WEBERN (1883–1945)

ERWIN STEIN

The works of Anton von Webern are suffused with an extraordinarily tender and intimate feeling. He is the composer of the 'pianissimo espressivo'. Most of his pieces are short and extremely transparent in sound, and his melodies are highly, sometimes ecstatically expressive. In his later orchestral works, strings and wind are used throughout as solo instruments, and the brass is always muted. In the 'Six movements for String Quartet', Op. 9, almost every note of a melody is given to a different instrument, and each note in a different tone-colour (harmonic, pizzicato, col legno, etc.). This, together with a rhythm that often lays stress on the weak beat of a bar, imparts to these pieces something unusually glittering and fluid. Schönberg's idea of a 'Melody of tone colour' may have influenced these features. It was a natural consequence of the composer's renunciation of the conventional formal means that these movements could not be allowed to assume large dimensions. They are melodies in one breath. Thematic development, climax and contrast do their share from the very beginning, as it were before the melody has lost its initial warmth. Thus are formed shapes of frequently less than ten bars, but of very concentrated expression, . . .

As a consequence of greater wealth of artistic means, the technique of an art is apt to be narrowed down and impoverished in other respects. This is not unnatural, for it is difficult for the ear, while occupied in becoming accustomed to new sounds, to grasp at the same time such things as complex forms. The harmonic richness of to-day is therefore frequently accompanied by simplified melodic and formal conceptions. Schönberg and his pupils, however, have not only revived the polyphonic principles of the old masters; they have adapted the modifications of motives and development of themes, the thematic and rhythmic variety evolved by the classics, to their new artistic media. This is undoubtedly a great enrichment of musical expressiveness; and if the hearer be unable to follow immediately, he should have patience and accustom himself to this music by hearing it frequently. It will not fail to reveal its musical worth to him in time.

Chesterian, Oct., 1922

ON ALBAN BERG (1885-1929)

ERWIN STEIN

The works of Alban Berg are symphonic in character. They consist generally of extended movements, where the thematic material is developed polyphonically and in very free variation. This explains, at the same time, their form, which is created by uniformity of the themes and clarity of cohesion. Thus, in the Orchestral Prelude, Op. 6, nearly all the manifold musical occurrences are evolved from a motiv of three notes. In other cases, a number of themes are placed next to or over each other from the very beginning. Contrasts, which in older music create a sense of symmetry of expression and form in large spaces, are here given a new function: the fact that they appear simultaneously—that is to say polyphonically—or nearly so, imparts a variety and an extent to the expression within which, as in the human soul, there is room for contradictory notions. The relation between the themes is, at the same time, of so intimate a nature, and they are so compellingly summarised in the working-out, that the whole, although rich in contrasting colours, makes an impression of the greatest unity. In Berg's String Quartet, Op. 3, for instance, three motives of entirely different character are opposed to each other in the first three bars; yet they are related to each other through some formal device or another, such as inversion, augmentation, or rhythmic completion, and the development unfolds their affinity; the common experiences of dissimilar relatives. 'Music describes the adventure of themes', as Schönberg says. . . .

The severe, tense forms of Berg's opera (Wozzeck) by

reason of the fact that they contain something organically necessary and are thus drama in themselves, create a sense of outward concentration of the dramatic moments. The species and the character of the pieces correspond, needless to say, with the action of each scene, but the wealth of form is equalled by the richness of sound, texture and expression of Berg's melodies.

Chesterian, Oct., 1922

PERCY A. SCHOLES (1877-   )

I. POLYTONALITY

There must be a good many people who are still asking themselves 'Whence and Whither?' They are aware of the need for patience with 'modern music'. They know they cannot at once hope to grasp the whole purport of music fashioned upon a new system (and for many 'The Rite' is still that), but, as every new style recorded in the history of music has grown out of an earlier one, and led to a later one, they would like some convinced modernist to explain to them his ancestry and forecast his posterity for the experience of apparently unrelated phenomena is always disturbing. After their failure to make themselves clear on the aesthetic side, on which I have already commented, can the modernists at least make themselves clear on the technical? Well, Milhaud, in an article, 'Polytonalité et Atonalité', in a recent issue of the admirable 'Revue Musicale' (3, Rue de Grenelle, Paris VIe), succeeds in giving a pretty plain exposition of two phases of the 'modernist' harmony, showing how they have evolved by perfectly logical processes out of the previously accepted system, and hinting, at the end of his article, at the nature of the further growth which is inevitable. He classes modernist harmony under two heads, 'Polytonality', or simultaneous use of different keys, and 'Atonality', or entire absence of key. I here summarize briefly his treatment of the one phase, and will do the same in my next chapter for his treatment of the other.

The harmony in which we were brought up was for the most part diatonic, that is to say, the notes making up a chord, or the 'parts' woven together into a contrapuntal fabric, all belonged to a definite (major or minor) key, and of keys there were twenty-four (twelve major and twelve minor). Necessarily, however, the music passed, from time to time, from one key into another. . The admission that succession of key, or 'modulation', was acceptable inevitably implied, says Milhaud, that, at some later stage, superposition of key ('Polytonality') would also be found equally acceptable. This hardly seems to follow, but the writer has omitted a stage in the argument, of a hint as to which I will make him a present. For thousands of years only unisonous (and octave) singing was tolerated, i.e., only succession of notes; then, at last, the practice of harmonic singing grew up, i.e., superposition of notes. Apply this, by analogy, and the missing link in the argument is, I think, supplied. Since, a thousand years ago, we began to pass from Homophony to Polyphony and accomplished the process successfully, there seems no reason why we should not similarly pass from Homotonality to Polytonality.

An astute suggestion is made by Milhaud to the effect that the device of 'canon' sometimes pointed to a polytonal future for music. . . .

What are called appoggiaturas, accented passing notes and suspensions, supply Milhaud with another argument, pretty obvious and by no means unfamiliar. At one period in history ears would only stand unison-singing, or, as an Irishman might say, one-note chords; next they tolerated two- and three-note chords, consisting of the simplest and most natural intervals (the third and the fifth); then they began to tolerate certain four-note chords (such, for instance, as the dominant seventh or certain 'suspensions'). So far, all the notes of a chord had been in the one key, but soon it became common to insert in a chord a note borrowed from another key, providing it quickly merged into its 'resolution'. Cut out the resolution and you have Stravinskyism, Satieism, Milhaudism—all of which, a purist might say, enforce the Sunday-school lesson of the danger of small steps in the wrong direction. Our dilemma is that if we decide to follow this purist we shall, to be logical, have to make an effort to thrust ourselves back into fifth-century unisonous singing, or, indeed, into (literally) monotonous chant; whilst, on the other hand, if we elect to act upon the Milhaud theory, we must, equally logically, in time pass into a condition where anything is possible, ... Other arguments I can only briefly mention. They are drawn from (a) the device of pedal, with modulations above it, as found commonly in the classics; (b) chords such as that of the ninth, eleventh, and thirteenth (here Milhaud, without knowing it, adopts the old 'Day theory', in which some of us who used Macfarren's Harmony were brought up—i.e., he considers such chords as being combinations of two different chords). And so on. It is all very alarming, as strict logic often is. But dare we say 'Down with logic'? Up to the present there is seen to have been a very strict logic governing the development of music, and it is probable that we cannot escape it.

II. ATONALITY

In the previous chapter I briefly discussed Milhaud's argument, based upon historical precedent, as to the propriety of Polytonality (or simultaneity of key), a principle which governs the harmonic structure of a good deal of music to-day. I need hardly say that no argument, however logical, can justify a piece of music; the music has to justify itself, but if the argument is sound it should have the effect of inducing us to exercise greater patience than we might otherwise have done, and so to give the music a chance of making its own appeal. To a musician who has several times heard Ravel's Sonata for Violin and 'Cello the Sonata probably becomes, in itself, an argument in favour of Polytonality, but until he has heard it several times it is quite possible that he may need to apply some logical argument about Polytonality in favour of the Sonata. History shows that composers do not as a rule first theorize as to harmonic systems, and then carry out their theories; rather they subconsciously feel their way towards new harmonic systems and then go on to discovery of the principles of these. That is precisely what is now occurring in the case of Polytonality and Atonality; they are systems already in active being, and the process of explanation and theoretical justification, which began some years since, is now working itself out pretty clearly. There will be written reams of thoroughly bad Polytonic and Atonic music, as there have been written reams of thoroughly bad Diatonic music. What we are interested in for the moment is not the value of the music but the soundness of the system. But in listening to the music, to-morrow or next day, it should be the other way about.

Having shown how Polytonality grew out of Homo-tonality by a perfectly natural evolution (canon, accented passing notes, pedals, etc.), Milhaud proceeds to show us how Atonality is already growing out of Polytonality. The argument is, briefly, this. Two or more perfectly regular diatonic melodies superposed, each going its way regardless of the other, produce a harmonic effect of Polytonality; horizontally considered, the music is Diatonic, perpendicularly considered, it is rarely so. Some few of the chords produced by the coincidence of the notes of these diatonic melodies may also, by accident, be normal diatonic chords, assignable to one key or another, and when this happens the effect is momentarily diatonic, otherwise the result is chromatic. The diatonic is the accident, the chromatic the rule, and Polytonality is thus harmonically a chromatic system. Presumably, if our ears were sufficiently trained to the appreciation of the effects, we should feel the two systems in use at one time, the one in each separate part, the other in their combination, and this is probably what happens with a genuine Polytonic composer; indeed, to him the pleasure of his music probably consists largely in the agreeable conflict thus introduced. Obviously the kind of listening required is an extension of the kind of listening required for the appreciation of a Byrd madrigal or a Bach fugue—the perception so to speak, of warp and woof at one glance. Now, chromaticism knows no key. The series D, D sharp, E, F, F sharp, for instance, is no more in any one key than in any other, whether it be used melodically or harmonically, and a good deal of Polytonality being harmonically chromatic, it is a small step deliberately to make the separate parts or voices or strands also chromatic, taking our separate melodies or parts from the keyless system. This done, we have something like a complete Atonality, or absence of key, the only reservation being that even now, by pure accident (or the merciful hand of Providence) a combination here or there may be a recognizable 'chord' of the old system, though, even in this case, two such chords, assignable to the same key, are little likely to occur in sequence, so that no key effect is set up, and we have complete Atonality.

For the practice of Polytonality, Milhaud gives simple but ingenious tables showing the combinations possible. Superposing all other possible major chords upon that of C major, we have obviously eleven combinations. Superposing all possible minor chords on it we have eleven more. Superposing all the major chords on the chord of C minor we have another set of eleven, and superposing all the minor chords upon it still another set. This makes forty-four Polytonic chords upon the one note C. As the same process can be repeated over C sharp,

D, etc., the forty-four can be multiplied by eleven = 484. Then come in the 'inversions' of all these chords, but already I tire of arithmetic, whilst when it comes to the combinations possible by superposition of three chords of four (and these not necessarily simple 'common chords', but also chords of the seventh, ninth, eleventh, thirteenth, etc.), I 'reel to and fro, and stagger like a drunken man and am at my wit's end'. And if all this is done in the green wood of Polytonality what shall be done in the dry of Atonality? Presumably a senior wrangler would make short work of the little sum called for, but its prospect leaves me staring wild-eyed into infinity.

Then comes the troubling question (and Milhaud never really faces it)—Will all this variety of resource give us, in practice, greater variety of effect? For the ear, to enjoy, has to classify; classification is, with the ordinary listener, subconscious, of course, but none the less it goes on. Then, of course, one not only classifies single chords, feeling them as major, minor, diminished, etc., but 'progressions' of two chords as dominant to tonic, tonic to subdominant, major to minor, and minor to major, and so forth. Is any such classification possible to our ears under the limitless new dispensation, and if not, shall we not simply experience a vague nondescript effect, one 'chord' being very like another, and one progression like another? What will be the composer's own method of selection of his effects?

Then how, in the wonderful days that are coming, will students in composition be trained? It is all very well for Milhaud to talk airily of 'complementary studies':

Polytonality and Atonality are not arbitrary systems. They are, the one a development from diatonic harmony and counterpoint, the other a development from chromatic harmony and counterpoint, and ought to be made the object of complementary technical studies.

How are these studies to be carried out? All that he proposes is obviously lawful. But when, from precedent to precedent the bounds of freedom have been broadened down to this extent, anyone can do anything, and nobody can say him nay. Which is all very right and proper, but art necessarily implying selection, a principle for the selection will have to be first felt and next discovered. Milhaud seems to imply a safeguard in a sort of *canto fermo* system:

The factor which will determine the Polytonic or Atonic character of a work will be much less the process of its composition ('le procédé d'écriture'—I don't quite follow) than the essential melody which will come from the 'heart' alone of the musician. It is the absolute and organic necessity of the initial melody which will prevent the progressions ('procédés') from congealing into a system otherwise still-born. The whole life of a work will depend upon nothing else than the melodic invention of its composer, and Polytonality and Atonality will do nothing more than furnish him with a vaster field, richer means of composition, a more expressive and complex scale, wherewith to employ his sensibility, his imagination, and his fancy. All very fine and large—especially the latter! And, after this, what next? Why, of course, a quarter-tone system, composition in which has already begun. And, after that—well, let us hope the resources here laid out for use will last our lifetime. Posterity must look out for itself!

Crotchets, 1924

SIR GEORGE DYSON (1883-   )

The word 'atonality' has recently been used to describe, presumably, developments which I prefer to define as modal, neomodal, or chromatic, respectively. My difficulty is that I cannot find a logical definition of atonality. If tonality means, as it surely does for most of us, the classical key-system, does atonality mean mere absence of this? Does it, therefore, include the old modes

as well as the new, or the one, or the other, or neither?
Does it cover the whole-tone scale? If it includes all this
it is useless for purposes of exact description. If its range
is narrower than this, then what is taken from it becomes
attached, logically, to tonality. I see no escape from this
ambiguity, which is the worst fault a technical term can
have. Chromaticism, on the other hand, is a well-known
and consistent historical tendency towards scalar expansion. The various stages in its progress are represented by
the fixed scales to which music has from time to time
attached itself. The end towards which all expansions
logically converge is pure chromaticism, as defined in
the text.

The New Music, 1924

CONSTANT LAMBERT (1905-   )

There is one objection to atonalism so simple and
childish that no one seems to have had the courage to
make it. Although atonalism has produced complicated
and objective fugal structures that can with justice be
compared with the 'Kunst de Fugue' of Bach, subjective
and neurasthenic operas that can be compared with
'Tristan and Isolde' or 'Parsifal', it has produced nothing
that we can set beside Chabrier and Offenbach, let alone
the comic operas of Mozart. The dance movements in the
'Serenade' and the Op. 25 Piano Suite, which are Schönberg's nearest approach to this genre, are sufficient proof
of the essential solemnity of atonalism. An atonal comic
opera is a chimerical thought, and though it is unlikely
that either Schönberg or Berg would in any case wish to
attempt such a genre, the mere fact that the task would be
impossible is a proof of the narrow emotional range
offered by their idiom.

Atonalism, though plastic in minor details of texture, is
in fact the least flexible and most monotonous of media,
and for that reason alone it is unlikely to play much part

in the music of the future. It will always remain a thing apart, having something of the hieratical solemnity and exclusiveness of a hereditary religious order; and the more we free ourselves from tonal prejudice and from the tyranny of textbook harmony the less appeal atonalism will have, because it is based on a direct reversal of academic method. Like blasphemy, it requires a background of belief for its full effect. Composers like Bartok or Vaughan Williams could no more become atonalists than a freethinker could take part in a Black Mass.

Music Ho! 1934

Appendixes

Their instruction in music and verse was not less carefully attended to than their habits of grace and good-breeding in conversation. And their very songs had a life and spirit in them that inflamed and possessed men's minds with an enthusiasm and ardour for action; the style of them was plain and without affectation; the subject always serious and moral; most usually, it was in praise of such men as had died in defence of their country or in derision of those who had been cowards; the former they declared happy and glorified; the life of the latter they described as most miserable and abject. There were also vaunts of what they would do and boasts of what they had done, varying with the various ages; as, for example, they had three choirs in their solemn festivals, the first of the old men, the second of the young men, and the last of the children; the old men began thus:

'We once were young and brave and strong'

the young men answering them, singing:

'And we're so now, come on and try'

the children came last, and said:

'But we'll be strongest by-and-by'

Indeed, if we will take the pains to consider their compositions, and the airs on the flute to which they marched when going to battle, we shall find that Terpander and Pindar had reason to say that music and valour were allied.

PLUTARCH, Lycurgas

CHRONOLOGICAL INDEX OF AUTHORS

378

380

(Since going to press the following authors have died.)

H. V. Jervis-Read
Thomas F. Dunhill
W. J. Turner

The excellence of music is to be measured by pleasure. But the pleasure must not be that of chance persons; the fairest music is that which delights the best and best educated, and especially that which delights the one man who is pre-eminent in virtue and education.

PLATO, *Laws II*, 658 e.

BIBLIOGRAPHY OF SOURCES

ARRANGED IN THE ORDER OF THE CONTENTS

JOHN DUNSTABLE:
> *Thomas Morley*; 'A Plaine and Easie Introduction to Practicall Musicke,' 1597

DR. CHRISTOPHER TYE:
> *William Rowley*; A Play

THOMAS TALLIS:
> *Dr. Charles Burney*; History of Music, 1776

'DEDICATION':
> *John Marbeck* or *Merbecke*; 'Concordance' (1547)

'THE TWO QUEENS':
> *Sir James Melvil*; Memoirs, pub. 1683

'REASONS FOR SINGING':
> *William Byrd*; Preface to 'Psalmes, Sonets, and songs of Sadnes and pietie, made into Musicke of five parts', 1588

WILLIAM BYRD:
> *Thomas Morley*; 'A Plaine and Easie Introduction to Practicall Musicke,' 1597
> *Thomas Peachum* or *Henry Peacham*; 'Compleat Gentleman,' 1622
> *Dr. Charles Burney*; History of Music, 1776
> *Rev. Dr. E. H. Fellowes*, Music and Letters, April 1923; Heritage of Music, Vol. II, 1933

'ON IGNORANCE':
> *Thomas Morley*; 'A Plaine and Easie Introduction to Practicall Musicke, 1597

THOMAS MORLEY:
> *Sir John Hawkins*; 'A General History of the Science and Practice of Music,' 1776
> *Dr. Charles Burney*; History of Music, 1776

JOHN WYNAL:
> *Epitaph*

'MUSIC AS A CURE FOR MELANCHOLY':
> *Robert Burton*; 'The Anatomy of Melancholy'

DR. JOHN BULL:
> *Dr. Charles Burney*; History of Music, 1776
> *Verse round the frame of picture*

JOHN DOWLAND:
> *Dr. Charles Burney*; History of Music, 1776

MONTEVERDE:
>   *Dr. Charles Burney*; History of Music, 1776
>   *Samuel Butler*; Note Books
>   *Sir Hubert Parry*; Paper read to the Royal Musical Association, 1916

'DEDICATION':
>   *Thomas Weelkes*; Five Part Madrigals, 1600

ORLANDO GIBBONS:
>   *Dart*; Translation of Epitaph, 'History and Antiquities of the Cathedral Church of Canterbury,' 1726

MR. JNO. JENKINS:
>   *Hon. Roger North*; 'The Musical Grammarian,' *c.* 1728

HENRY LAWES:
>   *John Milton*; Sonnets
>   *Dr. Charles Burney*; History of Music, 1776

THOMAS KINGSTON:
>   *Chapter of Lincoln Cathedral*; Minute Book

WILLIAM INGLOTT:
>   *Epitaph*

DR. BENJAMIN ROGERS
>   *Dr. Charles Burney*; History of Music, 1776

CHRISTOPHER GIBBONS:
>   *Anthony á Wood*; MS. Memoirs

CAPTAIN COOKE:
>   *Anthony á Wood*; MS. Memoirs

'A FAMOUS VIOLINIST':
>   *John Evelyn*; Diary, March 4th, 1656

'ITALIAN OPERA IN RECITATIVO':
>   *John Evelyn*; Diary, May 5th, 1659

'FRENCH AND ENGLISH MUSIC':
>   *John Evelyn*; Diary, January 11th, 1662

'THE QUEEN'S PORTUGAL MUSIC':
>   *John Evelyn*; Diary, June 9th, 1662

'A NEW INSTRUMENT':
>   *John Evelyn*; Diary, October 5th, 1664

'ITALIAN OPERA':
>   *John Evelyn*; Diary, January 5th, 1673

'A GREAT VIOLINIST':
>   *John Evelyn*; Diary, December 2nd, 1674
>   *John Evelyn*; Diary, November 20th, 1679

'A GOOD COMPOSER':
>   *John Evelyn*; Diary, September 3rd, 1680

'SOPRANO CASTRATO':
>   *John Evelyn*; Diary, January 27th, 1682

'LESSONS FOR MARY':
>   *John Evelyn*; Diary, February 7th, 1682

'An Excellent Singer':
> John Evelyn; Diary, January 27th, 1685

'Mary's Voice':
> John Evelyn; Diary, January 28th, 1685

'Panegyric to Mary':
> John Evelyn; Diary, March 10th, 1685

'Another Soprano Castrato':
> John Evelyn; Diary, April 19th, 1787

'The Most Excellent Singer We Ever Had':
> John Evelyn; Diary, May 30th, 1698

'On Psalm Singing in York Cathedral (sic)':
> Thomas Mace; 'Music's Monument,' 1676

'On the Value of paying Musicians':
> Thomas Mace; 'Music's Monument,' 1676

'Foreign Influence':
> John Playford; 'Music's Delight of the Cithren,' 166

'The First Conductor':
> Samuel Pepys; Diary, June 6th, 1661

'Domestic Music':
> Samuel Pepys; Diary, March 18th, 1662

'Innovations in Church':
> Samuel Pepys; Diary, September 14th, 1662

'A Royal Musician':
> Samuel Pepys; November 22nd, 1663

'A Slovenly and Ugly Fellow':
> Samuel Pepys; Diary, July 22nd, 1664

'More Domestic Music':
> Samuel Pepys; Diary, September 9th, 1664

'Effect of Domestic Music':
> Samuel Pepys; Diary, December 6th, 1662

'Beauty, Retire':
> Samuel Pepys; Diary, December 9th, 1665

'A New Viallinist':
> Samuel Pepys; Diary, June 18th, 1666

'Result of teaching the Maid to sing':
> Samuel Pepys; Diary, July 30th, 1666

'A Bad Singer':
> Samuel Pepys; Diary, November 10th, 1666

'A Naughty Singer':
> Samuel Pepys; Diary, December 26th, 1666

'A New Instrument':
> Samuel Pepys; Diary, January 23rd, 1667

'In Love with a Singer':
> Samuel Pepys; Diary, January 24th, 1667

'An Italian Opera Composer':
> Samuel Pepys; Diary, February 12th, 1667

'AN ARROGANT CRITIC':
: *Samuel Pepys*; Diary, February 13th, 1667

'TWO-PIANO MUSIC':
: *Samuel Pepys*; Diary, February, 16th, 1667

'A SINGING LESSON':
: *Samuel Pepys*; Diary, March 1st, 1667

'EUNUCHS':
: *Samuel Pepys* Diary, April 7th, 1667

'AN ENGLISH SONG UPON PEACE':
: *Samuel Pepys*; Diary, October 1st, 1667

AN INDIFFERENT TEACHER':
: *Samuel Pepys*; Diary, December 10th, 1667

'WIND MUSIC':
: *Samuel Pepys*; Diary, February 27th, 1668

'A PLEASING SONG':
: *Samuel Pepys*; Diary, May 7th, 1668

'WHAT A DAY!'
: *Samuel Pepys*; Diary, April 10th, 1668

'BAD MUSIC':
: *Samuel Pepys*; Diary, May 16th, 1668

PELHAM HUMPHREY:
: *Samuel Pepys*; Diary, November 15th, 1667
: *Samuel Pepys*; Diary, November 16th, 1667

DR. JOHN BLOW:
: *Epitaph*
: *Dr. Charles Burney*; History of Music, 1776
: *Sir John Hawkins*; 'A General History of the Science and Practice of Music,' 1776
: *Edward Fitzgerald*; Letter, June 12th, 1845

JOHN BERKENSHAW:
: *John Evelyn*; Diary, August 3rd, 1664
: *Samuel Pepys*; Diary, February 24th, 1662
: *Samuel Pepys*; Diary, February 27th, 1662
: *Dr. Charles Burney*; History of Music, 1776

HENRY PURCELL:
: *John Dryden*; Dedication to 'Amphitryon', 1690
: *John Dryden*; Dedication to 'King Arthur', 1691
: *Epitaph*
: *Hon. Roger North*; 'Musical Grammarian,' *c.* 1728
: *Dr. Charles Burney*; History of Music, 1776
: *Sir John Hawkins*; 'A General History of the Science and Practice of Music,' 1776
: *Sir Hubert Parry*; Oxford History of Music, Vol. III, 1902
: *Gustav Holst*; 'The Heritage of Music,' Vol. I, 1927
: *A. E. Brent Smith*; Music and Letters, April 1937

'ON PRE-RESTORATION CHURCH COMPOSERS':
>   *Thomas Tudway*; Dedication to second Volume MS. Collection of English Church Music
'ON ASSESSING MUSIC':
>   *Hon. Roger North*; 'Musical Grammarian,' *c.* 1728
MUDD
>   *Precentor of Lincoln Cathedral to the Dean*
'VOCAL CRITICISM':
>   *Stephen Jeffries*
STEPHEN JEFFRIES:
>   *Chapter of Gloucester Cathedral*; Minute Book, 1688
'THE BEGGAR'S OPERA':
>   *Dean Swift*; Intelligencer, No. 3
'OPERA':
>   *Colley Cibber*; 'Apology for His Life,' 1740
'USE OF BIRDS IN OPERA':
>   *Joseph Addison*; Spectator, March 6th, 1711
'ITALIAN OPERA':
>   *Joseph Addison*; Spectator, March 21st, 1711
'USE OF A MONKEY IN OPERA':
>   *Joseph Addison*, Spectator, April 2nd, 1711
'RECITATIVE':
>   *Joseph Addison*; Spectator, April 3rd, 1711
'PLAN FOR OPERA':
>   *Joseph Addison*; Spectator, April 5th, 1711
'BEHAVIOUR IN CHURCH':
>   *Joseph Addison*; Spectator, October 25th, 1711
'THE CAT-CALL':
>   *Joseph Addison*; Spectator, April 24th, 1712
'FAREWELL TO A SINGER':
>   *Joseph Addison*; Spectator, June 14th, 1712
'MUSIC IN CHURCH':
>   (*Henry Grove*); Spectator, December 8th, 1714
'MUSIC IS ALTERED':
>   *Rev. Arthur Bedford*; 'The Great Abuse of Music,' 1711
'PRIVATE BEHAVIOUR OF AN OPERA COMPANY':
>   *Sir Richard Steele*; Tatler, April 18th, 1709
'MOVEMENT AND MUSIC':
>   *Sir Richard Steele*; Tatler, May 5th, 1709
'BEHAVIOUR IN AN ORGAN LOFT':
>   *Sir Richard Steele*; Tatler, August 30th, 1709
'HUMAN INSTRUMENTS':
>   *Sir Richard Steele*; Tatler, April 1st, 1710
'HUMANS AS INSTRUMENTS':
>   *Sir Richard Steele*; Tatler, April 11th, 1710

'BUYING A TICKET':
>Sir Richard Steele; Tatler, May 2nd, 1710

'ITALIAN MUSIC':
>Sir Richard Steele; Tatler, November 2nd, 1711

'BEHAVIOUR IN CHURCH':
>Sir Richard Steele; Tatler, January 25th, 1712

BACH:
>Sir John Hawkins; 'A General History of the Science and Practice of Music,' 1776
>
>Dr. Charles Burney; History of Music, 1776
>
>Musical World; 1838
>
>Sir George Macfarren; Paper read to the Royal Musical Association, March 2nd, 1885
>
>Samuel Butler; Note Books
>
>J. A. Fuller-Maitland; Oxford History of Music, Vol. IV, 1902
>
>Sir Hubert Parry; 'Johann Sebastian Bach,' 1909
>
>W. G. Whittaker; 'Bach's Cantatas,' 1924
>
>W. J. Turner; 'Musical Meanderings,' 1928
>
>H. V. Jervis-Read; 'The Arrant Artist,' 1939

HANDEL:
>Lady A. Irwin; Letter, March 31st, 1733
>
>Francis Hare; Letter, December 18th, 1737
>
>Horace Walpole; Letter, February 24th, 1743
>
>Dr. Arbuthnot; 'Harmony in an Uproar,' 1754
>
>Rev. Thomas Morel; Letter written in 1764
>
>Sir John Hawkins; 'A General History of the Science and Practice of Music,' 1776
>
>Dr. Charles Burney; History of Music, 1776
>
>Rev. William Mason; 'Essays, Historical and Critical, of English Church Music,' 1782
>
>Fanny Burney; Diary, July 22nd, 1786; August 6th, 1788; February 10th, 1789
>
>Maria Edgeworth; Letter, May 1st, 1813
>
>George Hogarth; Musical History, 1835
>
>Edward Fitzgerald; Letter, February 6th, 1842; February 24th, 1844; June 12th, 1845
>
>Samuel Butler; Note Books
>
>Ernest Walker; 'A History of Music in England,' 1907

DR. MAURICE GREENE:
>Sir John Hawkins; 'A General History of the Science and Practice of Music,' 1776
>
>J. A. Fuller-Maitland; Oxford History of Music, Vol. IV, 1902

'WHAT IS A MASTER OF MUSICK?':
>William Tansur; Preface, 'A New Musical Spectator, or the Harmonical Spectator,' 1746

'Elementary Orchestration':
> Charles Avison; 'Essay on Musical Expression,' 1752

'On Adaptations':
> Rev. William Mason; 'Essays, Historical and Critical, on English Church Music,' 1782

Haydn:
> Dr. Charles Burney; History of Music, 1776; 'Verses on the Arrival of the Great Musician Haydn in England,' 1789
>
> Monthly Magazine; 1811
>
> W. Gardiner; A Life of Haydn, 1817
>
> Thomas Busby; History of Music, 1819
>
> William Bingley; Musical Biography, 1834
>
> Sir Hubert Parry; 'Evolution of the Art of Music,' 1893

'Dr. Johnson and Music':
> James Boswell; 'Life of Dr. Johnson,' 1791

Clementi:
> William Ayrton; Harmonicon, May, 1823; June, 1825

Mozart:
> Hon. Daines Barrington; 'Account of a Very Remarkable Musician'; Paper in the Philosophical Transactions of the Royal Society, 1770
>
> W. Gardiner; A Note in a Life of Mozart, 1817
>
> Thomas Busby; History of Music, 1819; Quarterly Musical Magazine, Vol. III, 1821
>
> Michael Kelly; Reminiscences, 1826
>
> Edward Fitzgerald; Letter after September, 1845; June 12th, 1845; March ?, 1873
>
> Samuel Butler; Note Books
>
> W. S. Rockstro; History of Music, 1886
>
> John Ruskin; 'Time and Tide'
>
> Sir Hubert Parry; 'Evolution of the Art of Music,' 1893
>
> E. J. Dent; Mozart's Operas, 1913
>
> Sir George Dyson; 'The New Music,' 1924

Samuel Wesley:
> Dr. Charles Burney; Paper in the Philosophical Transactions of the Royal Society, 1779

Beethoven:
> William Ayrton; Harmonicon, April, 1823

Overture 'Coriolan':
> William Ayrton; Harmonicon, June, 1823

Pastoral Symphony:
> William Ayrton; Harmonicon, April 1824; July 1825

Ninth Symphony:
> William Ayrton; Harmonicon, March 1825; April 1825

Pastoral Symphony:
> William Ayrton; Harmonicon, July 1825

BEETHOVEN (*cont.*)
  SECOND SYMPHONY:
    William Ayrton; Harmonicon, June 1826
  EROICA SYMPHONY:
    William Ayrton; Harmonicon, April 1829
  SEVENTH SYMPHONY
    William Ayrton; Harmonicon, May 1829; June 1829
  VIOLIN CONCERTO:
    William Ayrton; Harmonicon, May 1832; Quarterly Musical
      Magazine, Vol. IX, 1827
    Edward Fitzgerald; Letter, March 31st, 1842; December 24th,
      1871
    Samuel Butler; Note Books
    Lieut. H. W. L. Hime, Royal Artillery; Monthly Musical
      Record, October 1871
    Sir George Grove; 'Beethoven and His Nine Symphonies,' 1896
    Sir W. H. Hadow; 'Beethoven's Op. 18 Quartets,' 1926
    Sir John B. McEwen; Music and Letters, April 1927
'HIS IGNORANCE':
  Sir Walter Scott; Autobiography
'HIS LIMIT':
  Samuel Taylor Coleridge; Table Talk, July 6th, 1833
'A CHAPTER ON EARS':
  Charles Lamb; 'Essays of Elia'
'FREE THOUGHTS ON SEVERAL EMINENT COMPOSERS':
  Charles Lamb; 'Essays of Elia'
'APOLOGY FOR CHARLES':
  Mary Lamb; Album Leaf
DR. WILLIAM CROTCH:
  Author Unknown; Letter to Dr. Charles Burney, included in
    Philosophical Transactions of the Royal Society, 1779
'THE OPERA':
  William Hazlitt; Essays
SPOHR:
  William Ayrton; Harmonicon, May 1824
  George Hogarth; Musical History, 1835
WEBER:
  William Ayrton; Harmonicon, May 1826
  Samuel Langford; Musical Criticisms, 1926
BISHOP:
  George Hogarth; Musical History, 1835
CZERNY:
  William Ayrton; Harmonicon, May 1823
MEYERBEER:
  Edward Fitzgerald; Letter, June 8th, 1852; Monthly Musical
    Record, January, 1877

MEYERBEER (*cont.*)
>   *Sir Charles Stanford*; History of Music, 1916

ROSSINI:
>   Quarterly Musical Magazine, Vol. II, 1820
>   *George Hogarth*; Musical History, 1835
>   *Leigh Hunt*; 'Going to the Play Again'
>   *Francis Toye*; 'Rossini—A Study in Tragi-Comedy,' 1934

CIPRIANI POTTER:
>   Quarterly Musical Magazine, Vol. VIII, 1826
>   *William Ayrton*; Harmonicon, June 1826
>   *J. W. Davison*; The Times, May 29th, 1855
>   *W. H. Glover*; Morning Post, May 29th, 1855
>   *Sir George Macfarren*; Programme Note, Royal Philharmonic Society, May 3rd, 1869; Musical Times, June 1869

SCHUBERT:
>   *J. W. Davison*; Musical World, 1839, 1859
>   *Sir George Macfarren*; Programme Note, Royal Philharmonic Society, April 19th, 1869; Monthly Musical Record, January, 1875
>   *Samuel Butler*; Note Books
>   *W. S. Rockstro*; History of Music, 1886; Musical Times, February 1897
>   *Sir W. H. Hadow*; Oxford History of Music, 1904
>   *Eric Blom*; Music and Letters, October 1928

BERLIOZ:
>   *Rev. John Edmund Cox*; 'Musical Recollections of the last Half-Century,' 1872
>   *Francis Hueffer*; 'Half a Century of Music in England, 1837–1887,' 1889
>   *Samuel Butler*; Note Books
>   *W. S. Rockstro*; History of Music, 1886
>   *W. J. Turner*; 'Musical Meanderings,' 1928
>   *Tom S. Wootton*; 'The Hermitage of Music,' Vol. II, 1933
>   *J. H. Elliot*; 'Berlioz,' 1938

BALFE:
>   *Edward Fitzgerald*; Letter, October 10th, 1844; Musical Times, 1876

MENDELSSOHN:
>   *William Ayrton*; Harmonicon, June 1829, June 1832
>   *George Hogarth*; Musical History, 1835
>   *H. F. Chorley*; Athenaeum, 1837, 1840, 1842; 'Modern German Music: Recollections and Criticisms,' 1862
>   *Edward Fitzgerald*; Letter, August 16th, 1842; May 4th, 1848; December 27th, 1853
>   *Sir George Macfarren*; Programme Note, Royal Philharmonic Society, May 3rd, 1869

MENDELSSOHN (*cont.*)

> *Rev. John Edmund Cox*; 'Musical Recollections of the last Half-Century,' 1872
>
> *Ernest Walker*; 'A History of Music in England,' 1907
>
> *Alexander Brent Smith*; 'Studies and Caprices.'

CHOPIN:

> *E. Pauer*; Monthly Musical Record, June 1871
>
> *Sir W. H. Hadow*; Studies in Modern Music, 1894–5
>
> *Sir Hubert Parry*; 'Summary of the History and Development of Mediaeval and European Music,' 1904
>
> *Edward Dannreuther*; Oxford History of Music, Vol. VI, 1904

'REFORM OF CATHEDRAL MUSIC':

> *Samuel Sebastian Wesley*; 'A Few Words on Cathedral Music and the Musical System of the Church, with a Plan of Reform'

SCHUMANN:

> *H. F. Chorley*; 'Modern German Music: Recollections and Criticism,' 1842
>
> *J. W. Davison*; Musical World, November 1854
>
> *Sir George Macfarren*; Programme Note, Royal Philharmonic Society, April 5th, 1869
>
> *Rev. John Edmund Cox*; 'Musical Recollections of the Last Half-Century,' 1872; Musical Times, May 1866; Monthly Musical Record, May 1871, November 1873
>
> *Joseph Bennett*; Programme Note, Royal Philharmonic Society, March 14th 1889
>
> *Sir Hubert Parry*; 'Evolution of the Art of Music,' 1893
>
> *Sir W. H. Hadow*; 'Studies in Modern Music,' 1894–5

LISZT:

> Quarterly Musical Magazine, Vol. VII, 1825
>
> *Francis Hueffer*; 'Half a Century of Music in England, 1837–1887,' 1889

WAGNER:

> *George Hogarth*; Daily News, March 27th, 1855; Illustrated London News, March 31st, 1855, May, 19th, 1855
>
> *H. F. Chorley*; 'Modern German Composers: Recollections and Criticisms,' 1862; Athenaeum, March 31st, 1855, June 9th, 1855
>
> *Edward Fitzgerald*; Letter, December 9th, 1861
>
> *Henry Smart*; Sunday Times, April 1st, 1855, May 20th, 1855
>
> *J. W. Davison*; Times, May 3rd, 1854, December 11th, 1854; Musical World, March 31st, 1855; Times, June 12th, 1855; Musical World, June 30th, 1855
>
> *W. H. Glover*; Morning Post, March 28th, 1855, May 15th, 1855
>
> *John Ruskin*; Letter, June 30th, 1882
>
> *Samuel Butler*; Note Books

WAGNER (*cont.*)
    'KAISER-MARSCH':
        Monthly Musical Record, June 1871
    'THE MUSIC OF THE FUTURE':
        Monthly Musical Record, October 1871
    'DIE MEISTERSINGER':
        Monthly Musical Record, April 1873
    'DAS RHEINGOLD':
        Monthly Musical Record, May 1873
    'DIE WALKURE':
        Monthly Musical Record, June 1873
    SONGS:
        Monthly Musical Record, July 1873
    WAGNER FESTIVAL:
        Monthly Musical Record, June 1877; Musical Times, March
            1883
        Sir Hubert Parry; 'Evolution of the Art of Music,' 1893
        Sir W. H. Hadow; 'Studies in Modern Music,' 1894–5
        W. J. Turner; 'Facing the Music,' 1933
VERDI:
        H. F. Chorley; Athenaeum, May 1856
    'LA FORZA DEL DESTINO':
        Musical Times, July 1867
    'REQUIEM':
        Monthly Musical Record, June 1875
    'AIDA':
        Musical Times, July 1876
        Francis Toye; 'Guiseppe Verdi: His Life and Times,' 1928–
            1930
        Eric Blom; Music and Letters, October 1931
STERNDALE BENNETT:
        Sir R. P. Stewart; Monthly Musical Record, April 1875
'PHILHARMONIC':
        W. Gardiner; Note in a Life of Haydn,' 1817
GOUNOD:
    'TOBIAS':
        Musical Times, March 1866, August 1867
    'ROMEO AND JULIET':
        Monthly Musical Record,' June 1870
        Rev. John Edmund Cox; 'Musical Recollections of the Last
            Half-Century,' 1872
    'REDEMPTION':
        Musical Opinion, June 1833
        W. S. Rockstro; History of Music, 1886
    'MUSIC FOR GIRLS':
        John Ruskin; 'Sesame and Lilies'

'Music, What Kind the Best is':
  John Ruskin; 'Sesame and Lilies'
'Definition of Music':
  John Ruskin; 'The Queen of the Air'
'Perfect Music':
  John Ruskin; 'The Queen of the Air'
'Music in Greek Education':
  John Ruskin; 'Time and Tide'
'New Music':
  John Ruskin; 'Cestus of Aglaia'
'Nobleness in Music and Horses':
  John Ruskin; 'Rock Honeycomb'
'Originality':
  John Ruskin; Quarterly Musical Magazine, Vol. IV, 1822
Brahms:
  J. W. Davison; Musical World, May 1864
  Sextet for Strings:
    Monthly Musical Record, April 1871
  Serenade in D:
    Musical Times
  Requiem:
    Monthly Musical Record, May 1871
  Serenade in D:
    Monthly Musical Record, February 1872
  Piano Concerto in D Minor:
    Monthly Musical Record, April 1872
  Requiem:
    Sir George Macfarren; Programme Note, Royal Philharmonic
      Society, April 1873
  Requiem:
    Musical Times, May 1873
  Violin Concerto:
    Monthly Musical Record, August 1873
  Sextet in G:
    Monthly Musical Record, January 1873
  St. Anthony Variations:
    Monthly Musical Record, April 1874
  Serenade in A:
    Monthly Musical Record, August 1874
  Symphony in C minor:
    Musical Times, April 1877
  Alto Rhapsody:
    Musical Times, June 1877
  Requiem:
    Monthly Musical Record, October 1877

BRAHMS (*cont.*)
SYMPHONY IN D:
Monthly Musical Record, November 1878
VIOLIN CONCERTO:
Monthly Musical Record, March 1879, April 1879
Musical Times, May 1897
Sir Hubert Parry; 'College Addresses,' May 1897
J. S. Shedlock; Monthly Musical Record, May 1897
J. A. Fuller-Maitland; 'Brahms,' 1911
H. V. Jervis-Read; 'The Arrant Artist,' 1939
BIZET:
'CARMEN':
Musical Opinion, July 1898
TSCHAIKOWSKY:
PIANO CONCERTO IN B FLAT MINOR:
Monthly Musical Record, April 1876
ROMEO AND JULIET:
Musical Times, December 1876; Monthly Musical Record, November 1892; Musical Times, December 1893
Constant Lambert; The Listener, 1926
Gerald Abraham; Music and Letters, April 1940
DVORAK:
Monthly Musical Record, March 1879, November 1891
Sir W. H. Hadow; Studies in Modern Music, 1894–5
GRIEG:
PIANO CONCERTO:
Monthly Musical Record, May 1875; Musical Times, March 1877
SULLIVAN:
Musical Times, December 1866, June 1878
'RUDDY-GORE':
Monthly Musical Record, February 1877
Dame Clara Butt; South Wales Daily News, September 19th, 1895
'PRINCESS IDA':
Musical Opinion, February 1834, January 1901; Musical Times, December 1900
'PHILHARMONIC AGAIN':
Musical Times, August 1876
MACKENZIE:
Francis Hueffer; 'Half a Century of Music in England, 1837–1887,' 1889; Monthly Musical Record, November 1884, May 1888
PARRY:
Thomas F. Dunhill; Monthly Musical Record, November 1918

Parry (*cont.*)

> *Sir W. H. Hadow*; Paper read to the Royal Musical Association, June 17th, 1919; Musical Opinion, 1918
>
> *H. V. Jervis-Read*; 'The Arrant Artist,' 1939

Stanford:

> Monthly Musical Record, August 1884, June 1884
>
> *Samuel Butler*; Note Books; Musical Opinion, May 1924

Elgar:

> *Ernest Walker*; 'A History of Music in England,' 1907
>
> *Eric Blom*; Chesterian, June 1922
>
> *J. H. Elliot*; Sackbut, October 1931
>
> *Rev. Basil Maine*; 'Elgar: His Life and Works,' 1933
>
> *Constant Lambert*; 'Music Ho,' 1934

Puccini:

> *Cecil Gray*; Sackbut, October 1920
>
> *A. Walter Kramer*; Chesterian, January–February, 1925
>
> *F. Stephen Clark*; Monthly Musical Record, January 1925

Mahler:

> *Henry Boys*; Note for HMV Records, 1938
>
> *Herbert Antcliffe*; Dominant, March–April, 1939

Debussy:

> *Mrs. Franz Liebich*; 'Claude Achille Debussy,' 1908
>
> *Cecil Gray*; 'A Survey of Contemporary Music,' 1924

Delius:

> *Philip Heseltine*; 'Frederick Delius,' 1923
>
> *Sir George Dyson*; 'The New Music,' 1924
>
> *Edwin Evans*; Chesterian, September–October, 1934
>
> *Bernard van Dieren*; Monthly Musical Record, July–August, 1934

Sibelius:

> *J. H. Elliot*: Chesterian, January–February, 1931
>
> *Constant Lambert*; 'Music Ho,' 1934

Roussel:

> *Edmund Rubbra*; Monthly Musical Record, December 1932
>
> *W. H. Mellers*; Scrutiny, September 1938

Vaughan Williams:

> *Edwin Evans*; Musical Times, April 1920
>
> *H. C. Colles*; Chesterian, February 1922
>
> *E. C. Rose*; Sackbut, July 1926
>
> *A. E. F. Dickinson*; 'An Introduction to the Music of Vaughan Williams,' 1928
>
> *Rev. Basil Maine*; 'New Paths in Music,' 1940

Holst:

> *Edwin Evans*; Dominant, April 1928

Holst (*cont.*)
    Bernard van Dieren; Dominant, December 1928
    Richard Capell; Dominant, December 1928
Schonberg:
    Rollo H Myers; Chesterian, April 1922
    Andre Coeuroy; Chesterian, March 1928
    Constant Lambert; 'Music Ho,' 1934
Ravel:
    Norman Demuth; 'Ravel,' (in the press)
Bartok:
    Cecil Gray; Sackbut, November 1920
Stravinsky:
    Henry Boys; Monthly Musical Record, 1934
    Cecil Gray; 'Predicaments,' 1936
Bax:
    Eric Blom; Chesterian, February 1920
    L. Henderson-Williams; Sackbut, March 1931
Webern:
    Erwin Stein; Chesterian, October 1922
Albanberg:
    Erwin Stone; Chesterian, October 1922
Polytonality and Atonality':
    Percy A. Scholes; 'Crotchets,' 1924
'Atonality':
    Sir George Dyson; 'The New Music,' 1924
    Constant Lambert; 'Music Ho,' 1934

In America we blame the foreign conductors, who have no sympathy with native effort, but here (in England) they have only native conductors; Wood, Geoffrey Toye, Landon Ronald, Beethoven, Goossens, and yet ——————. It is certainly true that English music is as rarely heard in England as American music is—or was—heard in America.
                    '*Musical Courier*', June 26th 1919